OURS AS WE PLAY IT

Kate Flaherty is an ARC postdoctoral research fellow at the University of Sydney. She has published essays on contemporary Shakespeare performance in Australia with Rodopi (2011), Cambridge University Press (2010), and with *Contemporary Theatre Review* (2009).

OURS AS WE PLAY IT
Australia Plays Shakespeare
KATE FLAHERTY

UWA PUBLISHING

First published in 2011 by
UWA Publishing
Crawley, Western Australia 6009
www.uwap.uwa.edu.au

UWAP is an imprint of UWA Publishing
a division of The University of Western Australia

THE UNIVERSITY OF
WESTERN AUSTRALIA
Achieve International Excellence

This book is copyright. Apart from any fair dealing for the purpose of private study, research, criticism or review, as permitted under the Copyright Act 1968, no part may be reproduced by any process without written permission. Enquiries should be made to the publisher.

This book forms part of the Long Histories Series – initiated by UWA Publishing and the Australia Research Council Network for Early European Research (NEER) – offering intellectual exchanges on the long European influence in Australia and the history of cultural translation and transmission.

The moral right of the author has been asserted.

Copyright © Kate Flaherty 2011

National Library of Australia
Cataloguing-in-Publication data:
Flaherty, Kathryn
Ours as we play it : Australia plays Shakespeare / Kathryn Flaherty
ISBN: 9781742582627 (pbk.)

Includes bibliographical references and index.

Shakespeare, William, 1564–1616—Appreciation—Australia
Shakespeare, William, 1564–1616 Midsummer night's dream
Shakespeare, William, 1564–1616 As you like it
Shakespeare, William, 1564–1616 Hamlet

822.33

Cover image © Philip Le Masurier
Typeset by J & M Typesetting
Printed by Griffin Press

To Penny

CONTENTS

Introduction   1

Part I: *Hamlet*
1.   Madness and Masculinity in Australian *Hamlets*   23
2.   Play, the First Player, and the Idea of Theatrical Force   71

Part II: *As You Like It*
3.   Re-imagining Arden in Australian Space   95
4.   'Necessary tallness': Australian Rosalinds measure up   125

Part III: *A Midsummer Night's Dream*
5.   'I Pyramus am not Pyramus': 'true performing' and the magic within the magic of *A Midsummer Night's Dream*   161
6.   Power and Play: staging authority and subversion in *A Midsummer Night's Dream*   193

Afterword   235

Acknowledgments   241
Notes   244
Bibliography   261
Index   269

Introduction

> If you and I now start playing poker, we're using the elements of poker that have served for the last five hundred years. But the reality is nobody else's reality. It's ours as we play it.
>
> Peter Brook[1]

Shakespeare in Australia: unfinished business

One definition of 'play' has no usual association with theatre: the space provided within a mechanism for the movement of its parts. It is this definition of play that I conjure as a prompt and model for my exploration of Shakespeare in performance in Australia. Shakespeare's plays make constant reference to theatre, to audiences, to histrionic practice, to performance, and to art. From the most obvious instance of the play-within-the-play, to the eavesdropping scene, to the subtlest discourse on 'seeming', to uses, both comic and sinister, of disguise, Shakespeare's plays engage constantly and consciously with the predicament of theatre. This is Shakespearean metatheatre and it is this metatheatre that provides a space of play for the 'moving parts' of actor's bodies and audiences. This is because, in performance, each moment of metatheatre has the capacity to direct the actors' and audience's awareness towards themselves as participants in a specific performance event, in a specific time and place. Thus metatheatre offers a space of play for living cultural idiom, and therein the possibility of specific

Introduction

meaning and perennially renewable pertinence. The driving force of this book is a belief that metatheatre is what can make the reality of the play 'ours as we play it'.

In *Post-Colonial Drama: Theory, Practice, Politics*, Helen Gilbert and Joanne Tompkins touch upon the special significance of metatheatre in post-colonial productions by pointing to Derek Walcott's *A Branch of the Blue Nile* – a Trinidadian appropriation of *Antony and Cleopatra*. Gilbert and Tompkins see *Blue Nile* as characteristic of other 'post-colonial reworkings of Shakespeare' by virtue of 'Walcott's interest in metatheatre as a way of examining the problems of developing a performance aesthetic specific to the needs of the local culture'. They go on to explain that

> Metatheatre reminds us that any performance stages the necessary provisionality of representation. Although often playfully postmodern as well as strategic, it should not be seen as simply part of the postmodern intertextual experiment. By developing multiple self-reflexive discourses through role playing, role doubling/splitting, plays within plays, interventionary frameworks, and other metatheatrical devices, post-colonial works interrogate received models of theatre at the same time as they illustrate, quite self-consciously, that they are acting out their own histories/identities in a complex replay that can never be finished or final. In all this, the question of how Shakespeare might be fully appropriated remains disturbingly relevant.[2]

The insight that metatheatre has the potential to be purposive in a political sense, and not simply a postmodern aesthetic device, impels my study. However, the apparent discomfort with Shakespeare expressed in Gilbert and Tompkins' final sentence merits a moment's attention. The notion of 'fully' appropriating

Introduction

Shakespeare seems inconsistent with the authors' prior recognition that drama – and most pointedly post-colonial drama – is necessarily a kind of unfinished business. Most post-colonial scholarship would exclude a so-called 'straight production' of Shakespeare from this special category of unfinished business. Yet there is a strong case to be made that Shakespeare's plays are rife with the above-listed characteristics of metatheatre, and, as a consequence, also 'illustrate, quite self-consciously that they are acting out their own histories/identities in a complex replay that can never be finished or final' nor, I would add, fully appropriated.

The problem with the goal of 'full appropriation' is that it designates the plays' historical provenance, ownership and ultimately, meaning, as elsewhere. It belies the fact that the ongoing life of the plays as drama is and always has been the result of successive ploys of appropriation – none of which can be completely fulfilled, finished, or final. *The Tempest* proves an excellent instance in point: a play over which imperialist agendas have lost much of their appropriative control in the wake of the new uses found for it. *The Tempest*'s potential to question the act of colonisation, muted perhaps for centuries, has made it *the* play for exploring such systematic abuses of power in the post-colonial era. As a consequence, the kind of cultural work the play is used to perform has undergone a complete reversal. *The Tempest* is now indelibly layered with the cultural and political exigencies of our time. It would be difficult to imagine a contemporary production of *The Tempest* which did not engage with the problematic nature of colonisation. Caliban's dimensional and speaking subject-hood on stage is impossible to stifle. In the past, producing a plainly repellent Caliban to legitimate Prospero's domination was the status quo and understood as an inherent meaning of the play.[3] In the present, it would be seen as a perverse, even irresponsible, interpretative exercise. Such a reversal alerts us to the pragmatism of theatre; meaning is as much a function of the use to which plays are put as an essential ingredient. The reason why Shakespearean drama is unfinished business in the Australian context is that Australians still have uses for it.

To argue that Shakespeare's plays are necessarily unfinished business requires a specific understanding of the ways in which performed drama makes meaning within culture – ways that differ vitally from those in which printed literature makes meaning. My work concerns the vexed question of how Shakespeare's plays make meaning in performance, but resists the equation of their 'perpetual relevance' with the extraordinary prescience of the author or universal themes latent in the text. I base my argument on the theoretical position that 'meaning' in theatre is constituted by the qualities of a particular (and passing) encounter and not by the fulfillment of a hallowed original intention. In this vein, meaning is generated by intersections between the imaginative plenitude of the play-text and the conscious exigencies of the cultural moment in which it is performed. In this notion of 'cultural moment' I include all the moments which the cultural present holds dialogue with, reacts to, enfolds, and draws upon. James C. Bulman has formulated this intersection as

>...the radical contingency of performance – the unpredictable, often playful intersection of history, material conditions, social contexts, and reception that destabilises Shakespeare and makes theatrical meaning a participatory act.[4]

Proclaiming the 'unpredictable', the 'playful' and the 'participatory' in theatrical meaning liberates the scholarly task from the constraint to privilege textual meaning over what I will call 'performative meaning'. Yet this also problematises the analytical endeavour. If the text is not the source from which meaning is derived in a linear, exegetical manner, then what is the legitimate starting place for study? W. B. Worthen outlines some ramifications

Introduction

for scholarship by challenging our understanding of the sources of meaning and 'force' in performance:

> ...performance always takes place in present behaviour; throughout its stage history the ongoing vitality of Shakespearean drama has depended on the ability to fashion Shakespeare's writing into the fashionable behaviours indigenous to the changing tastes of the stage.[5]

When we attribute 'force' or 'power' to a performance, say, of Ophelia's 'mad' scene, we are applauding that performance's capacity to make vivid a contemporary, perhaps even local, conception of madness because that is the only kind of madness that 'works' – for a contemporary audience. The same might be said of any scene of pleading, grieving, cruelty, or love. Our own behaviours and knowledges of behaviour are as much the rubric for truthful, authentic, successful, or powerful performance as the play-text itself. To return to Brook's succinct summation: 'the reality is ours', not that of some hazy historical provenance.

Shakespeare's plays are preoccupied with what it means to act in both its senses – to take action and to perform. In accordance with Worthen's insight, we can assume that the content of these 'behavioural genres' in the context in which the play is performed will influence the meaning of the play just as much as the script does. Performance and text are, therefore, co-active in generating performative meaning. Worthen clarifies his radical formulation when he points out that 'acting isn't determined by textual meanings but uses them to fashion meanings in the fashions of contemporary behaviours', and furthermore that performance can never accurately recover meanings inscribed in the text because 'theatre does not cite text; it cites behaviour'.[6]

I would like to take this idea a step further by localising the popular analogy of the stage as the globe. If the stage is a

Introduction

microcosm of the world, then the 'fashionable behaviour indigenous to the changing tastes of the stage' must be deeply inflected by the particular part of the world in which the staging takes place. This has been confirmed for me repeatedly in my discussions with theatre practitioners who work in touring companies. The way in which a single production means, makes sense, or has force, differs noticeably from one audience to another, but even more from one location to another.

Roy Luxford, Producer for the widely touring British theatre company Cheek by Jowl, described to me ways in which he has seen plays affect different audiences and, conversely, the way different audiences affect productions. In 2004 Cheek by Jowl took a production of *Othello* to fourteen countries, including Nigeria. Nonso Anozie, who played Othello, is of Nigerian descent. Luxford perceived that this, among other aspects of the production, had a particular import in the Nigerian context that in turn influenced the nature of the relationships within the play:

> [A] lot of the references in the text about magic were very strongly picked up upon by the audiences and the fact that in Nigeria, a black man in that position is not uncommon, whereas I think that there is still a hang up in the whiter world of seeing a black man playing this character...particularly when you have Desdemona [Caroline Martin] who we cast as incredibly petite, white, and quite 'English rose'-like, – so the contrast both in their skin tones but also physically – Nonso was six foot six and Desdemona was about five foot something – so I think the reaction between those two characters was markedly different in Nigeria than it was elsewhere. And also, on an individual basis, if you're playing it in a country that is predominantly black, it's a very different scenario to if you're playing it say, in the UK or in Hong Kong. That was a very different scenario where there aren't many people of

Introduction

African descent in Hong Kong at all. So their relationship changed quite dramatically.[7]

Intimately connected with this tendency of the cultural context to influence the internal dynamics of the performance, Luxford also noted distinct differences in the response that the production generated from place to place. In Nigeria:

> there was a much more vocal response because that is their culture of theatre-going. You know, they interact very vocally with actors on stage…So it was quite, it wasn't boisterous, but it was a vocal scenario in which to perform the piece.
>
> It's curious, in New York, the biggest reaction to Othello and Desdemona was when Othello actually slaps Desdemona down to her knees and I think that had perhaps had reminiscences of the Mamet play, *Oleanna*, about that whole male–female relationship. That was quite an interesting moment because really, for New York audiences, for a man to slap a woman in that scenario is, you know, quite personal to them. And in London that actually didn't have such a resonance, which was really bizarre, because you'd think it would be about the moment when he strangles her, but in New York it was really the moment about a piece of physical abuse.[8]

A more local observation of the re-calibrations of emphasis which take place as a production tours was provided by Australian actor Robert Alexander when describing the Bell Shakespeare Company's *Richard III* and *Julius Caesar*:

> I can tell you that audiences do subtly vary throughout Australia…to take a production of *Richard III* from Sydney to Canberra – the reaction in Canberra was utterly different.

Introduction

> And one can only assume that they know more about politics with a hatchet – they certainly laughed more.
>
> *Julius Caesar* as well. When Mark Antony did his funeral oration in Canberra, they received it in a different way than Sydney audiences did. If we think of one city as cottoning onto manipulation and the humour of political audacity, do we also think that they might actually receive something that is more moving or sentimental? I'm not quite sure about that.[9]

These accounts reflect recognition that a performance is not a self-contained entity, that it is permeable to its contexts, and that the meanings it creates are generated through encounters with living culture. Such a realisation keeps astride of the recent theoretical movement called 'presentism'. Presentism, eschewing new historicism's emphasis on the inaccessible otherness of the past, posits continuities in the way that Shakespeare makes meaning through history. One element of this, as articulated by Terence Hawkes, is through play:

> The essence of playing lies in a symbiotic relationship with the audience neatly characterised by the metaphor of the trumpeter. Adjustable, responsive, shifting position to 'get an echo', it's far more concerned to interact with the material reality of the spectator's world than to impersonate a different 'reality' on the stage. In order to operate, it needs constantly to elicit a reaction so that it can acknowledge and reply to that with an unrehearsed flow of repartee, which itself invites and inspires further reaction and so on.[10]

The participatory and contingent nature of theatrical meaning remains one of theatre's continuities from Shakespeare's period to

Introduction

our own. The possibility of laughing at the contemporary political ironies elicited by a play's action is perennially the promise of that play's performativity. This was no less the case in Shakespeare's period than it is in our own, albeit that the contemporary significance is utterly our own. Shakespeare's plays are rife with such portals of performativity which, by generating different realities in different contexts, actually signal the multivalent performativity of the play.

Having nominated a focus on Shakespeare as contemporary performance, it may seem strange that this book confines discussion to theatre, excluding film and other contemporary media. The reason is aligned with my emphasis on examining the interaction of the plays within particular cultural contexts. A theatre production takes place at a time and in a location. In this respect all theatre, even the most stylistically avant-garde, shares the conditions of the theatre for which Shakespeare wrote by virtue of being a specific live and living event. A film, in contrast, is characterised by permanently fixed content that can be replayed anywhere on an infinite number of occasions. As Douglas Lanier has pointed out, film, as a preservable and repeatable cultural entity, can be subjected to the close-reading protocols of text. Film thereby harbours the potential to take on text's monumental authority:

> ...even as these media have democratised access to performances they have also shaped our sense of them. Video and film have encouraged us to assimilate performances to the condition of texts, stable artifacts rather than contingent, unstable, ephemeral experiences.[11]

Despite being a book, *Ours As We Play It* moves in a contrary direction by paying special attention to the conditions of theatre.

Introduction

Performing a response

This book examines three of Shakespeare's plays in performance: *Hamlet, As You Like It,* and *A Midsummer Night's Dream.* The criterion for this selection of plays is in keeping with my mode of inquiry: these are the plays that have enjoyed multiple productions in the past two decades, in parts of Australia where I have spent time, and of which I have an experiential awareness of culturally specific 'behavioural genres'. Each chapter commences with a brief glance at the play's wider legacy in the Australian or international context before exploring some cultural preoccupations that can be seen to intersect with that play across a number of recent Australian productions.

Part I examines Company B's 1994 *Hamlet* directed by Neil Armfield, Pork Chop Productions' 2001 *Hamlet* directed by Jeremy Sims, Bell Shakespeare's 2003 *Hamlet* directed by John Bell and State Theatre Company of South Australia/Queensland Theatre Company's 2007 *Hamlet* directed by Adam Cook. Two inter-linked cultural preoccupations lead my inquiry. The first is masculinity: I ask what it is about the Australian context that conspires repeatedly to fuse the question of Hamlet's masculine social role with the question of his madness. I then take up the issue of metatheatre in *Hamlet* and ask what conceptions of theatre and play each production drew upon to make the Player's Tale (act 2, scene 2) forceful. (This reference is to W. Shakespeare, *Hamlet* in S. Greenblatt, W. Cohen, J. E. Howard and K. E. Maus, eds, *The Norton Shakespeare.* Unless otherwise indicated, all subsequent references to Shakespeare's plays are also to this edition.)

Turning to *As You Like It* in Part II, I embrace Robert N. Watson's insight regarding the linguistic violence with which Arden is constructed and appropriated by characters in the play.[12] This leads me to ask how Australian productions have conceptualised Arden as wilderness or pastoral; colonised or shared space; literal or figurative space. It also leads to recognition of Rosalind's

INTRODUCTION

extraordinary rhetorical stature and to the question of how performance constitutes, and reviewers respond to, this stature in Australia. These questions about Arden and Rosalind are pursued through the legacy of the play in Australia and across three productions: Sydney Theatre Company's (STC) 1996 production directed by Simon Phillips, Company B's 1999 production directed by Neil Armfield, and Bell Shakespeare's 2003 production directed by Lindy Davies.

Part III takes up *A Midsummer Night's Dream*, in recent times the most popular play on the Australian stage. Against a backdrop of the play's international production history, special attention is dedicated to the Sydney Theatre Company's 1997 production directed by Noel Tovey; the Australian Shakespeare Company's touring productions commencing in 1988 and directed by Glen Elston; Bell Shakespeare's 2004 production directed by Anna Volska; and Company B's 2004 production directed by Benedict Andrews. I ask how the play's magic is given a performative reality by specific cultural traditions and conceptions of 'the magic of theatre'. I also examine how the hierarchies of gender and social order in the play are used to fashion meanings that operate within identifiably contemporary and Australian understandings of power.

The questions I raise for discussion of each play have been largely shaped by what I have discovered as I researched each production. In an attempt to grapple with both the macrocosmic cultural operations of each play in production and with the minutiae of the practices of dramatic interpretation, my research has included a wide range of activities.

First among my adventures was attending rehearsals and performances and interviewing actors and directors. In moving between rehearsal and performance, what became clear to me about theatre practice is well summed up in a comment by Gay McAuley:

Introduction

> ...every theatrical signifier was like the tip of a semiotic iceberg, with depths of meaning beneath the observed surface. I began to realise that most spectators who see a performance only once, see a very small part of what is there.[13]

In the case of productions where I observed the rehearsals, I was an audience member with a privileged perspective on the growth of the performance – a perspective that exerted force on my interpretation. I had been a party to the entire evolution of a decision to lower the voice or to sit down on a particular line. My 'inside knowledge' cultivated in me a sensitivity to what actors hoped to 'mean' in particular scenes – a sensitivity which conversely occluded my awareness of what that scene might convey to the audience in general. I also became aware that meaning is a fragmentary experience for everyone involved in its production, that being a party to one kind of meaning can entail exclusion from others. For these reasons I sought a broader base for my speculations about how performance makes meanings in culture.

The explicit aim of my book to comment upon how performances of Shakespeare's plays make meaning in the broader Australian context demands that it take into account discourses other than those specific to the enclosed world of theatrical culture. To this end I also sought out the material traces left by performances: to my direct rehearsal experience and interviews with theatre practitioners I added archival research. Theatre archives, in themselves, offer a curiously composed performance of meaning. Filed together in one box it is common to find designers' sketches of costume and set, scale diagrams of the lighting rig, prompt copies of the script complete with lighting and sound cues and stage directions, inventories of items to hire, pages of photographic proof-sheets, an audio or audio-visual recording of the performance, press releases and parcels of reviews.

Introduction

Because I was already very familiar with the productions themselves, reviews were less a source of information about the production and more a source of information about its reception within a particular cultural context. As a consequence, reviews are used throughout this book critically. In some instances comments from reviews are proffered to reinforce my observations. In other instances, however, I take issue with the reviews by identifying the codes of moral, social, and cultural authority that they invoke. In Part II in particular, I point out the questionable bases of the authority assumed by reviewers to appropriate the 'real' Shakespeare as a yardstick for a particular performance. Another respect in which archival research has proven valuable is in offering prompts to my memory of the performance experience. Looking at photographs and, in some instances, watching audio-visual recordings of a performance has provided me with conduits back to the moment of performance.

The final dimension of my task has been endeavouring to link the foregoing forms of creative and popular public discourse with critical scholarly discourse. To reflect the sequence of my research activities, I offer this discussion last. Rather than beginning with scholarly approaches to the plays or theoretical approaches to performance, I have chased up the veins of inquiry prompted by my experiences of the play in performance, my contact with its various participants, and the preoccupations evident in discourses of reception. This has produced a theoretically wide-ranging set of sources. I have drawn upon works of literary criticism, Shakespeare in performance, theatre history, performance theory, gender studies and cultural theory.[14] Each strain of thought has contributed something to my understanding of the meanings available from the play-text and the manner in which meaning is produced within and around performance of Shakespeare's plays.

Ours As We Play It is itself a performance. It engages in a temporally bound and situated moment of making meaning. As

Introduction

text its life will perhaps be understood as less ephemeral than a staged moment of meaning. Yet, as in a staged moment, the meaning in this moment of writing (or this moment of reading) involves drawing opportunistically on culturally inflected personal experiences and pre-established conceptions of the form 'book'. There are rubrics, patterns, contemporary fashions of thought and discourse in place that, actor-like, I invoke to mean, to do things, to be performative.

Framing the book as a performance is my response to the problematic nature of writing about theatre. Theatrical performance is a fractious subject for traditional scholarship because theatre is not enduringly present as an object to be pored over and known. Writing about the theatrical event is, to some extent, always writing about the self and indeed, performing the self in(to) a moment past. While a scholar of critical literature, fiction, or cell biology has her object of study perennially before her; the scholar of theatre performance has only the traces the event has left on herself, and the material artifacts previously described. Traditional modes of documentation see writing about performance as an effort of recovery and preservation; as if the performance is a thing, hanging in the air before its student and able to be consulted. From this comes the accusation that writing about performance is a totalising endeavour. However, Barbara Hodgdon delineates a brave new tack. Hodgdon looks at the discourses that surround the performance event and, instead of seeing them as secondary, derivative discourses, sees them as integral to the way in which the performance makes meaning:

> Rather than assuming that the performance text itself contains or produces immanent meanings, or focusing on the marks of its making and its makers, I want to consider its status as an event constituted by the concrete conditions of its spectators. For it is in the 'discursively saturated materiality'

of the historical circumstances in which a performance is seen that it makes its demands for narrative intelligibility.[15]

My book is similarly interested in the manifold ways a theatrical event is constituted; before, during and after, with the acknowledgement that the study itself is an attempt to constitute the events as well as grappling with their constitution. For this reason, *Ours As We Play It* is conceived as a performance in conversation with performance and as a collection of lived moments rather than a totalising and definitive critical edifice.

Shakespeare in Australia: invasion or space of play

This book is concerned with Shakespeare and performative meaning in the contemporary Australian context. As such, it grows out from a number of scholarly approaches and differentiates itself from others. The study's uniqueness inheres in aiming to combine wide-ranging speculations about cultural history with a detailed analysis of the practices of dramatic interpretation. In this two-fold profile it takes up the example of some excellent shorter articles mentioned throughout my chapters, but as a book-length work permits a uniquely detailed and comparative mode of scholarship.

Of particular value have been essays, books, or critical editions of plays that lend significance to choices made in performance while also performing a detailed critical reading of the text. These 'Shakespeare in Performance' collections and critical editions have been useful in offering accounts of the sense made of a particular scene or line of text across many productions and periods of history. An example, of which I make use in Chapter 1, is the advent of the now-standard interpretation of Hamlet's anger in the nunnery scene as being prompted by his perceiving the presence of Claudius and Polonius.[16]

Another kind of study that informs the design of this book is the type of article and essay that focuses on a particular place and/

Introduction

or period of producing Shakespeare's plays on stage. *O Brave New World: Two Centuries of Shakespeare on the Australian Stage* constitutes a collection of such studies contributed by scholars from around Australia. Together, these essays flesh out an analytical account of patterns of production and reception of Shakespeare in Australia. *O Brave New World* is couched by its editors as a kind of starting place for investigation of Shakespeare in Australia:

> ...no attempt has been made to undertake any systematic analysis of Shakespeare on the Australian stage. The aim of this book is to begin to correct this sorry state of affairs. The volume does not try to be complete and comprehensive, but to be impressionistic, and to encourage further work by offering a variety of approaches and pointing to areas of interest and research potential.[17]

I take up this invitation, accepting with it the recognition that the term 'Shakespeare in Australia' conceptualises a relatively new discourse, a discourse in formation. Prior to the 1990s Shakespeare studies was a discourse defined chiefly by geographical origins. To take part in that discourse was, as an Australian scholar, to assent to working at a remove from the source. Works such *O Brave New World* and Michael D. Bristol's *Shakespeare's America, America's Shakespeare*, published around the turn of the millennium, signal a postmodern awareness that cultural production is culturally contingent and, most refreshingly, that meanings worth examining are made outside of Britain, using Shakespeare.[18]

Also pertinent to Australian Shakespeare scholarship is the post-colonial scholarship that problematises the pre-eminent place of Shakespeare within Australian culture. Helen Gilbert and Joanne Tompkin's book *Post-Colonial Drama: Theory, Practice, Politics* has already been mentioned as offering insight to the role of Shakespearean metatheatre in post-colonial contexts and as taking

Introduction

up the issue of how Shakespeare might be pro-actively appropriated.[19] An earlier example of clearly articulated challenge to the ostensibly unquestioned place of Shakespeare in Australian culture is the collection of essays called *Shakespeare's Books: Contemporary Cultural Politics and the Persistence of Empire* edited by Philip Mead and Marion Campbell. This collection is defined by Campbell as 'not about interpretations of Shakespeare's texts, but about the uses that past and contemporary societies make of those texts'.[20] While I strongly dispute this division of 'interpretation' from 'uses', I acknowledge a debt owed to *Shakespeare's Books* for pinpointing the hitherto invidious division between the work of cultural criticism and Shakespeare scholarship:

> For professional cultural critics…who are neither ignorant nor indifferent but actively contestatory in their relation to Shakespeare, conservative critics reserve their greatest contempt. This debate is worth engaging in because it puts content back into the name of Shakespeare and destabilises his supposedly monolithic and univocal significance. This obliges all of us who engage in the debate to consider both the historical and contemporary conditions of Shakespeare's signifying power, and the costs of either reinforcing or eliminating his cultural, educational and theatrical pre-eminence.[21]

As these examples illustrate, the possibilities offered by postmodern cultural theory and theories of performativity decentralise the source of authority in Shakespeare studies. Geographical centres and margins – once the self-effacing assumption of Australian Shakespeare experiences – are recalibrated. Rather than being a derivative, second-hand kind of activity, the production of Shakespeare in Australia is gradually being recognised as a constitutive dimension of the ever-burgeoning field called 'Shakespeare' and as such, merits scholarly attention in its own right.

Introduction

In the past thirty years, the subject of 'Shakespeare in Australia' has received increasing amounts of critical attention. Unfortunately, in debates about the rightful or wrongful place of Shakespeare in Australian culture, performance activities, education, and popular perception are often conflated as one oppressive freight. In this blurry polemic 'Shakespeare' emerges an emblem of cultural imperialism. But what is this 'Shakespeare'? Often the word 'Shakespeare' comes to stand for a particular use to which a text – which is by its nature volatile, ambiguous, indeterminate, polyphonic, metatheatrical – has been put. Without question, this 'Shakespeare' has promoted oppressive imperialistic modes of thought. This 'Shakespeare' ought to be criticised, resisted, exposed, and even patrolled in any culture that cherishes its own vitality. The problem with this 'Shakespeare' is that it does not exist as a discrete entity. The actual experience of oppression, boredom, or injustice that a critic attaches to 'Shakespeare' is often the ineffable and affective colour of a moment past. Consequently, the attempt to deconstruct this 'Shakespeare' builds the monolith anew before beginning.

Despite their often exclusive preoccupation with the 'uses' to which Shakespeare is put (few cultural critiques examine the words of the plays in detail) critics of the growth of Shakespearean drama in Australia conceptualise Shakespeare chiefly as textual rather than performative: a text-bound, text-preserved, entity. Shakespeare is seen as a book, which, like the British, usurped space in this continent. This produces a generalising discourse about cultural imperialism, which makes an important contribution to our understanding of how literature operates within culture. However, this discourse falls short of accounting for the very distinct ways in which dramatic performance makes meaning within culture and, especially, the way a particular culture is always implicit in and necessary to performative meaning. It is a paradigm which

Introduction

understands the operation of text and performance as a simple set of power relations whereby performance cites the text: the meanings of the text 'govern' performance and the performance re-produces, disseminates, and therefore naturalises the imperialistic meanings of the text. Within this paradigm, the legitimate mode of resistance is also conceived as text-centric: politicised appropriations of the text: rereadings and rewritings. As a book, Shakespeare is a manageable cultural nemesis.

The present book is under-girded by an entirely different understanding of the way performance makes meaning in a cultural context. An invaluable insight offered by Andrew Parker and Eve Kosofsky Sedgwick is that 'Performativity…lives in the examples'.[22] While Parker and Sedgwick are not referring explicitly to theatre, W. B. Worthen has articulated convincingly the relevance of the concept of 'performativity' for theatrical performance. Worthen argues that the dismissal of theatrical performance as an important instance of performativity by the disciplines of critical and cultural theory relies, once again, on an oversimplified paradigm of theatrical meaning: theatre as proscenium arch, theatre as the citation of text, theatre as a one-way transaction.[23] But if, as Worthen suggests, performance fashions meanings from what is at its disposal – from what exists in the cultural moment in which it takes place – it is not at all surprising that the performance of Shakespeare has been used in Australia to perpetuate imperialistic habits of thought. Imperialistic habits of thought were and are here to hand in the cultural context and we have co-opted Shakespeare to performatively 'mean' them. Demonstrably, many other living facets of the contemporary cultural context have found their way into processes of 'meaning by Shakespeare' in Australia: problematising the status quo in race and gender relations, questioning the place of learning, challenging militaristic patriotism and so forth. To conflate 'Shakespeare' as a static icon of cultural imperialism with what the Shakespeare play has meant, can mean, and will mean in performance is too broad a stroke of criticism to be of any real use.

Accusing Shakespeare of cultural colonisation is a form of cultural critique that relies upon an oversimplified notion of the practices of production; as if 'meanings' intended by some nebulous early-modern sensibility were somehow disseminated in an inert Australian culture like a disease. By contrast, *Ours As We Play It* sees meaning in theatre not as transmitted, but as negotiated as part of the creative, contractual work of culture. Furthermore, if the force and authority of Shakespeare's plays are not seen as inhabiting the text, then the accusation of cultural imperialism becomes a slip-knot without an object. What or who is doing the colonising? The easy target is the name of the 'canonical' author; but what if what we are registering as a postmodern, post-colonial scholarly community is not a common enemy – yet another invader – but an enemy within? What if what we register when we look at the performance history of Shakespeare in Australia is a tendency to put plays to uses that, in retrospect, highlight our own cultural projects and prejudices? And if this is so, how better to identify those toxic ideologies and crippling cultural assumptions than to investigate the uses to which we have and do put Shakespeare in Australia? The ubiquity and continuity of Shakespeare in performance is the very condition of its usefulness as a barometer of social, ideological, and political change. With this lens, *Ours As We Play It* examines practices of producing Shakespeare in Australia and suggests that it is feasible to see Shakespeare's plays operating in Australian culture, not as an occupier of space, but as a space of play.

PART I

HAMLET

1

Madness and Masculinity in Australian *Hamlets*

> CLAUDIUS ...to persever
> In obstinate condolement is a course
> Of impious stubbornness, 'tis unmanly grief
> *Hamlet* act 1, scene 2, lines 92–4

> FRANK No thanks. If you blokes all want to go and get yourself shot, go ahead.
> SNOWY Well I'm not scared to die for my country Frank.
> FRANK Well good for you Snow, you go and sign yourself on.
> *Gallipoli* 1981

I open by linking the quotations above for two reasons. The first is that each stages a public test of qualities equated with masculinity in its particular context. Before the court of Denmark Claudius censures Hamlet 'unmanly' grief. In Peter Weir's film *Gallipoli*, in the company of rail worker mates, Snowy (Mark Argue) censures what he interprets as Frank's (Mel Gibson) fear of death in battle. The second reason is that by bringing these moments together, I flag the advent of the Australian Hamlet. It is widely acknowledged that by casting Mel Gibson as Hamlet in his 1990 film *Hamlet*, Franco

Zeffirelli in fact cast *Lethal Weapon*'s Martin Rigg thus creating a new kind of Hamlet – Hamlet the action hero. What is less well considered is the extent to which Zefirrelli cast *Gallipoli*'s Frank Dunne as Hamlet. In doing so, Zeffirelli imported a reluctant combatant cum exemplary Anzac into the texture of *Hamlet* and imported Hamlet into the Australian imaginary as a figure who exhibited both contentious and cherished versions of Australian masculinity. This chapter is not about Mel Gibson as Hamlet. Rather, I use this junction of *Gallipoli*'s Frank and Shakespeare's Hamlet as a departure point for discussing Australian Hamlets of the theatre. In doing so, I nominate productions which engage specifically Australian problematics of masculine identity – physical valour, militarism and violence; stoicism, anti-intellectualism and inarticulacy; gender division and social isolation; generational conflict; larrikinism and mateship; and the cherished pathos of the lost cause.

Hamlet's problem is 'the problem of being a man and dealing with a man's social role'. So suggested Richard Madelaine in a conversation with Neil Armfield about Armfield's much acclaimed production of *Hamlet* for Company B at Belvoir Street, Sydney in 1994.[1] Madelaine's comment highlights something that haunts all contemporary Australian *Hamlets*: the inextricability of his madness and dilemmas of masculinity – what is seen as the 'male role'. As Claudius' criticism in my opening reference illustrates, anxiety about the credentials of manhood is registered strongly within the play. Contemporary Australian productions of *Hamlet* have centralised that anxiety remarkably, producing *Hamlets* which are about masculinity: its dominant and alternative forms and their relational and social fields of expression.

To explore the link between Hamlet's madness and dilemmas of masculinity, I examine four productions of the play: *Hamlet* directed by Neil Armfield at Belvoir Street Theatre, Sydney in 1994; *Hamlet* directed by Jeremy Sims for Pork Chop Productions at Belvoir Street Theatre, Sydney in 2001, *Hamlet* directed by John Bell for the Bell Shakespeare Company at The Playhouse, Sydney 2003, and *Hamlet* directed by Adam Cook in a combined production for the State Theatre Company of South Australia (STCSA) and Queensland Theatre Company (QTC), Adelaide and Brisbane in 2007. I ask how two of Hamlet's relationships are interpreted in these productions as playing into Hamlet's specifically masculine madness: the relationship between Hamlet and Ophelia and the relationship between Hamlet and his fathers.

It may seem axiomatic that Hamlet's problem is one of fulfilling or resisting the expectations of his father and father-in-law respectively and that, therefore, his madness is inevitably linked to pressures of the 'male role'. Yet, this is to assume that the way of understanding gender encapsulated in the term 'male role' is both trans-historical and trans-cultural. As R. W. Connell has pointed out, the use of the theatrical metaphor ('role') 'as a technical concept in the social sciences, as a serious way of explaining social behaviour generally, dates only from the 1930s' and therefore, that 'in speaking of masculinity at all...we are "doing gender" in a culturally specific way'.[2] My question, then, is: what is culturally specific about the preoccupation with masculinity and 'male roles' in contemporary Australian productions and discussions of *Hamlet*.

The *Hamlets*

Neil Armfield's direction of *Hamlet* at Belvoir Street in 1994 was characteristic of his work in its stylistic economy and dedication to telling the story. The Upstairs Belvoir space, prior to renovations, seated three hundred and twenty people and was (and is) unique in the proximity it allowed each audience member to the action. The stage was an oblique wedge-shaped space formed by the meeting of two walls at a corner. Around this space the audience formed a stepped arc. Actors could enter via two tunnels that ran out from under the audience, or from backstage, or through the aisles.

Armfield's production embraced the naked characteristics of the space – originally a factory – as integral to the production aesthetic. Hence the concrete floor with a visible drain canal was left as such. The walls also had a concrete surface. The space was strikingly bare. In his interview with Richard Madelaine and John Golder, Armfield describes the way he and the designer Dan Potra arrived at design decisions. After sifting through a range of elaborate expressionistic suggestions, they arrived at the simplicity of the concrete floor. Armfield describes his reason for this choice:

> It's very important that the stage is essentially a platform for the play and it has to remain to some extent visually neutral, so that a human body within the space can have maximum focus on the stage.[3]

The one conspicuously colourful set feature was an intricately patterned, rectangular, red Persian rug which throughout the course of the performance was rotated, rolled up and moved on and off the stage.

There was great fluidity to the action and a conscious sense of theatrical activity within the performance. This was established at the outset when the whole cast appeared on stage and Horatio (played by Geoffrey Rush) stepped forward and gave a prologue comprising lines from the play's final scene. This direct address to the audience acknowledged the mechanisms of theatre, particularly the need for audience confederacy. In this acknowledgement inhered a particular kind of theatrical force which I discuss further in Chapter 2.

Like the design, the costumes facilitated, rather than distracted from, the story. The use of top-hats and tail-coats, dinner jackets and braces suggested a kind of European modernity and permitted clear differences in social rank.[4] This conveyed at once a pre- World War I society of crumbling diplomacy and impending chaos and, with the help of Jacek Koman's (Claudius) Polish accent, a subtle implication of contemporary Eastern European political strife.

Armfield's *Hamlet* received high critical acclaim and Richard Roxburgh, who played Hamlet, was the focus of this praise. Some of the qualities ascribed to his Hamlet were 'incandescence', 'brilliance', and being 'painfully sane'.[5] He exhibited a peculiarly Australian quality of wry humour – Golder and Madelaine describing him as 'lucid', and 'at ease in comedy'.[6] Roxburgh's physical energy and expressiveness, echoing that of Gibson, were seen as the special stamp of his Australianess. Katherine Brisbane commented upon his 'Australian way of behaving' and his 'use of a lot of action to demonstrate the restlessness of someone who doesn't know who he is or why he is behaving the way he is'.[7] In keeping with this vitality and volatility, Roxburgh's Hamlet was seen as being at odds with the traditionally assumed inertia and meditativeness of the role:

> This Hamlet is no moral philosopher: Roxburgh's Hamlet is alive to the fires of life. He is like a coiled spring, charged with action, who literally bounds and leaps across the stage and flings himself bodily against the wall crying 'Vengeance!'[8]

Figure 1.1 Richard Roxburgh (Hamlet), Geoffrey Rush (Horatio), *Hamlet*, Company B, Belvoir Street Theatre, Sydney, 1994. Photograph ©Heidrun Lohr Courtesy of Company B and Heidrun Lohr.

In 2001, another *Hamlet* was staged at Upstairs Belvoir Street Theatre – this time by Jeremy Sims' company, Pork Chop Productions.[9] Sims co-directed the production with Jason Clark and played the title role. One of the most obvious differences between the Armfield *Hamlet* and the Sims *Hamlet* was Sims' extensive cutting of the text. Sims' *Hamlet* ran for a little over two hours and was characterised by a great deal of splicing and rearrangement of scenes. Like Armfield's *Hamlet* it used the plainness and versatility of the Belvoir space to facilitate quick transitions between scenes. Sims made the choice to extend the performance space into the audience: he used the two corridors, aisles, and the space at the back of the auditorium as centres of action. Scene changes were very rapid, comprising swift cross-fades that left characters from the previous scene in dimmed light as if continuing their scene and permitting a meaningful resonance between one scene and the next. The effect was of a whole world in action or a Court of many chambers, terraces, and corners in which action was simultaneously building towards a climax.

The set, designed by Andrew Raymond, comprised two major features. The first was a large piece of vermilion fabric arranged and rearranged throughout the performance to act as a drape which, suspended from a point, swept the floor to form a rug, a stage curtain, and finally a shroud for Polonius who was shot while hiding behind it. The simplicity and flexibility of this property echoed that of the Persian rug in the Armfield production.[10] The second feature was a large, sturdy oval table, made of timber with an inset surface that resembled green marble. With papers spread across it this gave the immediate impression of a government office. However, it was later used in the players' scene as the platform on which the sleeping king is poisoned, and then turned on its side to form Ophelia's grave. This inventive use of simple evocative set features was integral to the fluency, pace, and story-telling focus of the production. In an interview with Judy Adamson, Sims explains how he sees objects operating in theatre:

> ...the great thing about theatre is that you can just drag anything you want into the room that will help you tell the story, and as long as you've thought it through, that's fine.[11]

The production aesthetic was boldly and deliberately contemporary. As in Company B's production, there was from the outset a deliberate disclosure of the means of theatre that functioned as a contract between the audience and Horatio (Jerome Ehlers) acting as a club DJ. The costumes were unobtrusively contemporary. They were clothes that people might be seen wearing on Belvoir Street in Surry Hills on any day of the week in 2001 – jeans, leather jackets, business suits, and t-shirts – as fitted the role or occasion of the particular character. The exception to this was Fortinbras and his 'squad' who wore contemporary military fatigues with berets and carried automatic weapons to evoke 'the volatile world of the contemporary Balkans'.[12] Contributing to the pace and energetic contemporary aesthetic of this performance was the original music written by Aya Larkin – keyboardist and lead singer of the Sydney band Skunkhour. Scene changes were always attended by atmospheric electronic music and a mixing/sampling style of sound effects.

Jeremy Sims as Hamlet had what can only be described as a quality of 'cool'. There was a strong sense in which this Hamlet was directing the show. He coached the audience, made them laugh at his own self-indulgence and exhibited an extraordinary capacity to clown. His excitement prior to The Murder of Gonzago was expressed as crazed and impetuous joking and railing energy and drew much laughter from the audience. To this, Jerome Ehlers' Horatio provided a foil in the form of an affectionate friend counseling him to be more subdued. This Hamlet was eager, excitable, warm-hearted, vigorous, very physically impulsive and dangerous. Introversion, despondency and brooding melancholy were antithetical to his nature. To see Hamlet as an energetic extrovert was to broaden the notion of his soliloquies from the voicing of internal, psychological torment and to locate the extraordinary physical dimensions of his language. Sims' Hamlet, like Roxburgh's was not the moral philosopher; he was always communicating, never ruminating.

In 2003 the Bell Shakespeare Company performed *Hamlet* at the Playhouse, Sydney Opera House. The different spatial arrangement of the Playhouse made this *Hamlet* distinctive from the two Belvoir productions. The Playhouse is a three-hundred-and-ninety-eight seat rectangle with a conventional end stage. Although the stage itself is equipped with high technology to accommodate diverse designs and lighting capacity, the performance space is clearly demarcated from the auditorium and there is very little versatility in this respect.

The Denmark of Bell's production had a detached grandeur to it. Designed by Laurence Eastwood, the playing space appeared to be a metal box with a myriad of square holes in every surface through which beams of light entered the space. The floor was steeply raked towards the audience. A small platform extended from the rake and directly above it was a corresponding box in the ceiling of the set, the front of which was inset with three television screens. Most of the lighting effects were generated from this box. The screens were intended to give the effect of closed circuit television – conveying an atmosphere of paranoia and suspicion. However, as one reviewer put it:

> [T]he video surveillance monitors are underused and distract because the idea is only half-heartedly embraced. The

> monitors are switched on to signal arrivals...It counters the surprise element and the purpose of catching people out.[13]

The costumes, designed by Matthew Aberline, were likewise at times effective and at times distracting. Generally, they seemed to be of Victorian/Edwardian vintage, opulent and of rich colours such as dark red and charcoal. Claudius, Gertrude, and Polonius all wore diagonal sashes implying aristocracy or political rank. These costumes underwent little change from the sketches shown in the first rehearsal. In contrast, the Players' costumes were devised throughout the rehearsal period in association with their improvisatory modes of working and contributed to an arresting and coherent group aesthetic.

Leon Ford played Hamlet in Bell's production and brought to the role an energetic youthfulness. Hamlet's crisis took on the quality of disillusioned adolescent idealism. He seemed cornered by his own extraordinary intellect and his all too rapid perception of hypocrisy and treachery. Ford was lauded for his 'agility, reckless enjoyment, tenderness and apparent spontaneity'.[14] Of all the Hamlets, Ford's was the most boyish.

Adam Cook's *Hamlet* – a collaboration between the QTC and STCSA – was performed at the Dunstan Playhouse in Adelaide and the Playhouse Theatre of the Queensland Performing Arts Centre in Brisbane in 2007. Although performed in an end-stage venue somewhat like the Sydney Playhouse, Cook's production contrived at a less concept-heavy and more intimate performance of the play. Both useful and articulate, the set (designed by Bruce McKinvern) comprised a broad-faced memorial pillar which opened into a stepped arena rimmed by jagged timber palings. In its two states it spoke the monument to military valour, war, death, then, when opened – battlements, the 'Wooden O' of the Globe theatre and the psychological confinement of 'this distracted globe'.

While evoking thematic intersections with the Australian context in a non-prescriptive way this set also functioned flexibly as places rather than as a sequence of defining concepts. It made the spaces of the play accessible to the audience, lent a compelling pace to dramatic transitions, and permitted concentration on the language as action rather than as effect.

The first thing the audience was confronted with on entering the theatre was a broad-faced burnished pillar containing columns of names. This war memorial contributed a direct resonance in the performance. A familiar sight in Australia, the war memorial cannot but evoke Anzac and all its complex associations with putatively nation-founding masculine wartime heroism. Cameron Goodall's Hamlet played against this locally recognisable ideological backdrop. He was a self-ironising, witty, intimate anti-hero whose sharpest capacity was in language. Goodall was universally commended by reviewers for his intelligent and dexterous expressiveness:

> His depth of understanding and his command of the stage had the audience on the edge of their seat from beginning to end. [15]

The Fortinbras plot was cut, producing, as several reviewers noted, a claustrophobic sense of familiar turmoil. This move was critiqued as removing much of the political intensity of the play[16] turning it into a domestic tragedy. Nevertheless, it was a domestic tragedy troubled by shadows of recent war and the measures of manhood they exerted.

Hamlet and Ophelia
'The concept [of masculinity]', states R. W. Connell 'is inherently relational.

'Masculinity' does not exist except in contrast to 'femininity'.[17] If Connell's insight offers any guidance for my inquiry into masculinity and *Hamlet* it is to direct attention to the male/female relational cultures established in each production's portrayal of the relationship between Hamlet and Ophelia. How Ophelia's femininity is constructed in each production will shape how Hamlet's masculinity is understood.

Hamlet's relationship with Ophelia is fraught with ambiguities. The play gives very little information about exactly what kind of relationship it is and that which is only hinted in the play is further obscured for the contemporary audience by social, cultural, and moral assumptions foreign to its own milieu. Immediate questions that arise regarding Hamlet and Ophelia's relationship pertain to its contractual status and whether or not it is a sexual relationship. Ophelia tells Polonius in response to his interrogation that Hamlet 'hath, my lord, of late made many tenders of his affection towards me'. When asked how she interprets this, Ophelia responds: 'I do not know, my lord, what I should think'. In defence of Hamlet's manner of courtship she says, 'My lord, he hath importuned me with love in honourable fashion', and insists, despite her father's dismissal, that Hamlet 'hath given countenance to his speech, my lord, with almost all the vows of heaven' (act 1, scene 3, lines 100–14).

Whether or not Ophelia really does know 'what [she] should think' is open to interpretation and provokes the question asked her later in the play: is she honest? She consents to obey Polonius' advice to cease to speak with Hamlet. Other places from which productions draw inferences about the status of the relationship are Gertrude's expressed wish that Ophelia had been Hamlet's wife (act 5, scene 1, lines 226–9), and the bawdy content of Ophelia's songs in madness which Richard Madelaine has perceptively observed 'are concerned with rejection after sexual giving'.[18]

Company B's production of *Hamlet* directed by Neil Armfield in 1994 has been described as offering 'an approach which focussed on power and its effects, rather than on sexual engagement or oedipal undercurrents…'[19] Armfield suggested that 'at the point where the play starts, sex has become very complicated' adding that Gertrude, Claudius, Hamlet, and Ophelia are all probably engaged in 'fairly guilty sex'.[20] Betrayal and the characters' inability to reach and connect with each other, despite their intentions, received emphasis in this production. 'Out of joint' proved an apt description of the dislocation of social and relational bonds through horrific abuses of power.

In the encounter Ophelia describes with the 'mad' Hamlet, Armfield saw the crisis point of the relationship and, in some sense, of the play:

> The moment of Hamlet going to Ophelia after he has seen the Ghost, which we tried to get into Ophelia's recounting in the description of it, shows that there has been such a misunderstanding on her part and such deep need on his part, and that's why he goes to her asking for something which he can't speak, because of the size of the emotion. And she just gets terrified and goes to exactly the wrong person about that.[21]

The mute Hamlet is an unfamiliar figure. Whenever we as the audience meet Hamlet, he is talking and Hamlet's poetic loquacity proves a conspicuous obstacle to his assimilation into broadly recognised forms of Australian masculinity. Yet in this unstaged scene, pressed for significance by Armfield, we see Hamlet needing something from a woman, unable to communicate with her and leaving her terrified. This rendering resonates with the distinctively separatist masculinity of Australian legend – a masculinity expressed and validated in relationships with other men but stifled and destabilised in relationships with women.[22]

Jacqueline McKenzie's Ophelia was disturbingly fragile, not through being a vague and ethereal presence, but rather in her 'too solid' mortality and the effective staging of her mortification. Paradoxically, the neglect this Ophelia suffered on stage contributed to her prominence. Armfield describes finding her soliloquy moment following the 'nunnery scene' awkward to accommodate in the flow of the play's dramatic action. He reasons that if Polonius and Claudius had been listening all the time, they would enter as soon as Hamlet departed, not pause for her poetic moment to be fulfilled.[23] Consequently he arrived at the radical and contentious solution of having Claudius and Polonius enter and speak over her soliloquy. This polyphonic moment was dramatically devastating, and had the effect of 'bells jangled out of tune'. Ophelia moved from one violent rejection to the comfortless presence of her father and the King who paced around utterly indifferent to her, speaking solely of political expediency and banning even the slightest interjection of her grief:

> How now Ophelia?
> You need not tell us what Lord Hamlet said,
> We heard it all. (act 3, scene 1, lines 177–9)

The sense conveyed was of two worlds simultaneously in motion. Claudius and Polonius' indifference seemed less deliberately cruel than a default mode of political expediency that elided the individual and the personal. In the consequent neglect of everything pertaining to her it was easy to detect the seeds of Ophelia's mental disturbance. Ophelia was so easy to ignore that when her deranged and desperate presence did finally make itself felt, it was almost unbearable.

Ophelia came on stage wearing nothing but her father's tailcoat and a pair of white underpants (see figure 1.2). Like her songs, this outfit revealed the chief sources of Ophelia's grief: the loss of her father and her naked humiliation at being rejected by her lover.[24] This epitomises Armfield's deliberately articulated principle of only using objects that help propel the story:

> ...everything you look at visually within the space somehow carries its history and carries its story with it, so that nothing comes onto the stage (including costumes) that doesn't help to tell the story.[25]

Ophelia's disturbance was substantial and registered: the large size of her father's coat on her small frame made her look like a lost child. The dramatic transformation was of a demure and neglected figure exerting the conspicuous physical presence of her grief.

Figure 1.2 Jackie McKenzie (Ophelia), Jacek Koman (Claudius), *Hamlet*, Company B, Belvoir Street Theatre, Sydney, 1994.
Photograph ©Heidrun Lohr
Courtesy of Company B and Heidrun Lohr.

To an even greater extent than the Company B production, the Pork Chop production directed by Jeremy Sims in 2001 dramatised and centralised the dislocation of Hamlet and Ophelia's relationship.

It did so in a way that produced a larrikin masculinity identified with inter-generational conflict and resistance to domestic entanglement. The production quickly established a sense of solidarity in youthful rebellion and subterfuge. Prior to Ophelia's account to Polonius of Hamlet's 'distracted' state (act 2, scene 1, lines 75–101), the lights came up on the young couple in the ecstatic stages of an energetic sexual encounter, accompanied by rowdy rock guitar. Hamlet's groan of pleasure became a laugh. He slipped down to his knees hugging Ophelia (Sacha Horler) before she, giggling, shooed him behind the makeshift 'arras', just before her father's arrival. When Polonius entered the audience laughed, fuelling Ophelia's savvy cover-up for her excited state: 'Alas, my lord, I have been so affrighted' (2.1.76). Her following speech, usually treated as a portrait of Hamlet's derangement, made a cleverly evasive account of their vigorous sexual encounter:

> He raised a sigh so piteous and profound
> That it did seem to shatter all his bulk
> And end his being... (act 2, scene 1, lines 95–7).

Ending with 'that done, he lets me go' (act 2, scene 1, line 97), Horler moved from the spot where the encounter had minutes before taken place. The double entendre was not lost on the school-aged audience[26] and an empathetic confederacy seemed to develop from this point between the young couple and the young audience who were privy to their secret. Ophelia's witty cover-up lent her real agency and unified her with Hamlet in using his 'antic disposition' as a smoke screen for their real intimacy. The generational divide was emphasised by the fact that throughout the scene Claudius remained seated at his table in shadow – effectively they were doing it all behind his back. The choice to nurture such a version of the play accords well with Jeremy Sims' theatre-making aims:

> Whenever we do a play we're always thinking: how can we get people into a theatre that wouldn't normally go? There are some nights at the STC (Sydney Theatre Company) when it's full of subscribers – they always buy subscription tickets and they have to come along tonight. The husband's just finished work, he's turned up and as soon as those lights go out he's (snaps his fingers) out like a light.[27]

Sims' production continued with this decisive and arresting interpretation of Hamlet and Ophelia's relationship. By feigning duty to her father through a penitent embrace, Ophelia signaled behind Polonius' back for Hamlet to leave his hiding place. Ophelia was not honest. As the scene shifted back to the government office context, Ophelia finished dressing Hamlet and they made gentle affectionate farewells in the shadows, rounding off the whole encounter and subsuming Ophelia's tale within a scene of action that revealed the exact nature of their relationship.

Scenes were cut and reshuffled so that shortly after this Polonius met Hamlet leaning smugly against the wall with his arms folded. Polonius asked 'How does my good Lord Hamlet?' (act 2, scene 2, line 172) to which Hamlet responded with what was obviously ironic understatement 'Well'. At this the audience laughed uproariously and applauded. The following warning from Hamlet about how Polonius' 'daughter may conceive' provoked Polonius to grab Hamlet's collar. Hamlet responded by grabbing Polonius and tipping him over. This interaction, following close on the heels of the sexual encounter, suggested that Hamlet's drive was paradoxically vital and dangerous.

The next meeting of Ophelia and Hamlet, following the 'To be or not to be' soliloquy by Hamlet, ushered yet another distinctive interpretative choice. Hamlet recognised Ophelia's entrance: 'The fair Ophelia! – Nymph in thy orisons / Be all my sins remembered' (act 3, scene 1, lines 91–3) and broke away from his thoughts to welcome her with a kiss and warm embrace. Then Ophelia began what seemed a cryptic speech given that she had no physical objects to return:

> My lord, I have remembrances of yours
> That I have longèd long to re-deliver (act 3, scene 1, lines 95–6).

Hamlet responded plainly with:

> No, no, I never gave you aught (act 3, scene 1, line 99).

Ophelia's intended meaning became clearer when at the end of the following speech she beseechingly took his hand and placed it on her belly:

> My honoured lord, you know right well you did…
>
> Take these things again, for to the noble mind
> Rich gifts wax poor when givers prove unkind.
> *There* my lord. (act 3, scene 1, lines 99–104).

Ophelia's request to accept the gift became a plea that he not reject her because she was carrying his child. Leaving his hand where she had placed it, Hamlet fell to his knees as if overcome by the realisation. He then began to question her as if in disbelief:

> Ha, ha, are you honest? (act 3, scene 1, line 105)
> Are you fair? (act 3, scene 1, line 107)

When he spoke the words 'This was sometime a paradox, but now the time gives it proof' (act 3, scene 1, lines 115–16), he made it clear through his gesture that 'this' was Ophelia's pregnancy. He seemed unable to accommodate the weight of the new idea. 'Get thee to a nunnery' (act 3, scene 1, line 122) was spoken in reproach, forcing Ophelia roughly away with his hand on her belly. 'Get thee to a nunnery' was an exasperated rejection. Ophelia approached to comfort him in his self-deprecation ('I could accuse me...'), (act 3, scene 1, lines 123–4) but this time he pushed her away even more forcefully, hurling her to the ground.

Figure 1.3 Sacha Horler (Ophelia), *Hamlet*, Pork Chop Productions, Sydney, 2001.
Photograph ©Wendy McDougall
Courtesy of Pork Chop Productions and Wendy McDougall.

The Pork Chop production omitted entirely the plot of the eavesdroppers. Hamlet's cruel treatment of Ophelia grew straight out of his own disturbed state rather than being a response to betrayal. At 'Farewell' (act 3, scene 1, line 133) Hamlet actually left the stage and then came racing back again prompting Ophelia to cry 'no! no!,' as if anticipating physical violence from him. He grabbed her tightly around the waist and made her 'jig and amble' at his side, parading her before the audience. When he finally departed the stage, Ophelia's expression of loss was highly credible and personal rather than the detached, lyrical tribute to Hamlet that it often becomes. Kneeling downstage in the posture he had left her, she followed him off with her eyes and revealed her own understanding of the situation: 'Oh what a noble mind is here o'erthrown!' (act 3, scene 1, line 149) (see figure 1.3).

By cutting the plot of the eavesdroppers, by explicitly establishing sexual intimacy between Hamlet and Ophelia, and by making Ophelia pregnant, this adaptation sharpened the focus on, and significance of, their relationship. As with Ophelia's recalling of the sexual encounter, her imagery – 'remembrances I've longed long to redeliver', 'rich gifts' – were transformed surprisingly and credibly into bodily events. This lent the poetry a muscular immediacy and shifted the play's centre of balance so that the rupture of the lovers became its central dramatic crisis. This in turn accentuated the issue of Hamlet's masculine identity. While heterosexual intimacy animated this Hamlet, fatherhood appalled him. As a man he experienced as treacherous, the capacity of Ophelia's body to make their union into something (or someone) more than themselves. And it was this ideological and emotional positioning – this embattled masculinity – that seemed to set him adrift amongst the other vicissitudes of the play's world leading to an escalation of violence and his (and her) eventual demise. Arguably, for this Hamlet, the ghost of his father was less psychologically destabilising than the ghost of his son.

In stark contrast to Armfield's and Sims' productions, Bell Shakespeare's *Hamlet* of 2003 made a distinctive choice to emphasise the extreme youth and sexual naivety of Hamlet and Ophelia. Publicity material in a synopsis of the play describes Ophelia as 'the object of Hamlet's adolescent love'.[28] Early in rehearsal, John Bell compared the current production to recent *Hamlet*s, expressing a desire to move away from the 'cynical, domestic, grunge, angry-young-man' image. He suggested that the play could be romantic – not in the sense of being sentimental but in its scale and spiritual dimensions. He expressed interest in 'young people having some kind of idealism that gets damaged' and of them '[becoming] capable of things by the end that they were not [capable of] at the beginning'. He also saw as significant the qualities of heroism and grandness and asked 'What are these qualities today?'[29]

These notions developed in a later discussion about the scene between Laertes and Ophelia (act 1, scene 3). There arose the suggestion that Ophelia was either 'flighty and provocative or guileless and naïve' to attract such a warning from her brother and her father. Having asked the cast 'Which is it?' Bell proceeded to suggest that 'If [Hamlet and Ophelia] are very young, there is more tenderness, mystery and ambiguity if they have not slept together'. To this Anna Torv (Ophelia) conceded: 'perhaps it is true as stated: letters and gifts'.[30]

In act three, scene one, where Ophelia returns to Hamlet the 'remembrances', Hamlet's anger was seasoned with tender friendship. When Hamlet said 'I loved you not' and Ophelia responded 'I was the more deceived', Hamlet relented and ran across the stage to give her a friendly embrace. This dispelled any sense of Hamlet calculating a rhetorical assassination of Ophelia. Within this embrace he began to accuse himself of 'such things, that it were better [his] mother had not borne [him]'(act 3, scene 1, lines 123–5). This was a sincere moment of seeking solace from a friend whom he trusted. However, as he took her more into his confidence, his physical affection took on a quality at once more needy and erotic, and Ophelia began to recoil, looking around her and revealing her awareness of the eavesdroppers. The moment of intimacy and trust lent great force to Hamlet's sense of betrayal at this point. He flung himself away from her and began to attack her bitterly. The first instance of Hamlet's becoming aware of the eavesdroppers is documented as the 1820 performance by J. B. Booth.[31] Since then it has become common-place to have Hamlet make this discovery at some point prior to or during his discussion with Ophelia, but before asking 'Where is your father?'(act 3, scene 1, line 126).[32] The distinctive choice in this production was to have Ophelia as a conscious – if unwilling – agent of the deception, give away the game through her own inability to conceal her fear. Even so, there were still remnants of tenderness in Hamlet's treatment of Ophelia: unlike Sims, Ford spoke the words 'get thee to a nunnery' as a compassionate solution rather than a dismissive taunt.

Leon Ford's Hamlet deviated in important ways from the preceding Hamlets. As I describe below, he was no less a clown than Sims – he held the audience with arresting energy and wit. However, he did not exhibit the traits of stereotypical Australian masculinity evident in Roxburgh and Sims: pent-up physical power, a need for action, and a constraining awareness of sexual difference. Rather, Ford's Hamlet exhibited a liminal masculinity and in keeping with this sought a shifting combination of childhood companionship and erotic acceptance from Ophelia. This Hamlet's force lay decidedly in his intellectual and imaginative precocity rather than in action and this in itself cast the revenge commission in an ironic light.

Cameron Goodall, who played Hamlet in Adam Cook's 2007 STCA/QTC production marked a further recalibration of Ford's counter-cultural Australian Hamlet. In Cook's production the relationship between Hamlet and Ophelia, like much else in the relational world of the play, was dwarfed in significance by the war monument and all that it represented:

> it was very much about setting the whole thing in some mausoleum and about providing a strong theatrical space

where you could see…that it was a country that was going to be at war and that had been at war.[33]

This emphasis on mortality received poignant pressure in the contrast between the tenderness and possibility evident in the encounter between Hamlet and Ophelia and its eclipse by fear and betrayal. Ophelia (Emily Tomlins) crept around the broad face of the monument to meet Hamlet. The monument was in one of its transitional states – partly open – so that the backdrop appeared as rows of names of the dead with a black chasm – death itself – split just wide enough to engulf the two lovers and, as the audience knew, to conceal the two eavesdroppers (see figure 1.4).

Figure 1.4 Cameron Goodall (Hamlet), Emily Tomlins (Ophelia), Bruce McKinvern (set design), *Hamlet*, State Theatre Company of South Australia and Queensland Theatre Company, Adelaide and Brisbane, 2007.
Photograph ©Shane Reid
Courtesy of STCSA and Shane Reid.

The thrust of Cook's approach was to render accessible and immediate the emotions of the characters. His approach is undergirded by an articulated belief that emotions do not date:

> Those elements in the periodic table of human nature don't change. The feelings that exist in human nature have always been the same – whether it's high passion or jealousy rage, murderous impulses, romance, envy – they have always all existed; its just the mix or the way they are calibrated in each person is different: everybody still falls in love, young people still feel that their parents don't understand them, relationships between lovers can be incredibly intense and mutually destructive and these things have never gone away.[34]

This left the production with a problem to solve: why does Hamlet treat Ophelia in the way that he does? The attitude towards women that Hamlet projects in his neurotic rant: 'Woulds't thou be a breeder of sinners?' and 'I know of your paintings' belongs to a set of socio-cultural assumptions which are abrasive to the contemporary Australian sensibility, as is Hamlet's sudden cruelty to Ophelia. How could this be made to read as contemporarily recognisable sequence of emotions? Cook's solution was twofold: first to give an immediate and plausible motivation for Hamlet's outburst in the nunnery scene, and second, to use the scene's imagery as a driver for action.

Hamlet's motivation came from becoming suddenly aware of the evesdroppers after a moment of tender intimacy with Ophelia:

> what we decided was that Hamlet knew at a certain point that they were being listened to and that she would be complicit in that infuriated him – knowing that she had allowed herself to be put in a situation where she betrayed her feelings or her loyalty to Hamlet to two eavesdroppers was the fuel that drove Hamlet to be so abusive.[35]

This awareness instantly reframed his seemingly safe and private moment as a kind of spectacle. A long moment of silence followed in which it was clear that both Ophelia and Hamlet had registered the rupture, in Cook's words: 'I can't believe you would do this to me'. When Hamlet put Ophelia to the test asking 'Where is your father?' Ophelia responded in a fatalistic monotone as instructed: 'at home'.

At this moment Ophelia seemed a sad and painfully sentient puppet: a living realisation of the otherwise bafflingly strange imagery of the scene:

> I have heard of your paintings, too, well enough. God hath given you one face and you make yourselves another. You jig, you amble and you lisp, and nickname God's creatures and make your wantonness your ignorance.

During the following speech he slammed her hard against the monument wall and hurled her from him. His physical action Cook also described as boiling up from the imagery of the scene again – 'images of sexual revulsion the whole panoply of toxic disgusted imagery'. Hence the psychological plausibility of Hamlet's cruelty to Ophelia became the focus of this production's interpretation of the relationship between the young couple. Hamlet's madness in this moment was quite distinct from his strategic 'antic disposition': his rage and derangement was prompted by betrayal and romantic disillusionment.

In his relationship with Ophelia, Goodall's Hamlet evoked distinctly contemporary and alternative masculine typologies:

> His interpretation of Hamlet as an Emo-like, dark young man with at once both a charm and nastiness about him is something to behold.[36]

The Adelaide Review also described Goodall's Hamlet as 'emo-like',

> ...with 'his punky black hair, his goth-dark coat with furry hood and frisky stage movement, he aptly suits Ophelia's report of – 'his pale feature of blown youth / Blasted with ecstacy'.[37]

Even the appellation of this recent term for 'emotionally troubled' suggests a potent recognistion of a contemporary form of cultural altereity. I suggested to Cook that Goodall's Hamlet was by no means the 'larrikin' and he agreed adding that in his conception, this was the very reason for Ophelia's attraction to him:

> I knew that Cameron would be one of those charismatic performers where you can see how a young woman would fall under his spell and, that kind of Nick Cave allure where he's dark and the teenaged girl wants the boyfriend who's unusual and different and not driven by testosterone only.[38]

Hamlet's relationship with Ophelia has been traditionally relegated to secondary significance in readings of the play – secondary to his relationship with his mother, with Claudius, with his father and with Horatio. Ralph Berry typifies this, reading Ophelia as a kind of dramatic spare wheel by claiming that the character's function is 'to divert the audience while the star is resting'. He likens Ophelia to 'a difficult child staying up late' and suggests that 'however her scenes are played – fey, pathetic, sexual, disturbing – there will be general agreement that enough is enough'.[39]

The Australian *Hamlets* discussed here radically reject this assessment, positioning the rupture of Hamlet's relationship with Ophelia as a psychological trauma that holds ramifications for his mental stability and the way he understands himself as a man. Rather than realising Ralph Berry's valuation of Ophelia, Armfield's *Hamlet* dramatised her assumed dispensability in a way that, paradoxically, drew her plight and her person to the audience's attention. As with other pivotal moments in the play, we experienced the shock of Ophelia's degradation as if with Hamlet's eyes. We saw her the way he might have seen her had he been there, and very differently to the puzzled and bemused melancholy with which the other characters on stage regard her. Sims' Hamlet plunged to the ontological heart of out-of-joint heterosexual intimacy: 'being' appalled him in the prospect of offspring as much as in his own life. Ford in Bell's production – at once a more brainy and childlike Hamlet – sought in Ophelia a genuine companionship of a peer not to be found elsewhere. Finally, Goodall's Hamlet was conceived as appealing to Ophelia because of his alternative masculinity and received readily by audiences as a distinctly contemporary type: a Gothic Emo.

As can be seen in the productions discussed above, Hamlet and Ophelia's relationship generates a productive dilemma for Australian masculinity. It confounds the simplistic binary that sets the self-contained stoicism of the 'masculine' against the needy and dependent 'feminine'. In his relationship with Ophelia, Hamlet demonstrates complex forms of vulnerability and need which (although arguably integral to the drama as written) contradict popularly held notions of Australian masculinity. This atypical need in Hamlets who exhibit other typically Australian traits produces a marked tension, heightening the importance of Ophelia's betrayal and of their relationship within the unfolding of the dramatic plot. This in turn splinters the myth of monolithic masculinity, producing, rather, a spectrum of masculinities at play amongst complex social and relational predicaments. In each instance, Ophelia and the nature of Hamlet's relationship with her was a crucial part of the socio-relational fabric in which Hamlet existed and to whose pressures he was expected to respond. In the section below I probe further into the weave of that fabric, examining other aspects of how each production's world conceived the 'pressures of the male role'.

Hamlet and his Fathers

In the opening scenes of *Hamlet* two tests of the protagonist's masculine attributes are staged – both by father figures. From his first appearance Hamlet is required to stand and unfold himself. His expression of grief for his father – which he asserts is integral to his identity: 'Seems madam? Nay it is, I know not seems' (act 1, scene 2, line 76) – is criticised as abnormal, willful and transgressive, daring the borderlands of insanity. Both his mother and his uncle – who insists on Hamlet's status as his 'cousin' and 'son' – use a range of rhetorical strategies to urge him from his 'obstinate condolement' (act 1, scene 2, line 93). His outfit becomes a metaphor for his undesirable disposition and by her glib pairing of the two, Gertrude makes the required change seem as easy as a change of clothes:

> Good Hamlet cast thy nighted[40] colour off,
> And let thine eye look like a friend on Denmark (act 1, scene 2, lines 68–9).

Claudius' assault upon Hamlet's identity is more comprehensive:

> To persever
> In obstinate condolement is a course
> Of impious stubbornness, 'tis unmanly grief,
> It shows a will most incorrect to heaven,
> A heart unfortified, a mind impatient,
> An understanding simple and unschooled (act 1, scene 2, lines 92–7).

Claudius systematically impugns Hamlet's masculinity, his morality, his emotional fortitude, and the calibre of his intellect. In this sense, Claudius, whose dextrous rhetoric 'seems' at this point to be maintaining the delicate balance required by a troubled state, exerts pressure on Hamlet regarding his social responsibilities, long before the Ghost's commission.

The second test Hamlet undergoes is the Ghost's injunction and it likewise touches on fundamental aspects of Hamlet's identity. The Ghost imputes dullness to Hamlet should he fail to stir in response to his revelation of murder:

> I find thee apt,
> And duller shoulds't thou be than the fat weed
> That rots itself with ease on Lethe wharf,
> Woulds't thou not stir in this (act 1, scene 5, lines 31–3).

Having harrowed Hamlet with the grievous tale of his murder, the Ghost gives the enigmatic advice 'howsomever thou pursues this act / Taint not thy mind' (act 1, scene 5, lines 84–5). There is a conspicuous irony in Hamlet's following avowal:

> Remember thee?
> Ay, thou poor ghost, while memory holds a seat
> In this distracted globe. Remember thee?
> Yea, from the table of my memory
> I'll wipe away all trivial fond records,
> All saws of books, all form, all pressures past,
> That youth and observation copied there,
> And thy command alone shall live
> Within the book and volume of my brain,
> Unmixed with baser matter... (act 1, scene 5, lines 97–104).

Hamlet wills a transformation of his mind. To Hamlet his mind is the first site of resolve and the core of all action. The fact that Old Hamlet's Ghost deems it possible to pursue such an action without 'tainting his mind' serves to illuminate the difference between himself and his son.

In the first scenes of the play, then, Hamlet's credentials of masculine fortitude are tested and these tests harbour an implied threat to his mind. It also becomes obvious that Hamlet's 'madness' and what he later defines as his 'antic disposition' involves resistance to the pressures of family expectation and cultural norms. For this reason it is important to recognise that the backdrop of cultural norms against which an early modern Hamlet invented his 'antic disposition' would have been very different from that against which any twenty-first-century Australian Hamlet invents his or hers. This is what makes the play enduringly compelling and provocative. The tension between Hamlet and the cultural system in which he finds himself can unwittingly produce a probing critique of the context in which it is performed. Hamlet is a character perpetually renewed in response to the cultural moment.

Now it is time to turn to the particular social and cultural concerns which inflect *Hamlet* in Australia. A preoccupation with defining masculinity is common to all cultures in that it is one of the ways in which each new generation defines itself against the former. However, in Australia, defining masculinity across generations evokes a specific set of problems that can be seen to have provided a conscious touchstone for Jeremy Sims' conception of the play and an engaging topic of discussion for the Bell Shakespeare cast. Judy Adamson recounts Sims' approach:

> Hamlet's father, instead of being remembered as a benevolent monarch is a – thankfully dead – warmonger and tyrant... Hamlet jnr., [said] Sims, is 'scared shitless of becoming his father. When I started from this point so many things in the play made sense that had never made sense before'.[41]

In the Bell production the cast found material for their discussion of masculinity in Hamlet's and Horatio's attendance of 'school in Wittenberg'. While Old Hamlet is shrouded in myths of wartime heroism, Young Hamlet is a scholar. John Bell raised the question: 'Is Hamlet out of his time? Too rational and modern for the Viking story of lust and revenge in which he finds himself? The "Renaissance man" in a different time?'[42] Such considerations engaged the young Australian cast in a long discussion about role models, masculinity, and generational divisions.

In both instances the discussion drew on myths of masculinity that have peculiar salience in the local Australian context. In the popular Australian imaginary, our origins as a nation are bound up with masculine wartime heroism. This fusion of nation-founding and war generates cultural tension and draws focus because it is as problematic and anomalous as it is entrenched. Before I continue my investigation of Australian productions of *Hamlet*, it is appropriate to draw attention to the link between war and nation-founding in popular Australian understandings of masculinity as expressed by the Anzac legend.

In 1915, Australian troops were deployed in a British strategy to assist in opening up an Eastern Front to the Great War. Turkey had offered no aggression to Australia and offered no feasible threat in the future. Nevertheless, in the service of Empire, Australia offered troops to be used at Britain's discretion and some of those troops were sent to Gallipoli to participate in a campaign which failed resulting in 8709 deaths and over 25 000 casualties.[43] Making meaning of this enterprise has been the Australian cultural work of the intervening century. The official bipartisan public stance is that Gallipoli provided an international stage on which Australia demonstrated its mettle – responding to national necessity with great courage and at great cost. However, as recent critics of the 'Anzac myth' point out, this echoes the laudatory British sentiments of the time and could equally be seen as a politically expedient recasting of a disastrous tactical error. The public discourse surrounding Anzac has evolved from the period immediately after the survivors returned home – when it was a deeply divisive issue – to the present, where it is deployed as a rallying cry for national unity and identity. An important observation to make in the present context is that the last of the men who saw action at Gallipoli have died and that the vast majority of those who 'celebrate' Anzac Day as a national day have not known war in their own lifetime or in their own country. Like Hamlet we live in a time overshadowed by myths of past valour when war is still taking place, but always elsewhere.

What is anomalous about the primacy of Anzac as a nation-founding myth is that is that it pertains to military action that took place on the other side of the world on behalf of the Empire with whose identity Australia's was at that time wedded. Arguably, Gallipoli was about Australia's lack of national identity and self-determination but 'Anzac' has, paradoxically, become synonymous for those qualities. Moreover, it pertains to action that involved primarily Anglo-Celtic Australian males, leaving women, Indigenous Australians and migrant Australians out of the nation-founding picture. The 'Spirit of Anzac' is the all-embracing mythological entity set usefully free from its historical and political particulars which continues to be popularly regarded as an anchor for Australia's cultural identity.

To add to this masculine birth-of-the-nation myth there is the more general backdrop of Australia's social and cultural history which, in the popular imaginary, is also predominantly masculinist. From the advent of white settlement, Australia was statistically over-populated by men: convicts, sailors, bush men, explorers, bushrangers, larrikin non-conformists, governors, and soldiers who died courageously. The statistical predominance of males deviates drastically from all international norms and imaginatively the gender imbalance continues into modern Australian life. Now we have surfers, lifesavers, and sporting 'heroes'. In this narrow band of cultural consciousness, Australianness *is* synonymous with masculinity.[44] The upshot of all this is of course that the individual

Australian male is forever beset with measures, foils, and models of masculine worth.

Much has been made of how these factors may have influenced what is popularly cherished as hyper-masculine characteristics of Australian manhood. The masculinity constructed by Russell Ward's influential *Australian Legend* is summed up by Linzie Murrie:

> Our man is practical rather than theoretical, he values physical prowess rather than intellectual capabilities, and he is good in a crisis but otherwise 'laid back'.

The other feature of Australian legend remarked upon by Murrie is the homogeneity of its masculinity – identity generated through sameness rather than difference.[45] Only in relatively recent times, in the wake of continual immigration, feminism, gay activism, increasing affluence and technology, and gradually increasing recognition of Indigenous Australians has the relevance of this monotonous cultural mythology been called into question. My conjecture is that, at least partly for these reasons, the 'problem' of masculine identity continues to attract popular zeal in parallel with the 'problem' of national identity.

In short then, the particularities of the Australian context produce Hamlets for whom the socio-cultural problematics of masculinity nascent in the play become full blown. Hamlet the student with the worker/warrior father elicits a rush of recognition because he has evolved as the champion of alternative Australian masculinity – the intellectual and the philosopher. By being an intellectual and a philosopher, Australian Hamlets transgress locally dominant tropes of masculinity in ways that a British, German, or American Hamlet never could. Hamlet's mental disturbance, however it is conceptualised, is in the Australian imagination almost inevitably paired with the pressure of a widely sanctioned and oppressive masculine stereotype. This takes me back to my first

MADNESS AND MASCULINITY IN AUSTRALIAN HAMLETS

observation: that for Australian Hamlets, madness has to do with masculinity.

In exploring the Australian Hamlet's 'madness' as linked to the socialising pressures of his context, it is important to think about how the character is understood to develop throughout the play. There are two popular narratives, evident in both critical and theatrical practice, and used to interpret his trajectory. The first is the traditional conception of Hamlet as maturing towards responsibility and an acceptance of the place of his actions within the tragedy. Ralph Berry reads the character in this way:

> The final scene is therefore Hamlet's coming of age. It is his rite of manhood...At the climax, Hamlet accomplishes his revenge and does what he can to bring about a smooth transference of power to Fortinbras. These are the actions of an adult, and they are social. The alienated figure of the first four acts is transformed into the public figure of the finale. What the audience has lost in intimacy it gains in respect. It is the triumph of the public figure that we applaud.[46]

This view of Hamlet sees him as moving from petulant, paranoid, and overly idealistic youth towards recognition of his own mortality and the operation of divine providence. In this conception, Hamlet is tested and found not wanting by the tragedy, rather than innocently caught up in an accident.

The second and more recently popular conception sees the play's tragedy in the gradual and indelible damage inflicted upon a young innocent man's idealism. This populist vision of Hamlet fits well with the late twentieth-century preoccupation with adolescent angst and makes Prince Hamlet into something of an Everyman. It is typified by what Bell articulated of his 2003 vision for *Hamlet* and found even more explicitly in Christopher Stollery's account of the character he played for the Bell Shakespeare in 1992:

> In the end he is a sacrifice. He is a sacrificial lamb. He takes up the cancer of his society and is killed by it; hopefully in order that society can learn from his story – the story which he is so adamant Horatio stick around to tell.[47]

In these two stories of Hamlet's development, we read nothing less than two masculinities mapping a generational shift in emphasis. Unsurprisingly, this runs parallel with the shifting beliefs about Australian masculinity as clearly charted in public discourse on the subject of Anzac. Early commendations of the Anzacs, such as those by the British journalist Ellis Ashmead-Bartlett who observed the Gallipoli landing, traded in terms and concepts such as Berry's 'coming of age' and 'rite of manhood'. Here is a sample:

> I have never seen anything like these wounded Australians in war before.
>   They were happy because they knew they had been tried for the first time, and had not been found wanting…

> There has been no finer feat in this war than this sudden landing in the dark and the storming of the heights, and above all, the holding on whilst reinforcements were landing. These raw colonial troops in these desperate hours proved worthy to fight side by side with the heroes of Mons, the Aisne, Ypres, and Neuve Chapelle.[48]

This rhetoric suggests that the blood shed by Australians and the Australian lives lost at Gallipoli partake of a vindicating narrative of maturity and respect and public triumph. The counter-narrative becomes evident in later accounts of Gallipoli – particularly that typified by Weir's film based on Bill Gammage's *The Broken Years* (1974) and other more recent individualised accounts of soldier experience such as Patsy Adam-Smith's *The Anzacs* (1978). The key words in this valuation are waste, futility, victim, innocence and sacrifice. As Marilyn Lake has observed

> In these new histories, Anzacs were no longer the aggressive and skilled wielders of the bayonet...but the victims of war – and of the British.[49]

Evidently, the masculinity of the Anzac myth is shaped by a temporally contingent narrative trajectory. While the 'Spirit of Anzac' itself is held to be a cultural constant, the story of its constitutive manhood changes to fit the sensibilities of the time. Likewise, there is a demonstrable plasticity to Australian understandings of Hamlet's journey, and the masculinities it is seen to uphold or critique. In the discussion that follows, I will explore how the relationships between several Australian Hamlets and their fathers illustrate this plasticity.

In Bell Shakespeare's 2003 *Hamlet*, Hamlet's separateness and difference from the court was registered at the play's outset by onstage groupings of characters. While Claudius' audience stood in an arc around him applauding his speech and raising glasses to him, Hamlet (Leon Ford) stood behind them all; downstage-left and facing the audience. His remoteness was accentuated by his rigidity of stance and his black Victorian-style frockcoat that contrasted with the opulent colours worn by the other characters.

Claudius (Christopher Stollery) spoke with a noticeably regimented stress pattern and Ford's Hamlet – separate and silent – evinced an instinctive dislike of Claudius from the outset. He shuddered visibly at Claudius' touch on his shoulder and remained in a sullen and rigid attitude throughout the entire scene. Even in his first soliloquy he seemed more dejected, 'stale', 'flat', and self-deprecating than passionately outraged. The irony of comparing himself to Hercules was born out touchingly in his own slender and awkwardly rigid physical bearing.

However, he underwent an extreme transformation of disposition in the course of the play. All rigidity gave way to an engaging, gangly, energetic and often comic youthfulness. Bryce Hallett interprets Ford's rigidity at first as a kind of slow start to his performance but later suggests its significance as part of a meaningful dramatic transformation:

> [Ford's] initially rigid bearing didn't inspire much confidence or indicate the impressive portrayal he would ultimately deliver. Ford grows on the audience just as Hamlet changes and grows, and my early misgivings were soon dispelled by the agility, reckless enjoyment, tenderness and apparent spontaneity of his performance.[50]

The first hint of Ford's capacity to realise other dimensions of the character came when Hamlet was left alone having been told of the appearance of his father's Ghost. Here he moved swiftly from a dull malaise to an appetite for revelation:

> My father's spirit[!] In arms! All is not well.
> I doubt some foul play. Would the night were come[!][51]
> Till then, sit still, my soul. Foul deeds will rise,
> Though all the earth o'erwhelm them, to men's eyes (act 1, scene 2, lines 254–7).

During this speech, side-lighting cast Hamlet's shadow in looming shapes across the otherwise darkened space. While adumbrating the appearance of the actual Ghost, this moment also illuminated the complicity of the audience's and Hamlet's imagination in generating ghostly forms.

Horatio's analysis of Hamlet's breaking away from his friends to follow the Ghost is that 'He waxes desperate with imagination' (act 1, scene 4, line 87). This enigmatic comment raises questions about what kind of reality should be accorded the Ghost. Despite the fact that Horatio witnessed the Ghost's appearance – or in the case of this production, the Ghost's voice – he still implies that Hamlet's idea of the Ghost could do more damage than the Ghost itself.[52]

Bille Brown's Ghost of Old Hamlet was a daunting spectacle. Appearing above the others on the outcropping platform, dressed in a massive fur cloak and surrounded by downward shafts of light, he had a self consciously performative quality. Like the Player King and the Gravedigger – also played by Brown – the Ghost had irresistible charisma. The Ghost was enormous and Hamlet was a dwarfed, cowering form in the dim foreground. Throughout the Ghost's speech Hamlet moved through a series of positions from reaching out to touch the Ghost's hand to folding himself into a foetal position facing away from the Ghost. Hamlet oscillated between love, unmanageable grief for the loss of his father, and being ignited with vindictive purpose. The foetal position suggested a tiny boy asleep – his dreams evoking a giant heroic father. Throughout, the Ghost remained aloof and left Hamlet's outstretched hand untouched receding into darkness with the resounding command 'Remember me'. This Old Hamlet embodied a masculine war-like heroism of mythical proportions. The Ghost's lack of connection with Hamlet served to reinforce the sense of Hamlet's isolation – the extent to which he was alone with his own imagination, memory and limitations – and the extent to which he differed utterly from his model father.

Ford's Hamlet was physically debilitated by the trauma of this event. Early in rehearsal Bell suggested that Hamlet's 'Hold, hold, my heart' (act 1, scene 5, line 93) could be indicative of Hamlet collapsing and Ford captured this in his performance; crawling and gradually trying to stand up as he spoke.[53] Once standing he leapt back onto the floor like a child to write into his notebook 'one may smile and smile and be a villain'. With the appearance of his friends he snapped into what would become his antic disposition – a capricious and manic mode of behaviour streaked with darkly comic insight. Physically it contrasted with his previous state, being characterised by playful contact with others, exuberant movement, juvenile postures, humourous impersonations, and much more eye contact with the audience. He exhibited a kind of elation, self-reliance and mastery of the situation.

Paradoxically, this identity functioned less as a disguise and more as a disclosure of Hamlet's bitter disillusionment and savagely witty insights into the society around him. His ensuing sarcastic defiance of Claudius and Polonius, his raillery and animated wit, won him great popularity with the audience and seemed less a deviation from normal behaviour than the very familiar antics of a highly intelligent and frustrated adolescent. In this sense Ford's 'madness' took on the nuance of rebellion. There were poignant moments such as the 'sterile promontory' speech with Rosencrantz and Guildenstern and his 'nunnery' scene with Ophelia, where he seemed on the cusp of revealing his real fear and seeking connection, but, finding his hearers unsympathetic, he retreated into his brilliant and dismissive sarcasm. Very rarely did Ford's disposition indicate serious psychological aberration. It seemed at all times the plausible response of a young man to uncontainable grief and moral outrage as he laboured under a commission from his dearly loved father that in essence conflicted with his own sensibility.

In the 2001 Pork Chop Productions *Hamlet*, Jeremy Sims established Hamlet as a culturally transgressive figure from the outset. Usually, as described in the 2003 Bell production, the court of act 1, scene 2 is located on stage. Various figures stand around listening to Claudius' speech as Hamlet stands conspicuously remote on another part of the stage. In Sims' production, Claudius' (Tony Phelan) speech – 'Though yet of Hamlet our dear brother's death / The memory be green …' (act 1, scene 2, line 1) – was delivered from offstage. His voice was heard as if amplified by microphone across a large auditorium adjoining the actual stage space. The light and sound from this event spilled from a doorway onto the actual stage, which consequently gave the appearance of being a dimly lit foyer or anteroom. In this space Hamlet wandered around restlessly playing darts and occasionally glancing into the offstage 'auditorium'. This had the extraordinary effect of making the stage space marginal to the action of the scene and to the mainstream of political events. An inventive and economical staging solution, this communicated the large scale of Claudius' political platform while concentrating the audience's attention on Hamlet's delinquent outsider status. This was further reinforced by the fact that, although he wore the formal attire of a dinner suit, Hamlet had taken off the tie and unbuttoned the collar as if having prematurely abandoned the event he was expected to attend. He began the play escaping into solitude rather than under public scrutiny.

The way in which Claudius' public speech was delivered gave further clues to Hamlet's behaviour. It was exaggeratedly monotonous and characterised by a very rigid stress pattern. The implication was that it was being read and, like most modern political speeches, had not been written by the speaker. The balanced rhetoric: 'one auspicious and one dropping eye', 'With mirth in funeral and with dirge in marriage;' (act 1, scene 2, lines 11–12) seemed utterly unoriginal, banal and vacuous, despite sprinklings of applause at appropriate moments. Applause rose at the end of the much-abbreviated speech, at which time Claudius, Gertrude, Polonius, and Laertes emerged from the 'auditorium' into the stage space.

Hamlet maintained his detachment – sitting on the table swinging his legs and looking out to the audience – as the business of Laertes's departure was transacted. When Claudius and Gertrude did address him there was a sense that Claudius found Hamlet to be a threat. Phelan's manner was strained and his pattern of speech, although different from that of his formal address, was tight and gesturally coercive. Hamlet's sitting downstage on the edge of the table with his back to Claudius gave him a status advantage as his attention was directed vaguely outwards while Claudius' and Gertrude's attention was concentrated upon him. One derived a sense of anger and thinly veiled violence between Claudius and Hamlet. Moreover, the context of this scene being less public than is usually the case, meant that there was less constraint for them to appear amicable. When Claudius attempted to approach Hamlet, Hamlet, rather than just flinching, moved away unrepentantly. Sims' Hamlet was much less straight-jacketed by the circumstances at this point in the play than Ford's and this was reflected in his greater physical freedom.

In terms of the kind of relationship expressed between Hamlet and the Ghost, Sims' production differed from Bell's. This accords with the interpretation articulated by Sims, in which Hamlet is afraid of becoming like his father. While Ford's Hamlet evinced obvious love, grief and admiration towards the looming figure of the Ghost, and possibly an imaginative confederacy in its invention, in Sims' production, the encounter was fraught with fear and confusion. The staging of the scene meant that instead of focussing on the Ghost the audience was compelled to focus on Hamlet. Torches held by the actors were the main source of light in the scenes with the Ghost. Consequently, the Ghost was a shadowy, indistinct figure. When Hamlet followed the Ghost away from his companions, the Ghost disappeared and only Hamlet's face was starkly lit as the Ghost spoke to him. Hamlet appeared disembodied – a head only – and frozen to the spot as he stared intently into the light with a mixture of fear and fascination.

At the end of the encounter, Hamlet returned to his body and to his friends via the startling stage stunt of throwing himself off the downstage-left platform and being caught by them below.

MADNESS AND MASCULINITY IN AUSTRALIAN HAMLETS

This physical impulsiveness offered a visual metaphor for his extreme mental state. In a dextrous manoeuvre he then explained his intention 'to put an antic disposition on' and warned his friends through a caricature not to give it away:

> That you at such times seeing me never shall,
> With arms encumbered thus, or this headshake,
> Or by pronouncing of some doubtful phrase
> As 'Well, we know,' or 'We could an if we would,'
> ...
> Or such ambiguous giving out, to note
> That you know aught of me... (act 1, scene 5, lines 174–9).

Sims aped this patronising treatment with hilarious precision causing the audience to laugh, perhaps with relief, that he had not lost his perspicacity and humour through his harrowing ordeal. These quicksilver shifts became the hallmark of Sims' unpredictable Hamlet. He was dogged, impetuous, physically daring, and seemed to wield power over those around him to the end. The charisma of his antics left the audience in his thrall, and him, more the subject of delighted fascination than pity.

In the play, Hamlet explains sending Rosencrantz and Guildenstern to their execution. The Pork Chop production implied that Hamlet killed them himself. In a cold light the three stood bundled in thick coats as if awaiting the ship that would carry them to England. As he concluded his soliloquy prompted by seeing Fortinbras, Hamlet slipped behind Rosencrantz and Guildenstern as they leant against the table. Deftly, and as he spoke, 'Oh from this time forth, / My thoughts be bloody or be nothing worth' (act 4, scene 4, lines 65–6), he took a gun that lay on the table. In the following blackout, there was a scream and two shots rang out. At this point in the performance it seemed clear that

Hamlet was extremely dangerous. He had taken on the brutality he loathed and in doing so become part of the culture of violence against which he had sought to distinguish himself.

Richard Roxburgh's Hamlet for Company B differed significantly to Sims' in the treatment of Hamlet's antic-disposition. While Sims' antics and charisma rendered Hamlet's internal reality somewhat opaque, Roxburgh's Hamlet seemed more transparent. As Armfield put it, '[w]ith everything that he does, we see the forces that create it. The point of the play is that it provides all the forces which work on his mind'.[54] The transparency of Hamlet's mental state was particularly evident in the scene where the First Player recites Aeneas' Tale for him. The audience tasted Hamlet's paranoia in actually seeing the Ghost in the First Player. This striking moment in performance is described and discussed at length in the next chapter. In discussing Hamlet, Richard Madelaine made the observation about Company B's Hamlet that the distinction between his 'antic disposition' and his actual mental disturbance was not made as clear as is often the case.[55] Armfield described his sense in which Hamlet's 'madness' is a sliding scale from moments when he is 'pretending to be ratty because he is playing a game' as with Polonius and Rosencrantz and Guildenstern, through to moments of real anguish and despair. Uppermost for Armfield was that the audience be able to 'follow clearly the passage of Hamlet's mind throughout the play'.[56]

A definitive moment in the 'madness' of Roxburgh's Hamlet was that following the 'Mousetrap' and the killing of Polonius, when Hamlet was finally found and brought before Claudius in a straight-jacket. This scene usually implies some threat of violence from Claudius towards Hamlet and a great deal of witty resistance on Hamlet's part. In Bell's production, Hamlet was at the zenith of his powers, making the audience roar with laughter as he leapt about offering evasive responses to Claudius' anxious questions. In Armfield's production the visual impact of Hamlet's being bound in a straight-jacket and of Claudius' farewell 'Judas kiss' provoked a much darker prospect of how the individual can be crushed to comply with political necessity. This sense was echoed by Armfield's account of how frightening this scene was to rehearse:

> ...there was a real chill in the room, of feeling that we're actually dealing with a play that is much closer to things that scare us about our own lack of control in the world, the kind of paranoia that exists in the world for what goes on in the corridors of power and those who get caught up in those corridors and are powerless within them.[57]

Armfield's directorial choices in this instance drew attention to the contrast between the way in which 'madness' is defined from the outside and experienced from the inside. The straight-jacket functioned as a restraint to a very physically energetic Hamlet and a metaphor for the legitimised means used by an oppressive regime to quell its arch opponent.

Figure 1.5
Cameron Goodall (Hamlet), Barbara Lowing (Gertrude), Sean Taylor (Claudius), *Hamlet*, State Theatre Company of South Australia and Queensland Theatre Company, Adelaide and Brisbane, 2007. Photographer Shane Reid.
Courtesy of STCSA and Shane Reid.

HAMLET

A striking feature of Cameron Goodall's performance in Adam Cook's 2007 *Hamlet* was its emotional directness. In act 1, scene 2 Hamlet's rejection of his mother's urging to 'cast off' his grieving with his black clothes is usually performed as a rhetorical stunt – matching Claudius and Gertrude's verbal dexterity by re-citing grief. In Goodall's performance, the grief was fresh in the words he spoke and in the way he spoke them. Rather than looking at Gertrude or Claudius to launch his clever rebuttal, Goodall's Hamlet, hunched on a step downstage, seemed to falter and weep as he explained to the audience: 'I have that within which passes show: these but the trappings and the suits of woe'. Pounded by Claudius' following diatribe 'to persever in obstinate grief...' Hamlet, continued to stare straight out at the audience.

The bond established with the audience in this way continued throughout the production. A strong characteristic of Cameron Goodall's delivery of Hamlet's soliloquies was a quality of authentic appeal to the particular people in that theatre. There was an intensely local exigency to everything he uttered – even to the point of tacitly recognising and responding to the oddly stratified matinee audience. In the first soliloquy he created a sense of intimacy rapidly by establishing the unlikelihood of Hamlet's matching the revenger role he has agreed to take on:

> The time is out of joint. O, cursed spite
> That ever *I* was born to set it right! (act 2, scene 1, lines 189–90).

By pressing the 'I', Goodall emphasised the absurdity of Hamlet setting right a 'time' in which – as the looming panels of names reminded us – militant strategies had already cost thousands of individual lives. How could one more act of retributive violence achieve a setting right? And how could such an act be performed by such a character – young, articulate, introspective and decidedly counter-cultural in the way he expressed his masculinity or, as director Adam Cook described it, someone with 'a deep and soulful approach to the landscape of human feeling'?[58] In drastic contrast to Ralph Berry's heroic Hamlet trajectory, this *Hamlet*'s revenge plot was doomed from the outset. Rather than being a rite of passage to true manhood and masculine valour, embarking on the revenge commission – even as reluctantly as he did – was this Hamlet's tragedy.

This emphasis was sustained throughout the Ghost scene, where, rather than pitching it as a supernatural sanctioning of violent action, Cook conceived of it as primarily an encounter between two suffering human beings. In Cook's conception of the scene, Hamlet registered rational incredulity and personal compassion: 'how can they have seen my father – he's dead? And how can I be seeing my father right now? And how incredibly sad it is to see the father so tormented and so tortured?'[59] The Ghost of Old Hamlet was, in this production, no prototype of military valour but a damaged and ashen figure that Hamlet pursued through a cellar of oversized low-hanging light bulbs. In an eerie sequence, each bulb flared and dimmed as the Ghost passed evoking a melancholy prospect of time passing, opportunities spent or misspent, light and life run its course.

Larrikin and post-larrikin Hamlets

In discussions of Shakespeare in Australia over the past two decades, the 'larrikin element' has provided a useful nexus. Larrikinism is a point at which the hyper-masculine expressions of Australian identity: anti-authoritarianism, physical action, gender polarity and anti-intellectualism among them, can be augmented by the self-conscious playfulness of many of Shakespeare's characters. In larrikinism and in Shakespeare's plays gender reveals the true contingency of the expression of playfulness – its seasoning by socio-political factors, by commonly held myths and narratives.

Larrikinism has therefore provided a fruitful way of making Shakespeare ours as we play it. The practice has been exemplified by the earlier work of John Bell with Nimrod and the early days of the Bell Shakespeare Company. As Penny Gay has pointed out, from the 1960s through to the 1990s, Australian performances of Shakespeare's male characters began to exhibit non-conformity to nineteenth-century effeteness and English refinement and an unapologetically energetic kind of masculinity; in short, a popularly recognised Australian form of masculinity. Gay lists important characteristics of this 'larrikinism' as

> a streetwise relation with the world and especially with authority, mateship (a culture of male bonding based on the pioneer bush man's ethos), egalitarianism, hedonism, and an emphasis on physicality.[60]

Although more naturally associated with comic characters, larrikinism, in this definition, has come to inflect the way in which all Australian Shakespeare male identities are understood. An example of this is the Anzac-inflected Hamlet of Zeffirelli's film and, on stage, Mel Gibson's Romeo for the 1979 Nimrod *Romeo and Juliet*. As Kiernander points out, Bell as director articulated an emphasis on 'colour, sex and violence, rather than something too lyrical'.[61]

There is, however, another chapter to the story of Hamlet's madness and masculinity in Australia which we can read in the shifting currency accorded larrikin masculinity in Australian culture. When first coined in the nineteenth century, the term 'larrikin' was a pejorative term implying resistant modes of masculinity – non-conformity to the normative social structures of family; recklessness, drunkenness and brazen monopolizing of public spaces.[62] However, as John Rickard suggests, in becoming 'lovable' the larrikin has become a hegemonic mode of Australian masculinity. Certainly the characteristics of larrikinism have meshed in animating ways with the character Hamlet, and his 'antic disposition' – amplifying his physical athleticism and energy as in Gibson's and Roxburgh's and his clowning brilliance as seen in Sims' and Ford's Hamlets. However, in the span of years covered by the productions discussed here, Hamlet's larrikinism has also been recalibrated to give expression to more complex and subtle, if equally recognisable, experiences of Australian masculinity.

While physical energy and agility were lauded features of each of these Hamlets, the psychological plausibility of their relational crises – particularly that with Ophelia, their introspective articulacy and emotional directness seemed to splinter rather than consolidate recognisable tropes of Australian masculinity. Leon Ford's Hamlet's occupation of 'outsider' status seemed firmly linked with his articulate intellectual brilliance and the physical as well as moral improbability of his conforming to a 'warlike' model. His enthusiastic engagement with the players, his ability to recite their work and his rapt fascination in the Player's performance made Ford's Hamlet more of a nerd than a larrikin. Likewise, Sims' choice to have the final duel between Hamlet and Laertes take place as a game of darts, while certainly fitting the larrikin model, reflected a self-conscious rejection of the trial of physical valour. In a world of automatic pistols, Sims' Hamlet demonstrated how little 'masculine' courage it took to end a life. In Company B's *Hamlet*, both Ophelia and Hamlet were subjected to striking forms of physical mortification. That Roxburgh's energetic force was subdued by the ugly device of a straight-jacket, rather than by any kind of competitive encounter with Claudius, prompted yet another re-evaluation of the operation of a priori codes and coercive measures of 'masculinity'. Cameron Goodall in Adam Cook's 2007 *Hamlet* branded 'Emo-like', evinced in his demeanour, costume, and emotional directness the most marked departure from larrikin masculinity.

Moreover, each of these productions emphasise the generational conflict in *Hamlet* in a manner which maps an evolving spectrum of masculinities in Australian public discourse. In reaction to the Imperial Hamlet – a stoic combatant whose unavoidable adverse circumstances offer a platform for the display of martial courage – Roxburgh and Sims invent the larrikin Hamlet who shares something with the 'Spirit of Anzac' as the courageous participant victim of a doomed endeavour. More recently, however, Ford and Goodall have emerged as new Australian Hamlets whose loquacity, physical bearing, and intellectual brilliance ironise the revenge commission and the militaristic world-view upon which it relies. These post-larrikin Hamlets extract from the predicament the expression of an alternative masculinity. In doing so, they stage equally recognisable experience of Australian masculinity: that of being marginalised for being intellectually curious, introspective and articulate.

Bruce Smith has observed that in Shakespeare's drama 'masculinity must be achieved. It is not given'. The scenes of anxiety about male identity in the plays, Smith continues, 'should make us hear with fresh ears the lines of an irresolute son who declares, "To be or not to be that is the question" (*Hamlet* act 3, scene 1, line 58)'.[63] For Smith, 'being' resonates with the significance of being (or failing to be) properly masculine. In Australia too, the enterprises of achieving nationhood and of achieving masculinity are peculiarly and inextricably bound up. 'Being' – as a nation and as a male individual – has been equated in the Australian cultural imaginary with a prescriptive set of stereotypical masculinist qualities. Recent Australian productions of the play produce *Hamlet*'s Denmark as culturally identifiable with Australia – a space in which gender is an ontologically determining force. 'To be' is to be a man. To qualify as properly masculine involves wrestling with a rigorous set of culturally peculiar measures. This wrestle generates the drama and is, in fact, the question *Hamlet* urges in the contemporary Australian context.

2

Play, the First Player, and the idea of theatrical force

> …I don't really agree with the notion of setting the plays anywhere in particular.
> When asked that question about *Hamlet* I tend to say that it was set on the stage.
>
> Neil Armfield[1]

Hamlet is a play deeply concerned with notions of play: the power of play, the danger of play and the threshold between play and reality. When a troupe of players arrives at the court of Elsinore, the hitherto dejected Hamlet makes an enthusiastic request that they perform for him immediately: 'We'll have a speech straight. Come, give us a taste of your quality. Come, a passionate speech' (act 2, scene 2, lines 413–14). To further prompt the Player's performance, he nominates and begins a speech himself. At this moment, theatre is consciously made the centre of the action. It is one of several instances of metatheatre in *Hamlet*. Others include Hamlet's advice to the Players (act 3, scene 2, lines 1–40), Hamlet's 'antic disposition', the The Mousetrap or play-within-the-play (act 3, scene 2, lines 80–248), and Rosencrantz's report of the success of the boy players (act 2, scene 2, lines 319–46).

These moments of metatheatre within *Hamlet* have been understood, by theatre practitioners and Shakespeare scholars alike, as precious sources of inside information. Hamlet's advice to the players is a prime example:

> Speak the speech, I pray you, as I pronounced it to you – trippingly on the tongue; but if you mouth it, as many of your players do, I had as lief the town crier had spoke my lines. Nor do not saw the air too much with your hands thus, but use all gently; for in the very torrent, tempest and, as I may say, the whirlwind of your passion, you must acquire and beget a temperance that may give it smoothness (act 3, scene 2, lines 1–7).

This speech is often appropriated by directors and actors as direct instruction from Shakespeare on the subject of acting. It has also been used to support the idea that in it Shakespeare puts forward an early manifesto of naturalism.[2] Likewise the play-within-the-play has been taken up repeatedly as a key to the dramatic dynamics of the play by which it is encased.[3] Hamlet's 'antic disposition' generates a spectrum of theories: Freud saw it as purposeful ploy of an integrated personality; Robert Weimann has identified it as a complex subversion of representational logic.[4] Finally, in the seemingly obscure reference to the child players whom Rosencrantz says 'are now the fashion and so berattle the common stages' (act 2, scene 2, lines 328–9), scholars have excavated a local cultural history of London and the competition Shakespeare's company was facing from the newly emerging children's companies.[5] Of all the examples of metatheatre in *Hamlet*, least attention is devoted to the impromptu performance of Aeneas' Tale to Dido that the First Player offers in response to Hamlet's request. However, it is this instance of play-within-the-play upon which I want to focus. I believe it offers a specific challenge for the production in which it takes place and, as examples will show, constitutes a pivotal instance of the performativity of Shakespeare's plays in contemporary Australian culture.

Before discussing three remarkable Australian treatments of the First Player's impromptu, it makes sense to consider the role the speech plays within broader discussions of *Hamlet*. In what ways is the speech considered significant, if at all? The relevant editions of *Hamlet* (Quarto 1, Quarto 2 and First Folio) vary considerably in the extent to which they include the speech given by the First Player.[6] This kind of variation in editions across the plays has been taken by some scholars to indicate revision of the play not only for theatrical purposes but also for publishing purposes. Advocates of Shakespeare as a 'literary dramatist'[7] have seized upon such instances to suggest that Shakespeare thoughtfully prepared manuscripts especially for printing by deliberately including or re-introducing passages which working prompt-books from the theatre may have indicated as 'cut' for performances. Jason Gleckman goes even further than this, finding evidence for speculation about such editorial practice within Hamlet's commissioning of the First Player's impromptu.

Gleckman argues that this moment reveals Hamlet as the connoisseur of literary drama, and Polonius, through his interjection ('This is too long'), as more attuned to the needs of drama as performance. Gleckman finds evidence in the fact that Hamlet requests of the Player a speech that was 'never acted, or if it was, not above once; for the play, I remember, pleased not the million' (act 2, scene 2, lines 416–18). Aeneas' Tale, Gleckman pursues, was perhaps encountered by Hamlet 'as an excerpt, a recitation, a formal rhetorical display that is precisely not acted but spoken, a work of art more appropriate perhaps to the printed page than to the stage.'[8]

The problem with Gleckman's argument is that it automatically positions 'speaking' and 'formal rhetorical display' – practices whose early modern vitality is inaccessible to print-saturated cultures such as our own – as quaint sub-genres of printed drama. My point is that, as an impromptu instance of play, the recitation is in fact a heightened instance of performativity – one that pushes play, its dangers and valencies, to a crisis. In a forceful performance by the Player this point is borne out by the onstage response to his unprecedented power and by the audience's empathy with this surprised response. As Polonius discovers, it is a mistake to equate 'recitation' with a contained and predictable outcome. In the productions under discussion, it is not the refined 'literary' nature of the speech that impresses Hamlet, Polonius, or the theatre audience. It is rather, the raw power of performance, despite its limited means, to compel.

The First Player's speech has a unique significance in the play's ongoing discourse of play. As an impromptu, the performance activates the manifold nature of play: 'play' as a game, 'play' as performance, and even 'play' in its technical sense, as space allowed for a 'moving part.' It is a staged moment in which both the fiction and the power of performance can be acknowledged simultaneously. As such, it sets up a test, not only for the First Player, but also for the actor and for the audience.

Hamlet requests of the First Player a performance of Aeneas' Tale to Dido which recounts Pyrrhus's violent slaying of ancient Priam, and Hecuba's grief and rage at her husband's slaughter. The Tale, as a story of grief and bloody revenge, has immediate implications for Hamlet's predicament and provokes Hamlet into a frenzy of self-abasement. The test that every production of *Hamlet* encounters at this juncture then, is whether or not the First Player can realise the *idea* of theatrical power. Hamlet's fervent anticipation, Polonius' dismay at the Player's force of performance, and Hamlet's ensuing soliloquy will only work if the Player's performance is, in fact, forceful. If the Player does not compel and astonish the audience, it will seem incredible that the on-stage audience is so deeply affected. While it may seem an elaborately clever and digressive theatrical 'in-joke', this scene is quite the obverse. It is an acid test for drama's capacity to compel.

The scene also harbours a challenge for the audience. The challenge is to see with what W. B. Worthen calls the 'double-vision' of 'theatrical seeing'. In his essay on *Antony and Cleopatra* he explicates this complex notion in a manner pertinent to the First Player's performance of Aeneas' Tale:

> The actor seems to inform and to stand apart from his 'character', and our task is to enable this double perspective to become part of our play, rather than a necessary failure of art, the falling short it may otherwise seem to be.[9]

While Worthen is describing Antony, his insight proves apt for the way in which the First Player 'informs and stands apart from' his narratorial persona. Whatever the First Player's resources are, his force must ultimately inhere in the 'falling short' of his ability to *be* Aeneas. His force resides in the poverty and transparency of his means for making theatre. Worthen's 'double vision' is not innate to modern audiences. Most contemporary dramatic mediums, such as film, sustain audience complicity through the creation of a complete, self-contained 'reality' – a seamless illusion. In contrast, Shakespeare's *Hamlet* is self-reflexive; it constantly draws attention to the greater reality by which it is encompassed: an audience in a theatre, watching actors perform as characters. The challenge for the audience then, is to remain consciously complicit – to submit to the fiction even while being aware that it is a fiction.[10]

Aeneas' Tale is a deliberately obvious contrivance and so functions to keep part of the imagination awake, as it were, to the powerful effects of a dream. Moreover, this microcosm of the theatrical moment reflects upon the overarching dynamic of theatre, compelling recognition of its simultaneous actor/character paradox. Hamlet the character uses the force of the Player's acting to berate himself for his own inaction. Here we see an ever more intricate spiral of self-reference. Hamlet's 'rogue and peasant slave' soliloquy (act 2, scene 2, lines 526–82) is of course no less a performance than the Player's Tale. Moreover, the close proximity and shared heightened style of the two speeches serve to reinforce their mutual status as performance. 'Now I am alone…' (act 2, scene 2, line 526), is ironic when addressed to a theatre full of people. With this phrase the actor who is playing Hamlet embarks upon his 'tale' for the audience, just as the Player has performed the Tale for him.

In his study on mimesis in *Hamlet*, Robert Weimann ably explains the complicated relationship between Hamlet as character in a play and as the *'actor-character* [who] revitalises, on the dramatic plane of stylised art, the legacy of the Vice actor as director and master of ceremonies theatrical'.[11] Most relevant to our inquiry is Weimann's point that Hamlet disturbs simple mimesis by being both its product and, consciously, its producer. Hamlet is 'a character performed in a role and one who himself performs and commissions a performance'.[12]

Weimann's work participates in an enduring legacy of 'stage-centred'[13] theorising that identifies metatheatre as an intrinsic dynamic of Shakespeare's drama. The various nuances of metatheatre as a theoretical concept have been long debated. However, the degree to which the play's metatheatricality is exploited, and the force of the First Player's impromptu are necessarily determined afresh by each instance of performance. In an attempt to address this fact, I investigate the very different uses made of this scene by three recent Australian productions.

The productions in question are *Hamlet* directed by John Bell for the Bell Shakespeare Company in 2003, *Hamlet* directed by Jeremy Sims for Pork Chop Productions in 2001, and *Hamlet* directed by Neil Armfield for Company B, Belvoir in 1992. Each of the *Hamlet*s under discussion reflected an awareness of the self-referential power of the scene but utilised that power in radically different ways.

Bell Shakespeare's *Hamlet*: show-business

In the Bell Shakespeare Production, the Players were marked out from their first entrance as belonging together and to a world different from the court. They created a distinctive stage picture – forming a line along the far horizon of the stage and then stepping forward to fill the space in a stately yet energetic manner. The moment of their arrival created a new warmth and sense of anticipation. Discussions during the rehearsal period had yielded an aesthetic loosely associated with 1930s Eastern Europe and drawing upon a notion of the poor and itinerant actor. Names circulated while discussing the aesthetic of the dumb show and The Murder of Gonzago were 'Berlin Cabaret', 'Kurt Weill', 'Fred Astaire and Ginger Rogers'. In a discussion of how actors' public and social identity had changed during the last century, Bille Brown and John Bell contributed their reminiscence of the time when an 'actor wore a suit and tie to rehearsals and a dinner suit to radio broadcasts.'[14] The Players' costumes gave the impression of formal attire that had become shabby with age. They carried a combination of old suitcases and assorted props. Bille Brown, who as First Player led the troupe on stage, had an ostentatiously theatrical style resembling popular images of Oscar Wilde. He wore a wide brimmed hat, a cravat and a short flowing cape.

The behaviour of the Players was brimming with delightfully recognisable modern 'show-biz' idioms. During the interval, while audience members returned from the foyer and found their seats, the Players 'warmed-up' on stage for their *Murder of Gonzago* performance. The First Player and Hamlet (Leon Ford) held conference downstage as if finalising details for the 'show.' Paul Eastway and Julian Garner practised sword fighting with wooden sticks and Luisa Hastings Edge, presumably the troupe's diva, stood in a silk gown alternating elaborate vocal scales with smoking a cigarette. The effect was a humorous inversion of the onstage/offstage divide, bringing the means of theatre to the audience's attention by performing, as it were, the chaos of the dressing room.

It is illuminating to trace the development of this cohesive troupe identity back to the distinctive rehearsal strategy employed for the Players. Most of the play's scenes were approached through the conventional progression from reading and discussion around a table followed by the actors getting on their feet to block the scene on the marked-up rehearsal floor. In contrast, the Players' scenes were deliberately permitted a period of formlessness. Even costuming and music decisions were allowed to evolve as the group identity of the Players evolved.

During the first week of text rehearsals, the Players spent afternoons working with Darren Gilshenan – an associate artist with the Bell Shakespeare Company recognised for his skills in physical comedy. Gilshenan led one session of improvising in which the Players were prompted to explore their identity as a troupe by preparing for a journey, travelling together, and arriving at Elsinore. The actors adopted objects and items of clothing as suited their storytelling. The text of *Hamlet* was not used at all in this particular session and very little of the improvised material appeared in the eventual performance, but it is important to note this practice as a fully embodied approach to interpretation. As such it reversed the usual format of intellectual engagement with the script before 'moving it'. The way play was used in the formation of the Players' identity contributed a force to their use of the play-within-the-play. In the First Player's playing of Aeneas' Tale to Dido this production realised on stage the idea of theatrical power prefigured in the text.

Bille Brown's evocation of Hecuba, grieving and raging through burning Troy, was an extraordinary transformation; all the more so for its physical improbability. Brown's shaman-like

PLAY, THE FIRST PLAYER, AND THE IDEA OF THEATRICAL FORCE

power consisted in the utter simplicity of his magic, in his gift for storytelling. For 'Pyrrhus's sword,' a member of the troupe handed him a cricket bat. Such was the power of the storytelling that even this ludicrous device seemed transformed to support it. Similarly, with Hecuba's 'blanket:'

> But who, O who had seen the mobbled queen –
> ...
> Run barefoot up and down, threat'ning the flames
> With bisson rheum; a clout upon her head
> Where late the diadem stood, and for a robe,
> About her lank and o'er-teemèd loins
> A blanket in the alarm of fear caught up – (act 2, scene 2, lines 482–9)

At this point the Player used his own cape – clutching it with a painfully feeble gesture in front of him. The Player's utter commitment to his story transformed him and the energy of the stage. It was as if he had become a vortex of intensity – winding in the unsuspecting court and the theatre audience. The performance feat was neither an act of mimetic impersonation nor simply one of narrative description but rather a kind of conjuring which included both.

The effect of this conjuring was intensified rather than diluted by Polonius' (Robert Alexander's) interjections. During the first part of the Tale, Ford as Hamlet set himself up as the model audience member. After his own applauded attempt at the speech, he made room for the First Player; crouching and watching with his arms across his knees in a posture of childlike curiosity. The first part of the Tale reached its climax:

> And never did the Cyclops' hammers fall
> On Mars his armour, forged for proof eterne,

> With less remorse than Pyrrhus' bleeding sword
> Now falls on Priam (act 2, scene 2, lines 469–72).

At this Polonius made his interjection: 'This is too long' (act 2, scene 2, line 478).[15] The mounting tension of the speech was at this moment attenuated by Polonius' inability to 'submit to the fiction'. Yet this breach in the Player's performance only served to emphasise the accumulated tension. The Player appeared to absorb Polonius' interruptions and proceed to the mesmerising climax of the Tale where Hecuba runs through burning Troy to find 'Pyrrhus make malicious sport / In mincing with his sword her husband's limbs...' (act 2, scene 2, lines 493–4). It was at this point that Polonius seemed to undergo a revolution. From being unable to 'submit to the fiction', he moved to being unable to see it as fiction. To re-invoke Worthen's terminology, he was not able to hold in tension 'the reality of the Player' and 'the reality of the characters' he played and so called a halt to the performance in a compulsive and frightened manner:

> Look whe'er he has not turned his colour, and has tears in 's
> eyes. Prithee no more (act 2. scene 2, lines 499–500).

Polonius seemed perplexed when the Player emerged from his role seemingly unscathed, pleased with himself and applauded by his troupe.

The 2003 Bell *Hamlet* exploited the way in which this scene models various versions of what Worthen calls 'theatrical seeing'. Hamlet recognises and later expresses perplexity at the enigmatic relationship between performer and character:

> Is it not monstrous that this player here,
> But in a fiction, in a dream of passion,
> Could force his soul so to his own conceit

> That from her working all his visage wanned,
> Tears in his eyes, distraction in 's aspect,
> A broken voice, and his whole function suiting
> With forms to his conceit? (act 2, scene 2, lines 528–34)

Yet it can hardly escape the audience's attention that the actor who is playing Hamlet is at that moment doing no less. Ford's performance of this speech reinforced the parallel between the Player's and his own facility. In rehearsing this scene, Bell worked closely with Ford – paying attention to the cyclic rhythms of 'winding up and crashing' within this speech. As an exercise, Bell directed Ford to 'make it about movement' and to 'exaggerate the polarities of the speech' by alternating between 'dragging' and 'stretching' and 'running' while speaking it.[16] In performance the effect was multi-layered. At one level the character, Hamlet, was grappling with the enigmatic idea of dramatic transformation. At another level the actor, Ford, was effecting transformation. Goaded by the changing tempo of his speech, he proved himself as capable as the First Player of a mercurial transfiguration.

Pork Chop Productions' *Hamlet*: mixing and sampling

Like the Bell Production, Pork Chop Productions' *Hamlet* of 2001 registered and exploited metatheatrical possibilities of the play. The actors continually gave the impression that they were playing: both playing a game with each other and playing as performers. The aesthetic of the production was directed at a youthful audience. Its energy and fast pace were facilitated by the absence of clear divisions between audience and performing space. Much of the action took place in aisles beside and behind the audience. The formality of the conventional scene-change sequence was challenged by a radically fluid grammar of stage movement, including rapid cross-fades used to 'turn on' and 'turn off' different parts of the space. Characters could step out of one scene and immediately into the next. Often, characters from previous scenes remained behind in shadow and these overlapped scene transitions, as well as being economical, allowed meaningful resonance between consecutive scenes. During the entire scene of Hamlet greeting Rosencrantz and Guildenstern, Polonius and Claudius could be seen in the shadows, sitting at a large table and sipping their drinks. As a consequence of this scene overlap, Hamlet arrived at the realisation that his friends were in fact 'sent for' against the sinister backdrop image of Claudius and Polonius' machinations.

The entire performance was framed by a device which drew attention to its status as performance and implied a recognisably contemporary form of audience/performer relationship. At the beginning of the performance, with the house lights up, a young man in jeans and a long brown leather jacket, a bag slung over his shoulder, dashed down onto the stage and took a moment to look around him. This produced giggles of uncertainty and a gradual hush across the audience. He then moved onto the downstage-left platform and stood at a set of turntables, switching on a desk lamp as the theatre lights dimmed. He put on a set of headphones, pulled some records from his bag, put them on the turntables and began mixing a heavy electronic beat with gothic pipe-organ sounds. Concentrating until he was satisfied with what he had set in motion and moving to the beat, he then raised his arms to the audience in peerless DJ style, receiving laughter and applause for his feat of 'cool'. A recognisably popular and contemporary mode of connection was immediately established between the performer and his audience. At this point, another man dressed in military fatigues, beret, and holding a pistol charged down the stairs yelling to the DJ: 'Where is this sight?' to which the DJ responded

> What is it you would see?
> If aught of woe or wonder, cease your search.
> ...

> And let me speak to th'yet unknowing world
> How these things came about. So shall you hear
> Of carnal, bloody and unnatural acts,
> Of accidental judgements, casual slaughters,
> Of deaths put on by cunning and false cause,
> And in the upshot, purposes mistook
> Fallen on th'inventors' heads. All this can I
> Truly deliver (act 5, scene 2, lines 306–7 and 323–9).

By cutting and sampling the script, Horatio (Jerome Ehlers) anointed himself the modern-day storyteller, the repository of the play's events and the mixer of its music. Moreover he made a self-conscious claim to the worth and reliability of his tale: 'All this can I / *Truly* deliver' (my italics). To this claim the uniformed figure, now revealed to be Fortinbras (Sims), replied:

> Let us haste to hear it,
> And call the noblest to the audience (act 5, scene 2, lines 330–1).

This interaction completed the inventive opening sequence or prologue that set up a direct, meaningful connection between a modern-day type of story maker and his audience.

The deliberate emphasis upon performance, and performance of stories, was furthered by the First Player's rendition of Aeneas' Tale to Dido, which diverged radically from the conventional playing of the scene. An airy electronic music – hitherto unused – ushered in a dim light on the downstage-left platform to reveal a young man with a shaved head wearing jeans, a T-shirt and running shoes, and adjusting a microphone stand. (This was the same platform upon which Horatio had mixed his music and upon which Hamlet had been recently abandoned after his encounter with the Ghost.) On the black wall behind the performer a large red skull was still visible: at once an enduring icon of mortality and a popular motif in contemporary skate designs.

Having adjusted the microphone the performer signaled to Horatio who stood, once again, at the mixing desk. Hamlet (Jeremy Sims) sat in the dark beside Horatio. These forms would have been immediately recognisable to younger audience members as preparations for performance in a bar or club. The performer – Aya Larkin from the Sydney band Skunkhour – may also have been familiar. Larkin performed Aeneas' Tale to Dido as performance poetry set to music. The piece began with Pyrrhus' state of paralysis:

> So, as a painted tyrant, Pyrrhus stood,
> And, like a neutral to his will and matter,
> Did nothing.
> But as we often see against some storm
> A silence in the heavens, the rack stand still,
> The bold wind speechless, and the orb below
> As hush as death, anon the dreadful thunder
> Doth rend the region... (act 2, scene 2, lines 460–7)

The 'silence in the heavens', was evoked by the quiet delivery of the lines and the eerily faint sounds of the electronic music. On the word 'thunder', the volume of the music increased and the performer was bathed in red light – making the skull behind him prominent and casting his shadow large against the wall.

The 'Player' introduced Hecuba: 'But who, O who had seen the mobbled Queen' (act 2, scene 2, line 482) with a marked intensity of grief in his voice. A distinctive funk beat was initiated which, from this point on, functioned as a leitmotif for Hecuba. As the Tale came to a close, the Player crouched, cupping the microphone in his hands and repeating the high-pitched and mournful appeal: 'Do you see her?' The intense commitment of the storyteller to his story was reflected in his capacity to transform; to sculpt his posture and his voice to the demands of the narrative. This innovative treatment of the Hecuba scene comprised a stylistic deviation from conventional interpretations yet captured in a contemporary mode the essence of the Hecuba moment – a moment where both the fiction and the power of performance can be simultaneously acknowledged.

Sims also found ways of challenging the traditional dynamics of the play and the theatre space in his performance of Hamlet's most famous soliloquy. 'To be or not to be' is a phrase that has been inscribed over time with the tenor of lofty philosophical musing. It is a fragment of Shakespeare with which almost every English speaker is familiar. In contemporary spoken English the phrase is such a common cultural possession that it is hard to imagine what it was to hear it for the first time or what kind of meaningful impact it may have carried. As Terence Hawkes aptly observes

> [i]n our society, in which *Hamlet* is embedded in the ideology in a variety of roles, the play has, for complex social and historical reasons, always already begun. And onto its beginning we have always already imprinted a knowledge of its course of action and its ending.[17]

Sims' treatment of the famous soliloquy, rather than trying to reinvent its significance, reflected an arch awareness of its common currency and thereby gave it back to the audience in a new way. After interval, Sims came down through the lit auditorium, distributing cushions on the steps in preparation for the next scene sequence that included The Mousetrap. He paused halfway and, beating the iambic stress pattern in the air like a conductor, said to the audience 'To be or not to…', to which the audience appended 'be!' with audible delight, followed by laughter. The audience's attention was fastened on Sims as the house lights dimmed and he descended to the stage to continue his speech. Having established a particular kind of casual energy, Sims proceeded to set up the stage for the next scene as he spoke. He took a corner of the large draped red cloth, and hooked it to a pulley on which it was hoisted to achieve the effect of apron space in front of a stage curtain. He spoke the speech in an energetic and demonstrative way as he worked, challenging its typical status as an abstract philosophical musing. To punctuate the line: '...to take arms against a sea of troubles, / And by opposing, end them' (act 3, scene 1, lines 61–2), he mimed pulling a gun from his jacket and shooting himself in the head. 'To grunt and sweat under a weary life' (act 3, scene 1, line 79), was likewise animated with a shoveling gesture. This demonstrative and self-conscious style employed by Sims cleverly acknowledged the inherently histrionic quality of the speech, while giving it a clear and specific physical meaning.

Company B's *Hamlet*:
'How all occasions do inform against me'

In their article 'Elsinore at Belvoir Street: Neil Armfield talks about *Hamlet*', John Golder and Richard Madelaine unearth a deep cognisance of metatheatre in Company B's 1994 *Hamlet*.[18] As well as documenting a conversation with Armfield and his assistant director, Greg McLean, Golder and Madelaine re-trace comments made in previous interviews and by reviewers of the production:

> A love of actors and the act of theatre are key metaphors in *Hamlet*, Armfield believes, because they elicit a recognition that the play is so much about a person's desire to act with absolute conviction, and the acting analogy is germane to it.[19]
>
> [Armfield] likened Hamlet himself to the 'method' actor trying to find the moment of pure inspiration where the body and mind join; one intuitive moment of truth where action is not calculated but 'natural' and 'felt'.[20]

PLAY, THE FIRST PLAYER, AND THE IDEA OF THEATRICAL FORCE

These comments reflect a consciousness of the play's intricate games of self-reference that resulted in an intelligent and highly articulate approach to its performance.

Like the Pork Chop *Hamlet,* this production had Horatio (Geoffrey Rush) open the play as storyteller. However, the full cast was also assembled on stage, reflecting an important principle of this production. It was not seeking to trick its audience about the means of theatre:

> Geoffrey Rush as Horatio came forward to deliver lines transposed from the final scene, together with lines from the play-within-the-play. This device established Shakespeare's world as uncertain, dangerous and violent: what this company of actors will enact for us is a disturbing miscellany of 'carnal, bloody and unnatural acts…accidental judgments…deaths put on by cunning and false cause'.[21]

Greg McLean expressed how this narrative moment of 'trying to find a language to tell the story' had resonance for the rest of the performance:

> We are struggling to find the spine of the language that we are inventing to tell the story with, and that is the actual key: we know the story essentially, but it is exactly that Brechtian idea of 'here we are as actors, the magic that you see will be just us'.[22]

While the function of the actors was made plain from the prologue, the physical means of this production were also pared back to a bare minimum. Rather than attempting to create an alternative reality or fully convincing illusion of 'another' place, this production embraced the characteristics of its actual physical setting. Upstairs Belvoir as the home of Company B is imbued with a certain imaginative heritage. Armfield exploited the extent to which this venue, without extensive set construction, was an evocative space. He expressed this aesthetic in the simplest terms:

> …I don't really agree with the notion of setting the plays anywhere in particular. When asked that question about *Hamlet* I tend to say that it was set on the stage.[23]

The main set feature was a vivid red Persian carpet that was rolled up, unrolled, moved on and off stage, and re-oriented on the floor by the actors themselves. In her review for the *Sydney Morning Herald* Angela Bennie went so far as to ascribe to it a cryptic quality, calling it a 'silent, blood-coloured but bloodless witness to the moving patterns of people and events that swirl around it'. She applauds the moment in performance when as Hamlet, '[Richard] Roxburgh in his fire has swept it up off the stage and hurled it around him like a cloak, its patterns cascading down his sides and across his body'.[24]

The carpet was a simple, malleable and yet intensely evocative piece of set design. The paradoxical wealth and economy of the carpet epitomises Armfield's notion of the link between transparency of means and the power of storytelling. Madelaine and Golder's interview provides evidence that this consistent preferment of clarity and simplicity pervaded production practices. A specific instance is recounted in the evolution of the Ghost.

The initial concept for portrayal of the Ghost was to project a filmed image of the Ghost in armour onto the wall. There would be no actual physical presence. However, as rehearsals proceeded, this technologically sophisticated version was abandoned in favour of a much simpler one described by Armfield:

> I asked Ralph [Cotterill] to do it and it was so powerful as a scene between the two actors that it seemed that, no matter

how effective the technology might be, if you only have Hamlet on stage something's going to be missing, and so it was really from here that I became more convinced in my heart that Ralph should be doing it.[25]

Ralph Cotterill's doubling as the Ghost and the First Player carried a revelatory dramatic force with the simplest of means. Rather than attempting to evoke a sense of the supernatural through effects, as the Bell and Pork Chop productions did, this production reinforced the fragility of the Ghost. Wearing nothing but a thin white grave cloth, he emerged from one side of the playing space and spoke while, with a hunched and halting gait, completing a tight arc around Hamlet to exit from the other side of the stage. All the while his eyes were fixed on Hamlet, creating a mesmerising intensity between the two actors.

Even more haunting than the Ghost in this production, however, was the ghost of the Ghost appearing before Hamlet and the audience in the form of the First Player. The Ghost's plain human presence on stage and Ralph Cotterill's doubling in the roles permitted an unprecedented resonance between this scene and the parallel narrative of Aeneas' Tale to Dido. As the First Player performing the Tale, Cotterill traced an identical trajectory to the Ghost's – circling Hamlet in a tight arc as he rendered the story. Consequently, the Player's power over Hamlet and over the audience watching Hamlet watch the Player, had an utterly harrowing effect. The poses and postures of the Player's performance minutely recalled those of the Ghost. A powerful precision of dramatic narrative characterised this moment and many others throughout the performance – as if the bare stage itself had become imaginatively engraved with the pathways and postures of the storytelling. The First Player's apparent ignorance of the power his story wielded was eerie, as was the moment when, looking at the Player, one saw the Ghost, and so gained access to the theatre of Hamlet's mind (see figure 2.1). The audience was herein permitted a special intimacy with the subjective – otherwise seemingly paranoid – vision that goads Hamlet to exclaim 'How all occasions do inform against me / And spur my dull revenge' (act 4 scene 4).

Figure 2.1 Ralph Cotterill (The First Player), *Hamlet*, Company B, Belvoir Street Theatre, Sydney, 1994.
Photograph ©Heidrun Lohr
Courtesy of Company B and Heidrun Lohr.

From the three productions discussed above, it becomes evident that metatheatrical moments in *Hamlet* contribute to the play's complex discourse on play by invoking the manifold and interrelated meanings of the word 'play'. Aeneas' Tale to Dido is at once a game, a performance, and figuratively, a space designed to accommodate a 'moving part' – the actor. Metatheatre as a form of self-referentiality might more normally be considered the province of postmodern cultural production. In *Hamlet* though, as in many of Shakespeare's plays, metatheatre functions to provide space for the 'moving parts' integral to drama. Metatheatre creates this space of play by provoking acknowledgement of the unique and temporally bound nature of each performance of the play.

Paradoxically, metatheatre within Shakespeare's play-text invites constant re-evaluation of what it is to perform with force here and now. If imported or outdated notions of forceful performance are relied upon, the production will buckle upon itself at this scene and become a sentimental tableau. Conversely, if the First Player does possess the power to compel, drama itself is vindicated and possible meanings of the play are vitalised in a new theatrical moment of being.

Each of the *Hamlet*s examined in the present chapter bears out this point in that each drew upon specific and recognisable conventions of performance to make the Player's Tale compelling. The Bell Company production drew on familiar features of twentieth-century theatre culture – the dressing room antics and 'warm-up' rituals, of a resourceful, rag-tag band of travelling performers. Pork Chop Productions seized upon a different, yet equally recognisable contemporary performance trope – that of late twentieth-century forms of club entertainment – music mixing and sampling and performance poetry. The Player's Tale within the Company B production drew its force from an even more immediate source – the particular convention of 'haunting' already established in the same production by the appearance of the Ghost. In each instance W. B. Worthen's insight is borne out; that 'performance always takes place in present behaviour', and that theatre does not cite text, it cites behaviour'.[26] *Hamlet* can therefore be seen as a play that toys with the instrinsic contemporaneity of the genuinely dramatic moment. In this light, it is not the space *Hamlet* colonises in our cultural imaginations but the spaces it opens up, that keep it playing.

PART II

AS YOU LIKE IT

3

Re-imagining Arden in Australian space

In 1863 Shakespeare's *As You Like It* was performed at the Theatre Royal in Melbourne. The production design received high praise for its faithful representation of Arden:

> There is scope in *As You Like It* for first-class ability in the production of the mimic scene, and it would be difficult to speak in terms too laudatory of the manner in which Mr Hennings, the artist of the Royal, has accomplished his task. His forest scenes have all the fidelity to nature which characterises Creswick's sketches. The representation of the wood of Arden, with its shaded knolls and leaping brooks, its sunny openings and grand old trees, becomes a palpable fact under his hand; and while looking at his umbrageous scenes, one could almost forget that the glare of gas is all around, and no light of heaven visible.
> *The Examiner, and Melbourne Weekly News*, 15 August 1863.

This review of Barry Sullivan's *As You Like It* gives us a taste for the way in which nineteenth-century Australian sensibilities shaped an understanding of Arden. The appraisal is steeped in the romantic value of verisimilitude whereby the greatest art achieves 'fidelity' in its replication of 'nature'. However, this reviewer finds himself in an aesthetic and geographical double-bind as he reviews an English play, evocative of the English pastoral setting, played on Australian soil. His yardstick for the production's 'fidelity to nature' is not nature, Australian or otherwise, but the work of a British landscape painter, Thomas Creswick. If verisimilitude is a paradoxical aim where extreme artifice is employed to *re*present reality, then this Australian instance of pastoral imagining adds paradox to the paradox. Removed by thousands of miles and many weeks' travel from England, the reviewer registers no disjunction in claiming the English pastoral mode as 'nature' by default. He presents this 'nature' as a universal constant. 'Nature' is an idea deployed to erase the difference between theatre and reality and between England and Australia. Arden is, moreover, made a kind of cultural embassy so that walking into the theatre effectively transplants the relieved settler on English soil for a few hours.

Since 1863 the story of *As You Like It* on the Australian stage has been one of challenging the identification of Arden with the English pastoral setting and the political ramifications that attend it. While the twentieth century offered the first radical re-imaginings of Arden's relationship with Australian physical and human geography, it was also characterised by intractable nostalgia on the part of theatre critics for English pastoral and pictorial realism. Such nostalgia, while appearing as a defence of the 'original' Arden is grounded more in the settler's sentimental ties with English theatrical tradition than in the play's altogether more complex and ambivalent discourses on nature. Contemporary Australian political and cultural developments have further inflected the meanings made possible through performance of the play and several productions from the late twentieth century and early twenty-first century reflect this: Simon Phillips' production for Sydney Theatre Company (1996), Neil Armfield's for Company B, Belvoir Street, Sydney (1999) and Lindy Davies' for Bell Shakespeare in 2003.

Shakespeare's Arden and Australia's *terra nullius*

Before taking a look at the re-imagining of Arden in Australia it makes sense to ask what kind of Arden we are presented with in Shakespeare's play. Shakespeare's Arden is not a self-evident physical location but a 'landscape'. As Paul Makeham points out 'landscape' is not a naturally occurring empirical reality. Rather, it is a human construction, a discursive formation related to – but distinct from – the 'land'. Makeham also observes that 'landscape… implies a viewer, a human presence whose description (representation) of the environment proceeds according to a vision shaped by a particular set of cultural orientations'.[1] By these definitions Arden is the quintessential landscape. It is a space constructed to fit the vastly varied visions of 'human presences': both the characters who inhabit it and the audiences who respond to it. In Australia, Arden has been formed discursively, that is to say, through the interaction of conflicting ideas. In 1863 Arden was employed to establish English pastoral on Australian soil and to cancel the dissonance of the Australian physical context. Since then we have witnessed a collective re-imagining of Arden as a landscape in which distinctly Australian conceptions of space and place are at play.

If there was anything authentic about Barry Sullivan's 1863 Arden it was not its faithful recoupment of Shakespeare's English pastoral but its capacity to fulfill a wish. Shakespeare's Arden is akin to the 'antipodes' in European Renaissance imagining in being a blank space onto which fears and fantasies are projected. Unlike, for example, the coast of Illyria where Viola actually begins her participation in the dramatic action of *Twelfth Night*, The Forest of Arden is prefigured as a mythical place; a beneficent 'other' space of Utopian dimensions. Charles reports to Oliver of Duke Senior

> They say he is already in the Forest of Arden, and many merry men with him; and there they live like the old Robin Hood of England. They say many young gentlemen flock to

him every day, and fleet the time carelessly, as they did in the golden world (act 1, scene 1, lines 121–6).

Charles's repetition of the phrase 'they say' signals the second-hand orality of the information that he himself performs with a kind of nostalgic lyricism. In Shakespeare's play, Arden is a landscape of the imagination conceived and constructed through verbal accounts.

Unlike Charles' imaginings of Arden, Rosalind's are full of apprehension. Arden's very distance from the court is coupled with a sense of danger:

> Alas, what danger will it be to us,
> Maids as we are, to travel forth so far!
> Beauty provoketh thieves sooner than gold. (act 1, scene 3, lines 112–14)

Rosalind links the journey's 'danger' with her and Celia's gender identity. Her parenthetical maidenhood is what builds 'danger' into the conceptual equation. But this is a double-sided quip. If gender can be constructed and deconstructed, disguised and disclosed, then perhaps the 'danger' of Arden can be disentangled too.

As Robert N. Watson points out, Duke Senior also partakes of an anthropomorphising tendency central to the paradoxical aspirations of the pastoral mode.[2] The Duke's attempt to eschew the artificiality, the 'painted pomp', of the court comprises an intricate linguistic appropriation of nature that ultimately distances him from it. He colonises Arden rhetorically by finding 'tongues in trees, books in the running brooks' and 'sermons in stones' (act 2, scene 1, lines 16–17). Duke Senior's 'wilderness' is a wilderness of androcentric linguistic construction.

Operating within the conventions of romantic love Orlando's attempts to inscribe the Forest with his own identity are predictably maladroit. He carves bad poetry on the 'trees': 'O Rosalind, these trees shall be my books / And in their barks my thoughts I'll character' (act 3, scene 2, lines 5–6). Yet, Orlando's inscription is a complex act. Ostensibly he is leaving his mark on nature but on the metatheatrical plane he is actually bringing nature into being. Whatever the actor playing Orlando has at his disposal becomes a tree when he says 'these trees'. On the Globe stage the word and the action might have made a tree of a column. With more literal and pictorial designs, the terrain is less volatile, and there is less the need for Orlando to make trees with words. Nevertheless, the language remains pregnant. The theatrical Arden is potentially born and re-born at each performance by that temporally bound act of speech.

Paradoxically then, Shakespeare's Arden is both empty and full: of substance chimerical but thick with myths such as Charles' 'golden age', fears such as Rosalind's that the journey there is fraught with terrors for women, and constructions such as Duke Senior's 'life more sweet'. In the Australian context, as a domain of questionable identity and contested ownership, Arden evokes issues of both historical and contemporary political exigency. Of immediate significance is the concept of *terra nullius* – land belonging to no-one – an ancient legal doctrine which for many decades served, in popular understanding, as a justification for white settlement in Australia.[3] In 1992 the 'Mabo' judgement by the High Court of Australia recognised the concept of native title in Australia – that Indigenous ownership of land precedes Crown ownership. This judgement articulated a formal and public rejection of the doctrine of *terra nullius* as a pretext for white settlement.[4] While the ramifications of the Mabo judgement have met with cultural and political resistance at many levels, it is fair to say that in the past two decades dominant (settler) definitions of land ownership have undergone both legal and ideological challenges. And if, as *As You Like It* suggests, words make places, then the reinvigoration of Indigenous place names in public discourse is intimately bound up with a much needed collective re-imagining of Australian space.

Along with *terra nullius*, the other conceptual intersection between *As You Like It* and Australian cultural history is the experience of exile. Exile to Arden has a potentially stinging pertinence in the Australian context because of Australia's history as a penal colony to which British convicts were transported. Many non-indigenous Australians have either ancestors who were transported or reasonably recent family histories of displacement through immigration. Equally pertinent to our discussion of kinds of Australian exile is the displacement experienced by Indigenous Australian, as a result of policy decisions by British and Australian governments. Exile of one kind or another is a ubiquitous part of the Australian psyche. Moreover, literal exile has a mirror image on the cultural plane: the 1863 reviewer's posture of 'cultural cringe' towards Europe.

Unsettling Arden: the late twentieth century

The re-imaging of Arden during the second half of the last century in Australia had a variety of expressions. These ranged from relocating the play setting indoors, to performing it outdoors, and from simply replacing the aesthetic elements of the English pastoral with those of the Australian, to deploying the pastoral problematics of the play to interrogate specifically Australian political circumstances. Unsettling Arden's meanings provokes a nostalgic backlash from reviewers and critical recourse to the idea of Shakespeare's original Arden. This pattern of reception is evinced most pointedly in response to the first Australian attempts to move away from what was essentially a Victorian 'sylvan' aesthetic.

In 1971 Jim Sharman directed the play for The Old Tote in Sydney. The design by Brian Thomas evoked a child's nursery complete with giant perspex cubes and an assortment of toys.

RE-IMAGINING ARDEN IN AUSTRALIAN SPACE

The young cast used the aisles as well as the stage space playfully. While one reviewer commended this production's 'infectious exuberance',[5] H. G. Kippax for the *Sydney Morning Herald* offered withering criticism. He accused the 'Messianic Mr Sharman' of turning 'the vintage champagne of *As You Like It* into ginger Pop'.[6] Notably his criticism pivots upon the production's putative mis-construction of Arden:

> What point can there be to the discussion of love when the lovers, as here, are babies playing at love? Or of responsibility and order when there is not an aristocrat in sight? Or of nature when the Forest of Arden with its cold winds and 'adversity' becomes a kind of Elysian playing field?[7]

In 1978 Aubrey Mellor directed the play for NIDA (National Institute of Dramatic Arts) at Jane Street, Sydney. This production came hard on the heels of the dismissal of Prime Minister Gough Whitlam by the Governor General and the retreat of ex-treasurer, Jim Cairns, from the political sphere. It engaged with a particular vein of disillusioned idealism. Mellor sought out direct parallels with the Australian political context:

> I just gave the audience something to hang onto very quickly by making the bad Duke very like the Governor General John Kerr who sacked Whitlam and…Jim Cairns was, you know, a bit of an old hippie – a Tweed jacket and talking about how wonderful it was in the Forest…Being in the city was…to do with survival of the fittest. Escaping from the regime was like: Do you actually leave Western civilisation behind? Do you actually start again? Do you drop…this terrible thing we've evolved to? And if you do start again, what is it?[8]

Reflecting on the production, Mellor oscillates between describing Australia and describing his Arden in a way that reflects his imaginative merging of the two. Mellor's typified a new approach to Arden – a specifically Australian politicising of its exile motif rather than a recuperation of the English pastoral. Arden became a useful tool for querying the idea of flight from urban-based political corruption. Trees and leaves were again banished in favour of a contemporary play space – 'a useful, open acting space, landscaped luxuriantly with hay coloured carpet, [that] had the visual effect more of a trendy rumpus room than a rich and dangerous retreat…'[9]

The 1981 Queensland Theatre Company production charted a return to the romantic aspirations of staging pastoral by performing in Brisbane's Albert Park. What is most curious about the critical response to this production is its lexical similarity to the reviews that praise the pictorial realism of the nineteenth century. Jean Sinclair in an article entitled 'Play in an ideal setting' makes the statement that 'there hardly could be a more perfect representation of the Forest of Arden'. Sinclair describes the 'Arcadian delight' of a production complete with 'weeping figs', 'pages ringing cowbells and four horsemen riding mettlesome steeds', 'baying bloodhounds', 'giddy gamboling goats', and ends in praising the 'picturesque spectacle' of the 'merry marriage scene'. Sinclair finds herself in the same aesthetic and geographical double-bind as the 1863 reviewer – praising an Australian production using the language of nostalgia for British pastoral.

In 1983 John Bell and Anna Volska directed a production for Nimrod Theatre in Sydney that took into account aspects of the Australian physical setting. The set, in contemporary fashion, resisted pictorialism while the costumes bore a distinctly Australian outback aesthetic. The play was set in the early depression years, contrasting the sinister urban gangland context to the Australian outback. For actor Robert Alexander, who played Jaques, this production was 'less specific' than Mellor's direct political comment but more 'dressed as Australia': 'It was very "Oz"...almost corks hanging from hats and that kind of thing.'[10] This comparison is informative. In being 'dressed as Australian', Bell's production accomplished something altogether different from Mellor's – it found a ready corollary for English pastoral in Australian pastoral.

This populist appropriation of Arden as one critic recognised, swapped distant myths for a new cache of local myths about settlement and landscape:

> Instead of the romantic pastorale of Arden, we have the Australian Utopian myth of the new country, fresh fields and untainted opportunity. And – Shakespeare's point – against it hard facts of wool-growing and weather'.[11]

While one critic deplored what he calls 'a hideous line-up of stark, leafless tree trunks beneath which "greenwood" nobody in their right mind would want to lie (let alone make love)',[12]

Kippax commended the possibility offered by 'Mr Eastwood's carved and leafless Arden, a forest seen as a cloister'.[13] The 'outback' of Bell's production fits Joanne Tompkins' observation about the receding signifying potential of the bush in Australian theatre. Tompkins suggests that by the 1960s, due to demographic shifts, the tendency to use the bush landscape to stand for Australia as a nation was succeeded by the use of the bush to stand for history and 'as a site for re-thinking national landscape and identity'.[14] While being much less overtly political than Mellor's Arden, Bell's stylised 'outback'-Arden met with critical resistance which is perhaps indicative of its participation in such 're-thinking'.

The Arden concept: Sydney Theatre Company, 1996

Sydney Theatre Company's 1996 *As You Like It* was a lavish and technically sophisticated production designed by Michael Scott-Mitchell (set), Nick Schlieper (lighting), and Simon Phillips (direction and costume). The conceptual coup, which drew both praise and censure from reviewers, was the use of words as physical denotation of the play's locations. The 'orchard' comprised a shallow stage with a row of black topiary animals along the rim and the word 'orchard' in glossy black on the matt black wall. The removal of this backdrop presented a deepened space with billowing blue silk scrim and lit flares emerging from the floor. Again, the location was signified literally by a large slanting brassy sign saying: 'COURT'. This was followed by a quick alternation between the orchard and the court before the final and most exquisite scenic revelation. The blue silk of the court backdrop disappeared into a trap in the stage to reveal a jumbled array of giant, tarnished-gold letters on a concentric double revolve. Despite the lazy tilt of the 'F' across the 'O', the 'FOREST of ARDEN' was discernable in autumnal disarray (see figure 3.1). In the centre a small ensemble accompanied jazz singer Kerrie Biddell in her sultry number: 'Under the Greenwood Tree'. Biddell's 'Come hither, come hither, come hither' was a direct invitation to the audience who applauded the striking and fluid transition.

Many reviewers praised the ingenuity of this design. John McCallum's review headlined 'Postmodern Bard matched by brilliant performers' praised the ironies, contemporary pop culture references, self-reflexivity, 'showbiz exuberance' and 'glorious pastiche' of the production. In doing so, he pointed to the congruence of the play and the postmodern aesthetic:

> Four hundred years ago this play took the Elizabethan conventions of the pastoral and revelled happily in them while at the same time exposing their unreality – a type of nostalgia

which we now like to think of a defining characteristic of postmodernity.[15]

Figure 3.1 Michael Scott-Mitchell (set), Nick Schlieper (lighting),
As You Like It, STC, Sydney,1996.
Photograph ©Philip le Masurier
Courtesy of STC and Philip le Masurier

Like that of many Shakespeare reviewers, McCallum's highest praise was reserved for the production's fidelity to what is assumed to be the play's original purpose. While less sophisticated critiques claimed universality of Shakespeare's 'themes' and made the tiresome quip that Shakespeare would have liked the production, McCallum registered a subtler affinity in the way that both the play and the production resisted generic classification.

Some reviewers placed emphasis upon the anti-pastoral implications of the design:

> This textual Forest of Arden is decidedly autumnal – no green world here. It starts out red, a jazz cellar which could be in another wing of the Duke's palace. There is at first no sense that the exiles have fled the court at all. They have

simply found a more congenial part of it. In the modern world there is no duality between the city and the forest.[16]

Brian Hoad for *The Bulletin* commented that

> ...the Forest of Arden is just that – writ large in giant letters of tree-like form, forever moving on a double revolve like some giant game of computerised Scrabble...Arden has become a sort of fancy-free nightclub where 'love is merely a madness'.[17]

The dissonance of this geometrical and autumnal forest was lamented in the *Newcastle Herald*, 1 February 1996:

> This production has a vaguely 1950s look and most of it is ugly. This is a comedy for the most part set in a forest, yet the only touch of green is in the opening orchard scene (and it's a green that's almost black).

Uncannily, such responses betray an assumption shared with the 1863 reviewer in his praise of the 'mimic scene' – that a design represents exclusively and fixedly what it most clearly resembles. In this paradigm of theatrical representation there seems to be limited awareness of what Tompkins has identified as the methektic approach to theatre space which permits it to signal multiple and overlapping realities.[18] In the mimetic framework the forest is understood exclusively as a jazz cellar or a nightclub. But this neglects the potential of performance and embodied language to transform the significance of space. The giant letters in Phillips' production were constantly imbued with transcendent 'tree-ness' through the performers' movement over and amongst them. There was a sense of fun, energy and physical adventure in the way actors disappeared through the letters or strolled amongst them that was far more suggestive of an outdoor context than a nightclub or cellar. Tangled through this is the wonderfully three-dimensional, Magritte-flavoured irony that this at once is the 'FOREST of ARDEN' and 'is not' the Forest of Arden.

The narrower appraisals of the production also miss the dynamic valence of speech, and, in this case, of dimensional text. Fortunately the audience did not. At the performance I attended there were gales of laughter when Anita Hegh as Rosalind entered saying 'Well, this is the Forest of Arden' (act 2, scene 4, line 15). For centuries actors have been walking onto stages saying 'Well, this is the Forest of Arden' when it is not. In this instance it actually was the 'FOREST of ARDEN' in a wittily denoted sense. The words were literally the substance of Arden. The logos was the logs. This should alert us to the way in which Shakespeare's drama plays with and upon and around the performative potential of language – the potential of language to bring things into being; 'to do things'.[19]

It is difficult to crystalise the meta-linguistic layering of this production into an interpretative unity. It sprawled. The sense of mischievous linguistic construction reached its peak at the end of the play. A figure dressed as Shakespeare descended from above on a giant quill to watch the nuptial celebration and went to work scribbling on a scroll. In an awkward pause he gestured offstage to an actor who entered uncertainly. The Shakespeare figure played by Paul Livingston (who, by this stage, was clearly the production's interpretation of Hymen) tossed the scroll to the newly arrived actor and urged him to read it. The scroll apparently contained the speech by the 'second son of old Sir Rowland' announcing the unlikely conversion of Duke Frederick to a religious life and the return of the lands to the exiles. Read and stumbled over with all due uncertainty as if for the very first time, these statements were met by howls of derisive laughter from the other actors. The actor 'playing' this second son responded by turning and pointing accusingly to Hymen (Shakespeare) as if to blame him for the gross improbability of this closure. There could hardly be a balder instance of deus ex machina than flying Shakespeare in from 'the heavens' to preside over and resolve the action of the play.

Figure 3.2 Paul Livingston (Hymen/Shakespeare), Michael Scott-Mitchell (set), with Lucy Bell, Raj Ryan, Max Cullen, Kerrie Biddell,
As You Like It, STC, Sydney, 1996.
Photograph ©Philip Le Masurier
Courtesy of STC and Philip le Masurier.

Phillips' production was brash and intellectually savvy in the way it invented Arden. Phillips, who previously directed a production of *The Tempest* set at the time of the First Fleet's arrival explained his approach: 'what I really look for is the element of the play that will bring it closest to [and]…give it the greatest pungency for the modern audience. But I don't think that as a general rule, I look at that with Australian specificity.' With *As You Like It* Phillips said

> I was interested in the liberation, the abrupt…sense of liberation that the forest gave all who entered it. I really focussed… on that jazz musical world…I'd always had…a feeling that it was almost a show that could be done by cabaret performers. It seemed to me that the clowns in the forest were a series of star turns for comedians.[20]

Phillips' production created a space unhinged from tropes of either the English pastoral or Australian landscape. It invented a palpably modern, culturally sophisticated space peopled by Australians – many of them well-known celebrities. This Arden negotiated with the broader western heritage of sensational pictorialism and with contemporary currents of postmodern pastiche taking the penchant for spectacularly literalistic forests a clever step further.

Backyard Arden: Company B, 1999

In an entirely contrasting manner, Belvoir Street's 1999 *As You Like It* directed by Neil Armfield also engaged with the play's production history and issues of contemporary cultural significance. While the Arden of Company B's production was relatively simple in its design features, it was interlaced with intricate political nuances. The kinds of meaning this production made available were intimately linked with a number of features: the physical space of the theatre and the micro-culture thereby influenced, the evocation of Arden, and the casting of Indigenous Australian actors. Belvoir Street theatre offered a more intimate, informal and communal space than the proscenium-arch design of the Sydney Drama Theatre and, because the stage was flanked on three sides by audience, there was little facility for elaborate apparatus of illusion. That being said, the space was a flexible one. Actors could enter and exit from many directions beside, beneath, and through the audience. The positioning of the three sets of audience stalls meant that the front row members of each stall could rest their feet on the edge of the stage. The seating consisted of long cushioned benches and from any point in the audience the audience member had other audience members in her direct field of vision. This contributed a sense of communal experience.

Set designer Robert Cousins and lighting designer Mark Howett arrived at a structurally simple space whose evocative potential rested upon one major scene change and the flexible effects of innovative lighting. Conceptually it was a fluid and cohesive design. The opening scenes of the play, set in Sir Rowland's orchard and various places around Sir Frederick's court, were typified by limited light and 'specials' operating in a largely bare space. The naked walls of the factory with their streaked concrete were a strong feature – softened by warmer lights in scenes between Rosalind and Celia and made to resemble an urban alley in the combative encounters between Orlando and Oliver. The wrestling scene was played in a coldly spot-lit square chalked on the canvas floor. All of the early scenes of the play were either dimly lit or lit intensely in parts leaving large areas of the stage in darkness.

This contrasted sharply with the daylight quality of the forest scenes initiated by the simple and miraculous transition to Arden. At the end of act one scene three, about thirty-five minutes into the performance, the court became the forest. What had been up until this point the grey canvas 'floor' of the stage was hoisted on poles to form a star-littered blue canopy over the entire stage space. The newly revealed stage floor appeared as a sunlit lawn, scattered with eucalyptus leaves. The transition was mechanically simple – effected by the actors themselves attaching lowered hooks to the canvas, and accompanied by music (composed by Alan John). As in Simon Phillips' production, the transition to the forest ushered a new dynamic between performance and audience. The flood of warm light spilled over into the audience giving a greater sense of inclusion.

The way in which the grassy open space was used also conveyed a sense of liberation from physical and social constraint. Most of the characters had bare feet and spent their time sitting or lying upon the inviting space of the grass. When the Duke's company was joined by Orlando (Aaron Blabey) and Adam (Ralph Cotterill) they shared their feast with the front rows of the audience. Rosalind and Orlando's interactions were characterised by playful and relaxed physicality: chasing and tickling (see figure 3.3). The mood of the forest stood in sharp relief to the chicanery of the court, the brutality of the wrestling and even the intense, rapid word wit of Rosalind and Celia's opening exchanges. Arden was established not only as visually and sensually contrasted to the court, but also as an utter change of pace and sensibility.

Figure 3.3 Deborah Mailman (Rosalind) and Aaron Blabey (Orlando), *As You Like It*, Company B, Belvoir Street Theatre, Sydney, 1999.
Photograph ©Heidrun Lohr
Courtesy of Company B and Heidrun Lohr.

In the final scenes, the spatial identity of this Arden was confirmed as being closer to a suburban backyard than a wilderness. The lighting shifted to skim across the grass and reflect from the stars in the canopy, giving the impression of a lawn on a summer evening. After all the matches were made the cast broke into a joyous gospel-style version of 'Wedding is Great Juno's Crown' accompanied by a guitarist (Wayne Freer). Freer then interjected as the 'second son of old Sir Rowland' before accompanying the cast in a jubilant rendition of 'There was a lover and his lass'. All the players danced together as Adam / Hymen set a sprinkler going on the lawn amongst them. When the water stopped, the footlights remained skimming the stage as a night–lit lawn. The laughing Rosalind, in a white summer dress with a hibiscus in her hair, addressed her prologue to the audience. Her mien encompassed authority without hauteur, warmth, passion and a kind of familiarity as if among friends.

Much was made of this playful closure and many reviewers saw it as an explicit stamp of the production's Australian identity. Julietta Jameson for *The Daily Telegraph* described the production as '[a] fabulously frolicsome argument for getting in touch with your inner child, Australian style, which is to go for a metaphorical romp in the backyard'.[21] Armfield himself explained the design choices in similar terms. Despite the obvious trend of comparisons with the *Hamlet* he directed four years earlier, Armfield drew an imaginative link with the much-loved Australian *Cloudstreet*; a novel written by Tim Winton, adapted for stage by Nick Enright and Justin Monjo in 1998, and directed by Armfield:

> The set has a sense of not moving into a forest at but moving into the backyard of *Cloudstreet*…To me this production is derived more from doing *Cloudstreet*…than *Hamlet*…The forest is a kind of released imagination. It is a speculation on

what the potential of a person is once the pressure of fear is taken off them.[22]

That Armfield's production of Shakespeare's play should be likened to *Cloudstreet* suggests a fond and potent identification with the setting. Armfield evoked an Arden that Australians recognised as personal and local.

The most significant feature of all in Company B's Arden was the immediacy of Australian concerns raised by casting Indigenous Australians; Deborah Mailman as Rosalind and Bob Maza as her father the deposed Duke. The cast also included two other indigenous actors: Bradley Byquar playing Dennis and Sylvius, and Irma Woods playing Phoebe. These casting decisions and the kind of a cultural junction they represented were the subject of much discussion. Some commentators saw it as announcing a new era of 'colour-blind casting' while others concentrated on the specific political implications made by the production. Conversely, many reviewers made no reference at all to the casting. In an interview recorded during the rehearsal period Mailman expressed her indigenous identity as having a two-fold significance in relation to performance:

> I think there's your personal development as an artist as well as concern for the social development of the community. The two go hand in hand...My choices have to be quite smart in the respect that it's not just me on stage but it's the rest of my people, too. At the moment, when we walk on stage it's a political statement because of where we are as a country in terms of race relations and reconciliation. So it can't only be Deb Mailman. It's Deb Mailman and a lot of history.[23]

Mailman expresses consciousness of the fact that as an Aboriginal actor in the contemporary cultural climate in Australia, her physical presence has a political resonance of its own. In interviews, Mailman and the other indigenous performers relate experiences of playing or being asked to play 'token blackfellas'[24] remarking that *As You Like It* was different. While, Armfield describes his casting decisions with reference to land: 'I don't know an indigenous actor who doesn't bring with them a strong sense of connection with the land...',[25] his production resisted an oversimplified polemic. As Helen Gilbert and Jacqueline Lo have identified:

> [B]y transforming the Forest of Arden into a suburban backyard rather than a more iconically 'indigenous' (outback) setting, the production avoided suturing Aboriginality to landscape, even while drawing on the body cultures of the indigenous actors to suggest their characters' connection with the land and to link the Duke and his daughter's exile to the historical dispossession of Aboriginal Australians.[26]

Rather than focusing upon the obvious external ramifications of having black actors in conventionally white roles, Armfield's comments focused upon the internal qualities and imaginative resources brought by all actors:

> An actor's Aboriginality can inform a story really wonderfully, and in that way no one is neutral and everyone brings a kind of cultural meaning into their presence on stage'.[27]

An example of the activation of this specific 'cultural meaning' was offered in the banishment of Rosalind by Duke Frederick. This moment was injected with chilling dramatic power through Mailman's Aboriginal identity and her choices in performance.

She bore his outrageous rebuke in stony silence, standing remote from him. This in itself differed from other productions where the character falls on her knees to plead clemency. Celia, played by the diminutive Kirstie Hutton, ran at her father in a rage, thrashing at his chest and wrapping herself around his feet in pleading. Rosalind remained still, making her case in a cool manner until the point where Frederick implied that her fault was inherited and lay in being her father's daughter. At this Rosalind turned and addressed him with fury: 'So was I when your highness took his [kingdom]; / So was I when your highness banished him' (act 1, scene 3, lines 53–4). Changing the word 'dukedom' to 'kingdom' gave the line a more general and readily recogniseable significance. A 'kingdom' is more apt to be construed poetically as representing abstract qualities of identity and space than a 'dukedom.' Rosalind became for that moment, as Mailman hints, the voice of her displaced people. The speech, which is often given as a placatory, rhetorical stunt showcasing Rosalind's resourcefulness, became a searing indictment of a specific Australian injustice.

Armfield's production levelled imaginative redress at a range of overly simplistic conceptions of Australia. It played with the malleability of the Forest of Arden, unsettling its accustomed pastoral implications by repositioning it within distinctly Australian spaces and experiences. The *terra nullius* myths of Arden and of Australia were challenged at once by the casting of Indigenous Australian actors. At that juncture of history, seven years after the Mabo judgement, Aboriginal Australian characters dwelling as exiles in Arden provided a pressing reminder of the abuses and ideological impositions involved in the act of settlement. Moreover, prior to the official Australian government apology to the Stolen Generations, Mailman and Maza in their respective roles as Rosalind and exiled Duke Senior gave particular dramatic poignancy to the experience of displacement.[28] At the same time, the playful comedy of love between a white Orlando and an Aboriginal Rosalind and the final evocation of a suburban backyard infused the play's resolution with communicable kinds of innocence and the possibility of reconciliation. Far from conjuring a fantastical and exotic escape from society, this production charted an enlightened return to a familiar location.

An actors' Arden: Bell Shakespeare, 2003

If Company B's 1999 *As You Like It* was criticised for being too light-hearted, then Lindy Davies' 2003 production for the Bell Shakespeare Company suffered the opposite vein of criticism. This production, like Simon Phillips' – designed for the large state theatre spaces – was sumptuous and elaborate. However, unlike Phillips', it was intended to tour to a number of locations. To create a set adaptable to a range of venues, sculptured fly-screen wire was used as the main structural element. On different stages this yielded differing results. When effectively lit from behind, as was possible in the Playhouse at the Melbourne Arts Centre, the layers of sculpted fly-wire gave an appealing impression of layered depth, evoking the enchanted forests of pantomimes. In contrast, on the much shallower stage of the Playhouse at the Sydney Opera House, the crumpled fly-wire was chiefly lit from the front, resulting in a more opaque textural quality that resembled the inside of a cave.

Reviews of Davies' production of *As You Like It* articulated a perplexing range of understandings of its Arden. It was lauded as 'mysterious and glimmering', and criticised as 'the territory of nightmare', and 'a very personal pantomime version' characterised by esoteric symbolism.[29] Examining the imaginative aspirations that shaped Arden during the rehearsal process offers some explanation for this distinctive splintering evident in reception.

On the first day of rehearsal for *As You Like It*, it became obvious that Davies' vision for Arden was much informed by her vision for the rehearsal room. Arden, like the rehearsal room, provided a space to escape determinism and to renew creative autonomy:

> The court is a place of collusion. Every day we have the choice to collude or not to collude. I think that's what the forest is about – a place where people find authenticity. That is the frame. That's how it is for me today. It might change.[30]

Authenticity was both the goal and means of the creative process in Davies' rehearsal room. Actors were challenged not to jump to interpretative solutions early in the rehearsal process, and not to make decisions about character 'intention', but rather to maintain their individual creative autonomy and a spirit of 'active receptivity' towards each other and towards the language while working. This had ramifications for how Davies saw her own work as a director. To the actors she said, 'I do not want to impose a world. I want the world to come out of you in your reading of the play. What is your personal connection with the material?'[31]

In contrast to the conventional model of blocking, Davies' rehearsal period was characterised by long periods of seemingly shapeless, exploratory activity or play.

In the 'abstract' phase in particular, actors were urged to appropriate physical properties and interact with the space as they saw fit while working 'hands free' from a script projected overhead. Set and costume decisions as well as patterns of movement within the space emerged and were 'imprinted' using this physical process rather than being 'blocked' and 'rehearsed'.

One result of this distinctive process was some actors felt very physically and imaginatively at ease with the set – seeing it as an organically evolved and collaborative work of creativity. Catherine Moore who played Celia described the set as supportive and flexible emphasising the benefits of working with set elements throughout the rehearsal period. When asked about the difference between the court and Arden as expressed by the set, Moore gave the following response:

> Moore: It becomes a home, the set...In terms of me relating to it and feeling at home in the world, it's fantastic.
>
> Flaherty: Does [the set] give you what you need to feel the different location of the court and the forest?
>
> Moore: Yes it does, but you also have to remember that I'm projecting that as well. It's in us and we hope that the audience sees that in us. And we're in different costumes. You endow each other and you endow the set and you endow the audience. It's really supportive in that way.[32]

In contrast, Robert Alexander, who played both Duke Frederick and Duke Senior in Davies' production, expressed a sense that the forest did not adequately provide a place of change and refuge from the court. He described this Arden as more enigmatic and European than those evoked by the productions in which he was previously involved:

> Aubrey [Mellor's] was a place of sunshine, the Nimrod production – John Bell's – was a place of much more realistic Australian bushland...and of course Lindy's [Davies's Arden] was a place of enchantment. But I found it to be a place of gloomier enchantment.
>
> ...Whereas the Nimrod set was a forest of trees, but of gum trees and various props were improvised from the Australian bush and there were billy cans – things that were very Oz. In Lindy's not so – it was much more European in many ways...

> Even though it was blue and silver and it had the magic of light being used, I never felt as if the forest was a place of refuge and change from an unpleasant and oppressive court.[33]

Unlike Phillips' or Armfield's productions, Davies' production did not alternate scenes between court and forest – the objective being to complete all the court scenes and then make a complete transition to the forest. The transition to the Forest of Arden was achieved by a combination of mechanical technology and manual adjustments performed by the actors. It took a considerable amount of time and was intended as a metaphorical adjunct to the play's other kinds of transformation. As Davies expressed, the transformative influence was not simply that of the forest upon the characters: 'When we move into the forest, the forest will be transformed by us in many ways.'[34]

First, a chandelier suspended above the stage shattered releasing a flurry of silver and blue metallic fragments. 'Foresters' appeared on stage carrying a large piece of netting to which shards of reflective blue and silver plastic were attached. This, the foresters attached to hooks on lowered ropes. The net was then hoisted up to form an impressive canopy of flickering shards. The fly-wire that formed the backdrop was lit from behind, lending added depth to space, and a shaggy carpet of black and blue strips of fabric was laid out to cover about a third of gently raked, silver-panelled floor. Foresters also manipulated the fan-shaped screen of bamboo poles to form a kind of enclosure that was soon revealed as Duke Senior's hideaway. The music, composed by Alan John to accompany the transition, included glassy, chiming sounds in keeping with the cool enchanted aesthetic of this particular forest space.

Responses by reviewers were typified by diverse opinions. Bill Perret for the *Sunday Age* praised the appealing inventiveness of Jennie Tate's design:

One of the real stars of the show is Jennie Tate's outstanding design. The forest is a mysterious, glimmering place with shadowy caves and glittering highlights in the ice blues and silvers which are the signature of this production…It also makes the forest what it must most importantly have been to Shakespeare, a place which is a magical, utterly unreal refuge from the nastiness of the 'real' world of cruel politics and capricious meanness.[35]

Interestingly, praise and criticism of the production alike revolved around references to fixed notions of genre and the perceived authority of Shakespeare's own pastoral vision. Recourse was made to the way Arden 'was meant to be'. Helen Thomson for the *Melbourne Age* stated:

[The set] appears more like the setting for a tragedy than a comedy, a dark cave that becomes a forest by the addition of funereal strips of cloth. It looks like the territory of a nightmare, not of comic liberation, which is surely the way the forest was meant to be. In fact, if ever a production was killed off by its set, this is it. All the energy seems sucked into the dark walls; all its sparkle is extinguished by what seems the habituation of trolls, not humans.[36]

Ken Longworth for the *Newcastle Herald* made a similar comment:

The lack of cohesion is also evident in Jennie Tate's designs. As a piece of stagecraft, the set is impressive, but its blacks and greys make it look more like a gloomy cave than a protecting forest.[37]

The contrast between the court and the forest was a focus for critical comment – Stephen Dunne claiming that '[c]ontrasts between the natural idyll of the forest and the artificial, human world of the court are central to the play, and the treatment of this is central to the disappointment of Davies's production'.[38] Yet, as Robert N. Watson has pointed out, the distinction between the 'natural' and the 'artificial' is anything but clear in Shakespeare's Arden. While the play's use of the pastoral genre seems always to elicit a fervent belief and investment in the 'idyll', this is not what the play itself delivers. Under closer investigation it becomes obvious that in the popular imagination, Arden is still anchored firmly to an eighteenth-century sensibility of pastoral ideal made 'palpable' through some spectacularly literal or pictorial staging. This reflects the recorded advent of the play's stage life – David Garrick's 1723 much adapted version called *Love in a Forest*,[39] and its subsequent popularity in the era of pictorial staging – not Shakespeare's pastoral vision.

In this light, one obvious reason for the criticisms of Davies' Arden is that she consciously sought to eschew the simplistic binaries – dark and light, artificial and natural, evil and good, court and forest – with which Arden is so fondly associated. In her program notes Davies expresses an explicit intention to disavow the usual polarities in her production aesthetic:

> The times we are living in are times of polarity and as we struggle to make sense of the extremities of violence in the world, extremities manifest by insistence upon black and white, right and wrong, it becomes clear that we need to embrace paradox.[40]

On the first day of rehearsal Davies explained to the cast the symbolic significance of the set elements. The chandelier and its shattering in particular encapsulated her sense of the prismatic – of multiplicity of perspectives.

In Davies' production the aesthetic principles out of which

Arden grew were not simply principles of decoration but principles that informed its modes of practice and definition of acting. If Arden, like the rehearsal room, was to be a space of unprejudiced, renewable possibility and inventive play, it could not afford to represent a particular place or even a fixed territory of the popular imagination. The result was an Arden that, through its censured ambiguities, served to highlight the Australian investment in Arden as a stable exemplar of comic pastoral.

Armfield's Arden, despite being in some senses equally iconoclastic, found a comfortable place in the collective imagination. The 'backyard Arden' satisfied certain instincts about the familiar in that it was both recogniseably Australian space, and carried the sanctioning literalism associated with the play's stage life – real grass. Davies' production, on the other hand, generated an estrangement from Arden that, if rich in philosophical implications, was mostly received with sarcastic reproof:

> In Jennie Tate's design, resembling nothing so much as the set of M*A*S*H with the camouflage webbing in violet shades, Davies delivers a very personal, pantomime version where symbols may be meaningful to her but no thought is given to making these choices clear to the audience.[41]

The production's chief transgression is here identified as one against a contemporary Australian sensibility – one that values transparency, artistic legibility and the putatively shared vision over the esoteric 'personal'. The philosophically contemplative character of this production was not warmly welcomed on the Australian stage.

A survey of recent Australian Ardens presents us with a legacy of flux. The play itself presents us with a volatile and contested domain. Arden is imaginatively appropriated, shaped and reshaped according to the needs, fears, and desires of individual characters. In the Australian context, Arden has accrued further ramifications as a site of conflict. Despite its instability within the play, what Arden is 'meant to be'[42] is constantly made recourse to as the definitive mark of the production's success or failure. Critical responses to all productions of *As You Like It* place marked emphasis upon getting Arden right. This can be partly explained by the fact that Arden references a dearly cherished, if problematic, genre of pastoral.

Another reason that Arden becomes the fulcrum for critical assessments of the play in production could be the sense in which it invokes a concern with origins: both authorial and ontological. Belief in an original Arden – an Arden that Shakespeare invented and intended – discloses a whole system of assumptions about the interpretative work of theatre. It is a belief that bears uncanny resemblance to belief in a pre-lapsarian or Edenic world. When reviewers imply belief in a state of Ardenic wholeness or pastoral perfection as authorised by Shakespeare's original vision, they betray a nostalgic impulse that owes more to the stage legacy of Arden than any identifiably essential feature of the play.

In Australia, the staging legacy of *As You Like It* is indebted to the long shadow of colonial British traditions and also to a newer more defiant ethos of making Shakespeare Australian, or as Elizabeth Schafer has aptly put it, of 'playing Australia.'[43] The three productions under close scrutiny reveal a range of solutions to the Arden enigma. Simon Phillips' glamorous production for Sydney Theatre Company offered a wood of words, taking up the challenge of the play's innate metatheatricality and the postmodern problematising of textual authority.[44] Neil Armfield's production for Company B at Belvoir Street was less arch in its conception. The playfulness of the Australian 'backyard Arden' was countered by the invocation of matters of profound political and cultural significance. The casting of Indigenous Australian actors, although not in any simply predictable way, lent a force to past failures of the collective imagination and present political debate. To a much greater degree, Lindy Davies's 2003 production for the Bell Shakespeare Company was castigated for its gloomy Arden. This production strove to blur the usual polarities associated with the play in favour of a more prismatic vision of Arden. In each instance, Arden was as much a response to or reaction against contemporary and even very local sensibilities, as it was a search for Shakespeare's supposed pastoral. This shaping of Arden by Australian contingencies reflects a new stage of the evolution of Shakespeare in Australia.

The 1863 review of Barry Sullivan's Arden evinced an aspiration to be transported by *As You Like It* to another world, to 'forget' being in the theatre in Australia. The productions discussed in this chapter exhibit a markedly different intention. Each in its own way has imagined Arden as an accessible present of theatrical invention. It is this imaginative evolution towards embracing a localised and particular theatrical moment that permits the concerns of the play to be vivified by those of our own time and place and in turn permits us to see our own habits of thought in a new light.

4

'Necessary tallness': Australian Rosalinds measure up

Miss Essie Jenyns was simply charming as Rosalind. She had all the necessary tallness of figure of which we are reminded by Shakespeare in his reference to 'Cleopatra's majesty', and she was thus enabled the more easily and the more satisfactorily to assume the male disguise. She had much of the grace and the sweetness attributed to the rose from which her name is compounded, and indeed was in every respect, if not actually, at any rate approximately, the personification of Shakespeare's imaginary princess.

'The Criterion Theatre', *Sydney Morning Herald*, 28 November 1887

She's not elfin and impossibly pretty – the audience will accept her in drag without too much straining of credulity.

Sydney Morning Herald, 19 December 1995[1]

Separated by over a century, these two accounts of Australian Rosalinds share a common requirement: that the actor playing Rosalind be tall enough to make her male disguise credible. This expectation reveals an assumption that relates distinctively to Rosalind, is detectable across reviews of countless productions, and is particularly concentrated in Australian reception of the role. That assumption is that the role exerts an authoritative set of specifications – that there is a 'real' Rosalind – to which any individual actor must attempt to measure up. While performers of other of Shakespeare's chief roles – and Hamlet provides a strong example – are routinely commended for re-inventing their characters in the light of the times, Rosalind's dimensions are set in stone.

In her article 'Shakespeare's Rosalind and her Public Image', Mary Hamer draws attention to the accretion of certain expectations around the character over time. Hamer explains the persistence of terms such as 'charm' and 'enchantment' in descriptions of Rosalind from the late eighteenth century onwards in the following way:

> Interpretation does not seem to be an issue, there is no drive to rediscover or redefine. Rather the question is one of approximating to an ideal whose outlines are in principle agreed.[2]

Hamer also points out that it is only from the point of the play's rediscovery in the eighteenth century that we can date prevalent perceptions and assumptions about Rosalind. These assumptions Hamer articulates incisively:

> What can be observed is the development of a myth. It is a myth of femininity, in which weakness and potency are reconciled, feminine allure and mystery reassuringly garbed in masculine attire. This involves the metamorphosis of traditionally female vices. Talking too much and being a bit bossy are with Rosalind transformed into signs of capacity and power.[3]

Hamer's identification of patterns of expectation is an engaging method of analysis. It comments not only upon the performance of the role but interprets patterns of reception. This interpretation offers insight into what we as a post-Victorian, English-speaking culture need from Rosalind. I extend and focus this kind of investigation by applying it to the Australian context.

Before looking at some Australian Rosalinds, however, what can be said about the myth of the 'real' Rosalind? Rosalind of Shakespeare's *As You Like It*, like the Forest of Arden, has fallen prey to ownership by forms of collective imagination. Reviews of productions regularly resort to the inherited consensual authority of this collective imagination as a measure of the production's success. The 1887 reviewer's irritatingly hesitant commendation of Jenyns as 'in every respect, if not actually, at any rate approximately, the personification of Shakespeare's imaginary princess'[4] exhibits a slavish assent to this authority as if it were continuous with both his own and Shakespeare's imagination. The unwillingness to accord this Australian Rosalind definitive status also reflects an obsequious attitude towards the geographically distant authority of London. Reviewers' responses to more recent Australian Rosalinds echo these sentiments in surprising ways.

It is important to recognise that comments which trade in notions of 'real' versions of any of Shakespeare's characters ignore the conditions of specific and ephemeral embodiment which make meaning possible in dramatic performance. With Rosalind, the myth of a 'real' Rosalind is particularly tenacious and particularly problematic. Successful assays of the part are repeatedly construed as part of a continuum that stretches back to Shakespeare's own time and by extension to the authority of 'Shakespeare's imagination'. Yet this accustomed habit of thought is glaringly ironic in the case of *As You Like It* for a number of reasons. The first is that there is no continuum. *As You Like It* is a play for which there is scant evidence of performance before 1723. Even at this date it was brought back to the stage – or rather introduced to the vastly different stage of Drury Lane – in a jumbled appropriation called *Love in a Forest* that included excerpts from many of Shakespeare's plays.[5] The second reason is that the role of Rosalind was written to be played by a boy. This means the prescriptions for the representation of 'femininity', so rampant in reviews of the play, cannot lay claim to the sanctioning force of authorial origins. Nevertheless, critical reviews such as the two which follow, are often entangled in this double-bind: claiming authority to comment upon the signifying power of the female body in the name of a mythical Shakespearean provenance that – no matter what it 'really' was – could never have included female bodies.

H. G. Kippax, in his scathing criticism of Jim Sharman's 1971 Old Tote production in Sydney, presents 'Shakespeare's Rosalind' as a set of fixed superlatives which damn the performance in question: 'Rosalind, most mature, witty and passionate of the comic heroines, goes down the drain'.[6] Conversely, in praise of Aubrey Mellor's 1978 NIDA production at Jane Street in Sydney, Robert Page claims that

> [a]t the centre is Rosalind, Shakespeare's most magnificent female – pretty, witty, wise, perceptive yet also playful, loving and frail. Angela Punch's beautiful yet lean figure, her large eyes one minute sparkling, the next doleful, her athleticism and vivacity, served the part better than I have seen in many a day.[7]

Although lauding Punch's performance, Page's syntax reveals a curious imaginative disjunction – it separates 'Shakespeare's most magnificent female' from the actor, who figures belatedly in the following sentence. Moreover, Punch's physical attributes are inventoried and described as having 'served the part'.

'NECESSARY TALLNESS'

In critical reception, the 'real' Rosalind is not hinged with any particular consistency to Shakespeare's period. Legendary, usually British, Rosalinds of the past can supplement 'Shakespeare's Rosalind' by partaking of her authenticity. Vanessa Redgrave is a case in point, whose 1961 performance is evoked with remarkable frequency in assessing the calibre of more recent performances.[8] Nevertheless, if we look at the contemporary reception of Redgrave's performance, it too epitomised the tension between the authoritative, if static, Rosalind template and the iconoclastic, if compelling, Redgrave:

> Perhaps it is not playing fair to Shakespeare to turn his Rosalind into a twentieth-century gamin, a fantasticated Bisto kid, a terror of the lower fifth. Miss Redgrave's Rosalind is like all these things. It may be, on the other hand, that *As You Like It* has had to wait until the 1960s for someone to appreciate that this is what Rosalind is.[9]

The reviewer vacillates between submitting to a notion of the essential qualities of '[Shakespeare's] Rosalind' and a kind of mutiny that attributes Redgrave's performance with definitive status. Discussions of Rosalind in performance consistently reveal this ongoing tension between the definitive fixities of the past and the living, embodied forces of the present.

What we observe then, in public discourse surrounding performance of the role, is a need for, and belief in, self-evident continuities. However, what we observe in longitudinal studies of the role played is Rosalind appropriated in the service of a diverse range of ideological projects over time.[10] At one end of the spectrum we have Rosalind working to reinforce the dominant and morally sanctioned expression of social class and gender representation. Reviews of Helen Faucit's numerous performances in the role throughout the nineteenth century suggest that she was just such a Rosalind: 'She is never less than the high-born and high-bred gentle-woman'.[11]

At the other end of the spectrum, the twentieth century, while opening up new modes of dialogue between artists and commentators, has seen Rosalind played by actors who articulate a consciously polemical stance. Juliet Stevenson, who played the role for the Royal Shakespeare Company in 1985, offers an example. In her interview with Carol Rutter she articulates a challenge to authority; both the authority of 'Shakespeare' and the traditional hierarchy of the rehearsal room:

> ...I argued that we couldn't have choreography that simply enacted conventional gender roles – the men strong and butch and doing a lot of lifting, and the women helpless and decorative, flopping around in the men's arms. Having spent three hours challenging notions of gender, we couldn't then end with a final stage picture that was clichéd and stereotypical, which threw the whole play away. Adrian [Noble] did point out to me that, whether I liked it or not, Shakespeare was a monarchist, a reactionary, a bourgeois and a conservative, but I said, 'I think it's irrelevant what Shakespeare was. The fact is that the *play* asks the most anarchic questions. It doesn't attempt to resolve them, so why should we?'[12]

Stevenson as artist uses both the character and the stage as a site for contesting contemporary paradigms of theatrical practice and gender representation.

Offering a different twist altogether, Declan Donnellan's Cheek by Jowl all-male production of 1991 completely eliminated the female presence. Paradoxically, this production was seen as both restorative of Elizabethan staging traditions and as offering a challenge to contemporary notions of gender identity.[13] In discussing the production, Peter Holland is cognisant of the varying political nuances made available. First he claims that the effect of the production was that

> [g]ender became a construct of performance, and sexuality was placed within the control of character, not actor. Adrian Lester's astonishing performance as Rosalind, sensuous and winning, was never simply a pretext for exploring the play's homosexuality…The problem of love and desire was defined here as lying beyond gender, simply coming into being, irresistible and unaccountable.

Simultaneously he is aware that

> [t]he rejection of the female voice could be seen as the rejection of the particularities of female desire, its separateness absorbed within a dominant male discourse of Shakespeare, of Donnellan and of the male cast and by extension of a patriarchal society.[14]

One thing that comes to light in examining these accounts of performance is that the fixed notions of gender identity – 'the necessary height', the charm, the sweetness – rehearsed in reviews of performance are complicated and contradicted by the bodies of actors as they play the role in particular times and places. As Anthony B. Dawson points out, the way in which the actor's body signals meaning is always unpredictable:

> The body does carry messages, no question. But those messages are so heterogeneous and dispersed that they are difficult to trace. To smooth them out in ideologically inflected ways tends to turn the body into one term in a polarity, rendering it newly invisible in that it comes to stand for something else, for culture's way of defining gender hierarchy, for example.[15]

In keeping with Dawson's insight, I pay attention the discourses at play around the character while recognising and exploring the unique force of the individual actor's body in performance. In this way, the 'body' of Rosalind might be seen as both a territory of dispute, and a flexible plane that promises renewable meaning and challenge to rehearsed myths about the character.[16] As accounts of the four Australian Rosalinds below reflect, the 'real' Rosalind, much like Hamlet, is animated by flux. The epistemological shifts brought about by the arrival of women on stage, and the much later challenges of feminist literary theory and post-structuralist approaches to meaning, have contrived to unmake and remake Rosalind's body, to constrain and liberate the signifying potential of the character's language and the identity of the actor who plays her.

The real Essie Jenyns

Despite her high-profile success, nineteenth-century Australian Shakespeare star, Essie Jenyns, was virtually owned by her stepfather, William Holloway. As a member of the actor-manager's family troupe, Jenyns had no fiscal independence and no scope to advance her prospects by performing for other companies. Her apprenticeship throughout her teenage years was arduous by her own account and after three years of unparalleled public popularity between the beginning of 1886 and 1888 she secretly quit the company, ran away to Sydney, married a wealthy man, and retired from public performance altogether.[17]

This raw list of biographical details may provoke speculation as to Jenyns' personal happiness and unhappiness. Unfortunately, little evidence is readily available to support or refute such speculation. Janette Gordon-Clark, who has had access to personal papers, diaries, and photographs of the Jenyns family, speculates that Jenyns' belonging to the Holloway company was the source of her early retirement and the occasion of great loss to Australian theatre.[18]

'NECESSARY TALLNESS'

What Jenyns' documented actions do reveal is one instance of marked defiance of the power structure and culture in which she found herself. For the present purpose, Jenyns' biography offers some telling intersections with Rosalind, the character that she played and for which, as we have seen, she received a warm, if tentative, tribute.

Figure 4.1 Portrait of Essie Jenyns as Rosalind, Collection of theatrical portraits of Australian actor Essie Jenyns 1884–1888.
(nla.pic-an23447530) National Library of Australia ©
PIC PIC/7097/6 LOC Box PIC/7097

In her work on Jenyns, Gordon-Clark differentiates the actor from her female predecessors by emphasising the special quality of her individual popular celebrity. It seems that the 'real' Jenyns had taken root as a character in the popular imagination and had thereby fallen prey to the dictates of collective cultural expectations. According to one source, 15 000 photographs of Jenyns dressed as various characters had been purchased in the three years from 1885 to 1888 (see figure 4.1). The writer of a nineteenth-century feature article on Jenyns for the *Centennial Magazine* comments that 'no other resident artist, whether Australian born or otherwise, has ever come within half this number'.[19] This form of popular celebrity suggests that Jenyns wielded unprecedented power of appeal. Paradoxically, it also implies that Jenyns was not only owned fiscally by her stepfather's company but also owned imaginatively by the Australian public. Further evincing this ownership are Thompson's opening comments:

> Miss Essie Jenyns claims special attention in these pages as a representative Australian actress. She has achieved fame where most she prizes it — in her native land; and whatever fortune may have in store for her elsewhere, here she will always be welcome.[20]

Jenyns, as is still often the case with Australian 'stars', is spoken of as if she were the mascot for a small provincial town. She seems to have activated the articulation of a number of normalising narratives and preoccupations which persist in close relation to players of Rosalind in Australia today. These include the notion of a witnessed growth to fame in the spotlight of popular appeal, a preoccupation with the body of the actor, and an effort to confirm Australian authenticity through description of an idyllic, preferably outback, childhood.

'NECESSARY TALLNESS'

First, Jenyns' long apprenticeship with the Holloway company permitted her exposure to the Australian public in a range of dramatic genres from the age of twelve. Her first speaking role was page to the King in an 1878 production of *Richelieu* with the famous William Creswick playing the title role. This was followed by a gradual ascendancy to more important roles in both popular Australian melodramas and in plays of Shakespeare.[21] Jenyns' association with popular forms of theatre and her perceived gradual and publicly witnessed growth to competence and talent is a narrative cherished in Thompson's account.

Secondly, we discover a marked focus on Jenyns' youth as manifest in her body – even including mention of changing dietary habits and physical development. Thompson mentions a picture taken in 1884 in the following way:

> Miss Jenyns' own unflattering description of herself as comparatively 'plumpy and stumpy up to the age of 16 or 17', is here in some measure borne out. There is little sign of the tall and lissome figure and the commanding intelligence which distinguished her beauty a few years later.[22]

Finally, to increase the sense of intimacy and put the sanctioning stamp on Jenyns' Australianness, the article offers a romantic description of her background:

> Long, lonely walks through the fragrant bush before the sun was fairly up, dreamy days over a book half-read in the drowsy heat, and early to rest in preparation for the morrow's gallop... Essie gave promise at this time of a stouter growth than she realised at maturity. 'In those days I could eat anything, from bread and butter to dough-nuts', is her explanation of the phenomenon. I daresay most of us would prefer to think of

our heroine gracefully bending from the saddle to stain her lip with the scarlet quondong...[23]

Thompson both sentimentalises and eroticises Jenyns' imagined childhood flagging up the degree to which the 'real' Jenyns is a 'heroine' captive to the framing of how 'most of us would prefer to think of her'.

Another noticeable characteristic of Thompson's account is the way in which he idealises and conventionalises Jenyns' relationship with her family. Her submissive and loyal relationship with her stepfather or 'kind master' is promoted as yet another of her winsome attributes.[24] In tandem with these narratives that contain and construct Jenyns' identity, her sojourn to Europe is described as providing the necessary sophistication for a respected artist in Australia:

> Mr and Mrs Holloway now felt they had done all that was possible in Australia towards the advancement of their daughter's education, and that to promote it still further a visit to the art centres of the world would be necessary.[25]

Jenyns, as presented in this article, is the product of an identifiably patriarchal and Anglo-centric Australian idealising impulse. Thompson's account rehearses a narrative of the Australian female performer's emergence from simple origins, fidelity to those origins and to her conventional family structure, a self-effacing attitude to her own physical appeal, and the formative influence of a European experience.

The 'real' Essie Jenyns as constructed by Thompson is like the 'real' Rosalind identified by Hamer: they have both been appropriated to reinforce public hegemonic discourses of gender identity, power, and ownership. As Rosalind has been for centuries, Jenyns was at the centre of two volatile strands of public discourse – the source of authority in the performance of Shakespeare's plays, and the politics of representing gender, both on and off-stage. The construction of the 'real' Jenyns seems culturally unexceptional given the vintage of Thompson's article. What is more striking is the pervasive evidence of similar mythologising impulses in responses to contemporary performances of the role in Australia. It is as if the threat of Rosalind's mutinous independence, self-determination, and disruption to systems of identity needs to be diminished by absorbing the actor's body into a rehearsed narrative of the familiar.

Anita Hegh

Anita Hegh, who played Rosalind for the STC production in 1996, was described by director Simon Phillips as having 'sufficient reserves of melancholy to make the discovery of joy a great experience'.[26] Her performance was characterised by a quality of gravity and internalised struggle.[27] The connection between Rosalind and Celia (Lucy Bell) seemed, as is often the case, far more profound and robust than any of the play's romantic bonds. Reviewers evinced a marked interest in the love between the women:

> At [the play's] centre is the relationship between Rosalind and Celia, played through to the end with passion, energy and intelligence by Anita Hegh and Lucy Bell. This is no mere girlhood friendship. Their love and closeness becomes the moral core of this play about the alarming suddenness and inevitable failure of romantic love.[28]

Director Simon Phillips was even more explicit about the relationship's breadth of possibility, claiming that Rosalind's male dress offered a kind of liberation that allowed Rosalind and Celia to 'explore their mutual sexual attraction'.[29]

Surprisingly however, Hegh herself rejected the notion of consciously expressed 'romantic' love between Rosalind and Celia:

> I can see how some people might find it erotic, especially with me in my braces and pants, it could provide some fantasy element. Certainly they love each other but it's not in a romantic way. It's more in the way of an extremely close friendship.[30]

Figure 4.2 Anita Hegh (Rosalind), Lucy Bell (Celia), *As You Like It*, STC, Sydney, 1996.
Photograph ©Philip Le Masurier
Courtesy of STC and Philip le Masurier.

Rosalind and Celia's first appearance was made as they broke away from a group of dancers moving in an eerily stylised routine. Their solidarity was expressed shaking-off of the stifling encumbrance of court formality and heterosexual pairing. It was a 'dance' in which neither wanted to participate. Hegh as Rosalind sat on the floor in a simple long black dress giving a sense of quiet grief and pent-up strength. When promising to render back in affection what Duke Frederick had robbed from Rosalind, Celia

'NECESSARY TALLNESS'

slid her hands down Rosalind's bare arms – a strikingly intimate and creative gesture which contrasted with the cold, fixed hold of the dancers. To compound the intensity of her oath – 'By mine honour I will, and when I break that oath let me turn monster' (act 1, scene 2, line 18) – Celia hurled it upstage in angry defiance at the now departed entourage of dancers.

Having rid themselves of formal constraints, Rosalind and Celia threw off their shoes and sat together on the floor. Their conversation was accompanied by a rough and playful mode of interaction. At one point Hegh straddled Bell, pinning her arms to the floor. Even in her dress, Hegh's Rosalind evinced stereotypically masculine characteristics of action: physical strength and roughness. The physical energy and agility of both actors from their first appearance was all the more striking for the fact of their female garments. The sense emerged that Rosalind need not 'put on' Ganymede but that a physical strength and energy integral to her particular femininity had been suppressed by codes of social and sartorial propriety and was allowed fuller expression when she changed her clothes.

This liberating shift was also registered in Hegh's voice. While wearing a dress, in both the early scenes and in the epilogue, Hegh delivered her lines in what appeared to be a more self-consciously formal, forced, and stagey manner. As Ganymede, however, her voice seemed more flexible and her manner more relaxed and confident. Ironically, for this particular actor, the frock was the disguise – 'Rosalind' was the adopted persona and 'Ganymede' the organic identity. As I point out below, this provokes a notable contrast with Alice McConnell's Rosalind for the Bell Shakespeare Company in 2003.

Hegh as Ganymede evinced a crisp, almost choreographed form of physicality. In this she recalled Juliet Stevenson's Rosalind, whose dance-like movement gave a sensuous fluidity to her performance.[31] In neither instance did the stylisation preclude a beguiling self-revelation. Rather, it emphasised the sense that Rosalind is self-consciously a performer. Rosalind, with her changes of costume and her successive naming, her posturing as a 'saucy lackey' and her adoption of rhetorical conceits, evinces an insatiable appetite for the gaze of her audiences—both off-stage and on. Rosalind, like Shakespeare's other clowns and fools, is a pointedly metatheatrical invention. She constantly draws attention to the junction between playing and being. Her many roles bring a paradoxical transparency to the act of performance and consequently to the actor playing the role.

Hegh's stylisation took on a particular nuance in keeping with the aesthetic of the production. The large playing space of the Sydney Opera House Drama Theatre's proscenium stage is best equipped for fourth-wall naturalism. However, Phillips' production exploited its other stylistic possibility – a self-consciousness 'big stage' spectacle more readily associated with the musical. The 1930s vintage of the costumes and jazz performances that interjected and overlapped the stage action accorded well with this vision. Individual performances were characterised by a self-conscious archness that animated both the self-reflexivity of the play and a sense of Broadway brashness. One of the clearest instances in point was the interaction between Orlando and Rosalind when they met in the Forest of letters.

Hegh as Rosalind used a range of stock performance gestures with the result of parodying both masculine and feminine stereotypes. When exclaiming to Celia 'Do you not know I am a woman? When I think, I must speak' (act 3, scene 2, line 227), rather than investing the line with honest exasperation, Hegh adopted a mock femininity. Propped lazily against the lowest lip of the 'E' she slid down until she knelt primly and spoke while fluttering her eyelids. Shortly after this, on first sighting Orlando (Paul Bishop), she struck a stereotypically masculine pose – one

'NECESSARY TALLNESS'

foot propped on the curving front leg of the letter 'R' – and her hands in her pockets.

In a sequence of similarly self-conscious attitudes and postures she delivered her speech about 'time' to be rewarded by Orlando's warm applause. This self-conscious performer/spectator conceit then dissolved deliciously as they shook hands and looked into each other's eyes until they were both unsettled. The performer/spectator dynamic was then reversed when Orlando, reclining on the lower curve of the 'S' became the subject of Rosalind's gaze and earnest inquiry: 'But are you so much in love as your rhymes speak?'(act 3, scene 3, line 357). Orlando responded 'Neither rhyme nor reason can express how much' (act 3, scene 3, line 358), without looking at her – allowing her to look appreciatively at him. Then with a visible shudder of excitement she exclaimed: 'Love is merely a madness' (act 3, scene 3, line 359), before recollecting herself as the saucy Ganymede and kicking Orlando off his comfortable perch. This playing of the interaction was distinctive in that Rosalind's exclamation ('Love is merely a madness') – often played as a didactic part of her disguise – was made a self-revelation.

In defiance of the self-contained mode of naturalism, Anita Hegh and Paul Bishop used the audience as a constant and conscious reference point: each dramatic revelation reinforcing a triangular dynamic inclusive of the audience. When Rosalind advanced her outrageous plan: 'I would cure you if you would but call me Rosalind and come every day to my cot and woo me' (act 3, scene 2, lines 381–2), Orlando paused, shooting a quizzical look at the audience, before agreeing to the scheme. This was met by laughter. The couple continued to register their emotions with the audience in a very deliberate manner. In their following encounter, during the mock/real wedding ceremony the couple kissed on Rosalind's line: 'I take thee, Orlando, for husband' (act 4, scene 1, line 118). Immediately after the kiss they sprung apart and swung momentarily out to the audience in shock. In perfect symmetry they then strode in opposite directions across the front of the stage, Orlando perplexed with his hand to his lips.

The dynamic of being drawn together and leaping apart continued throughout the scene with a consistent emphasis upon its dimension as a performed and witnessed spectacle. The ground of their interaction kept shifting between an evolving sense of attraction and intimacy and a taking refuge in adopted roles. This was instanced most clearly as the scene drew to its close. Rosalind warned Orlando of how she would regard him if he failed to come at two o'clock. She punctuated each of her adjectives – *'pathetical* break-promise', *'hollow* lover', and *'unworthy'* – by prodding Orlando backwards by the shoulders; a gesture guaranteed to provoke aggression. Orlando's response to this bullying was surprising. He gently raised a hand to her face, saying that he would keep his promise: 'With no less religion than if thou wert indeed my Rosalind' (act 4, scene 4, lines 168–9). Momentarily it seemed as if he saw Rosalind. Rosalind gave ground visibly, made expectant by his tenderness. Having caught her off-guard and just at the moment when she clearly anticipated a kiss he said 'adieu', and gave her strong retaliatory shove backwards by the shoulders before running off. This again provoked surprised laughter from the audience. It revealed an Orlando and not just a Rosalind who was prepared to play with assumed attributes of his gender role. This accords well with what director Simon Phillips said of the relationship between Rosalind and Orlando:

> [I]t was really about opening up the avenues in the rehearsal room for every permutation of the potential of sexuality to be employed. The play just offers up a chance for everyone to explore an element of their sexuality that they might not have otherwise explored...They can role-play. And of course the same thing happens with Rosalind and Orlando. There

> are obvious homosexual complications in that relationship for Orlando because he is attracted to the being that is Rosalind… almost regardless of her sexuality…There just seems to be a hell of a lot of fun and a kind of beauty in what the play opens up there.[32]

Despite the lively intelligence and popularity of Hegh's performance, she was not accorded status as the star feature of the production. Apart from an interview by Cec Busby for the free street publication *Beat*,[33] there were no articles featuring Hegh alone. Lucy Bell was interviewed about her career and identity as daughter of John Bell and Anna Volska of Nimrod and Bell Shakespeare Company fame.[34] Paul Livingston, known in Australia for his comic character 'Flacco', was interviewed about his new experience playing a number of roles in a play by Shakespeare.[35] Penny Biggins and Bruce Spence were interviewed as actors with recognised profiles outside of the Shakespeare and theatre context.[36] Australian jazz singer Kerrie Biddell's appearance also drew notice for its novelty. In each case, actors were singled out for their recognised and established status in the entertainment industry in Australia. This fitted Phillips' vision of the play as 'a show that could be done with cabaret performers' with the clowns in the forest as 'a series of star-turns by comedians'.[37]

The reviewers' approaches to Hegh's appearance as Rosalind differed markedly. While most emphasised Rosalind's centrality to the play, the commentary's emphasis was upon Hegh's almost unexpected competence in the role as a young performer and recent drama school graduate: 'Though fresh out of NIDA (1994), Hegh gives a performance fit for any stage'.[38] The previously identified theme of 'home-grown' and in fact 'home owned' talent also pervaded the reception of Hegh's Rosalind: 'Sydney theatre has a fine new talent in Anita Hegh'.[39] Other instances of reporting on Hegh as Rosalind bore uncanny parallels with reception of the earlier work of Essie Jenyns. Narratives used for both 'actresses' are characterised by a deserved growth to fame accompanied by the necessary blessing of innate physical beauty:

> Anita Hegh appears from amongst the clatter of the cafeteria dressed in earth colours. She has the typically flawless skin and elegant poise of an actor. This is Anita's first Shakespearean role outside of NIDA and lo and behold she has won Rosalind, one of the strongest female leads Shakespeare has ever written.[40]

This cafeteria narrative packages the actor's body, talent and body of work for easy consumption. It makes the real Hegh and the 'real' Rosalind into contained and recognisable, albeit fabricated, entities.

Deborah Mailman

Deborah Mailman was praised unanimously for her energy and audience appeal in the role of Rosalind for Company B, Belvoir in 1999. Her characterisation attracted the following epithets: 'a delight of verve and spontaneity', 'feisty and cheeky', 'a splendidly lumpish country boy', and, perhaps more conventionally; 'irresistibly charming'.[41] Mailman was in fact 'more than common tall' – much taller than Kirstie Hutton's tiny Celia and noticeably taller than Aaron Blabey's Orlando. Mailman's height, her rambunctious energy, and her Aboriginality defied smooth, symmetrical pairings and were registered in media discourse as anomalous for Rosalind. According to Joyce Morgan, reporter for the *Sydney Morning Herald*, even director Neil Armfield registered the fortuitous unusualness of casting Mailman as Rosalind:

> Director Neil Armfield acknowledges that his decision to cast Mailman as Rosalind – 'the Gwyneth Paltrow role' – rather

than her comic sidekick Celia was unusual. He sees Mailman's ability to move from physical comedy into tender, lyrical sadness as a way of opening up the play.

'Deb has the ability to make you glad you're alive…it's such a bracing and generous energy', says Armfield.[42]

While the STC production relied on a sophisticated and crisply stylised repertoire of self-revelations, Company B's production was characterised by casual intimacy with the audience and more organic and spontaneous kinds of clowning. Mailman was at the very forefront of this dynamic, evincing a beguiling mixture of self-assurance and generous-spirited self-irony. In contrast to the humour of Hegh's plucky, self-defensive strategies and postures, Mailman's Rosalind seemed a relaxed and confident comedian.

While it is a traditional feature of characterisation for Rosalind to 'betray herself', and reveal her love 'despite herself', Mailman walked no such tightrope of propriety. Mailman's Rosalind relished unabashedly opportunities for physical contact with Orlando. After the wrestling scene she followed Celia to approach him but soon interposed herself between the two, achieving an intimate proximity with Orlando. Early during their first encounter in the Forest, Rosalind revealed her physical desire for Orlando when enumerating the markers of a true lover. Adding 'a lean cheek, which you have not' (act 3, scene 2, line 338), she touched his face and halted speaking as if arrested by the sensation. While sitting side by side on a bench with him, Rosalind claimed she could wash Orlando's 'liver as clean as a sound sheep's heart' (act 3, scene 3, line 378) and reached sideways to gesture to his liver. Inadvertently, her hand slipped into his lap where she left it for some time – fixing her gaze ahead, with a gasp and momentary pause. This frankness of desire and the way it unsettled Orlando caused much audience mirth. The humour of Mailman's Rosalind's desire inhered more in its artlessness than in the more common kinds of coquetry and self-denial associated with the character. Her anger at Orlando for his lateness in act 4, scene 1, was not peevish, sulky, or of long duration. They joked and tangled and swung each other around using his scarf. Rosalind lingered delightedly on the idea of Orlando 'out of his apparel' (act 4, scene 1, line 75), much to the embarrassment of Celia, who, watching on from the bench by the wall, pulled her hat down over her eyes.

Like Hegh, Mailman seemed liberated rather than disguised by her Ganymede identity. Unlike Hegh's and Stevenson's dapper and tailored appearance in crisp white shirt, linen trousers and braces, however, Mailman wore shabby clothes. Her face was smeared with dirt and for most of her performance she wore an oversized shirt, knee length breeches with braces dangling from the waistband, bare feet, and a battered felt hat. The simplicity of this and other costumes suited the 'backyard' aesthetic of the production – the turf stage floor and blue cloth canopy of stars. The flat and evenly lit plain of the grass seemed to establish equality between the characters – both proscribing and suggesting particular possibilities of movement. In the scene where Jaques and Rosalind meet and talk (act 4, scene 1, lines 1–33), they lay at perpendicular angles on the grass taking alternate bites of a carrot. This gave the interaction an air of leisurely musing rather than competitive wit. On a conventionally glossy stage surface there is an obvious contrivance in having characters lie down or sit on the 'ground'. On the inviting grassy plot of Company B's Arden, sitting, lying, chasing, and playful skirmishes had a fresh dramatic viability.

Mailman's physically relaxed and playful mode of performance as Ganymede often veered towards crowd-pleasing slap-stick. Spying Orlando in the Forest for the first time, she screamed and took refuge in the audience. Her 'clowning' Rosalind was much commended in reception of the play, one reviewer going as far as to say she is the play's 'key clown'.[43] Mailman's Rosalind won the audience's sympathy and laughter throughout the performance and the robust simplicity of this bond between audience and performer was attested at a climactic moment of the play's dramatic development. In act 5, scene 2 Rosalind reports to the forlorn and wounded Orlando news of Celia and Oliver's match. Aaron Blabey's Orlando, poignant in his dejection, would not be urged from his sad humour. Preoccupied, and with his eyes downcast he told Rosalind: 'I can live no longer by thinking' (act 5, scene 2, line 45). At this point Rosalind, saddened by his sadness stepped over to the audience and whispered 'Shall I tell him?' to which the audience responded in an urgent whisper 'Yes!' Rosalind with a glance back at Orlando then inquired of the audience 'Now?' – to which they gave an even more emphatic 'Yes!'

Mailman was a popular Rosalind and more than that – a star – seen to carry representative functions in popular discourse far beyond her role in the play. Somewhat akin to Essie Jenyns in her popular identity, Mailman was treated as an Australian 'character' in her own right. Prior to *As You Like It,* Mailman had played a number of Shakespeare roles including Cordelia for the Bell Shakespeare Company's famously controversial *King Lear* directed by Barrie Kosky. In Sue Rider's 1994 production of *The Taming of the Shrew* for La Boite in Brisbane, Mailman played Katherina – a performance whose political implications bore parallels with her performance as Rosalind. As Elizabeth Schafer has pointed out:

> Making Katherina the unfavoured and Aboriginal daughter coloured the undervaluing and indeed demonising of Katherina, and evoked the troubling histories of the taming/abuse of Aboriginal women in Australia.[44]

Mailman was also the first Indigenous Australian to win the Australian Film Institute's award for best actress – for her performance as Nora in the film *Radiance*. In uncanny parallel to the much-pictured Essie Jenyns, Mailman was the subject of a portrait by Evert Ploeg that won the People's Choice Award in the 1999 Archibald Prize (see figure 4.3). The Archibald Prize – Australia's most famous art prize – functions as a dynamic platform for the formation and expression of popular cultural identity. Because Australian actors and artists are the most frequent subjects of

Figure 4.3 'Deborah Mailman' by Evert Ploeg © oil on jute
167.0 x 137.0 cm
National Portrait Gallery, Canberra
By kind permission of the artist.

portraits entered, the Australian public who vote at the exhibition are in a sense nominating favourite national personalities as much as discriminating between works of art. Other winning portraits of John Bell (by Nicholas Harding) in 2001, and David Wenham (by Adam Cullen) in 2000, suggest that to win either the official prize or the People's Choice Award the subject of the work needs to have a popularly recognised and sanctioned quality of Australianness. However, in a comment which mirrors the tendency to contain and dilute the force of Australian Rosalinds, Mailman's portrait was described as 'a portrait of an award winning actress, dressed in a flimsy calico nightie'.[45]

Also drawing on her popular appeal, promotional material for Belvoir's production featured a portrait of Deborah Mailman. The postcard and program present a head-shot: Mailman's face chalked white with a penciled black moustache and eyebrows, topped by a clown's mop of curly black hair. This image references both the

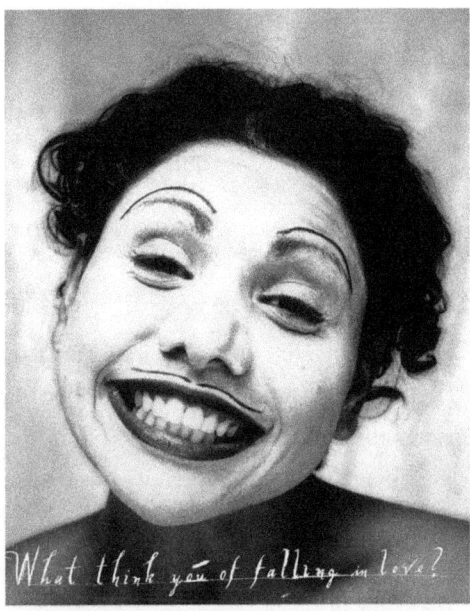

Figure 4.4
Deborah Mailman (Rosalind), publicity poster for
As You Like It, Company B, Belvoir Street Theatre, Sydney, 1999.
Photograph ©Julian Watt
Courtesy of Company B, Julian Watt and Deborah Mailman.

vaudevillian roots of Australian theatre and performs a brilliant inversion of the black and white minstrel stereotype. Offset by the scrawled line 'What think you of falling in love?' and Mailman's enticing smile, the photograph issues a playful and multi-layered challenge to fixed definitions of both gender and ethnic identity.

In reviews of the production, Mailman was also designated a representative function in relation to her Indigenous Australian identity. As discussed in Chapter 3, her prominence as an assertively outspoken and orchestrating female figure in the play, combined with the presence of a number of other Indigenous Australians in the cast, made the play a conduit for questioning and revising beliefs about both cultural and gender identity. Mailman, while registering awareness of the political statement made simply by walking on stage,[46] also articulated a resistance to having her individuality engulfed by political and ideological rhetoric: 'It places a lot of weight on us as indigenous artists…(but) first and foremost it's about me. I love what I do and I wouldn't be doing it if I didn't love it'.[47] By unapologetically asserting herself with her specific Australian cultural legacy and her own particular talents and idiosyncrasies, Mailman uncovered new possibilities for Rosalind in the Australian context. The unpretentious manner in which she describes her involvement in the production and her innate sense of fun belie the 'more than common tallness' of her achievement.

Alice McConnell

In her direction of *As You Like It* for the Bell Shakespeare Company in 2003, Lindy Davies saw the rehearsal process as one of ongoing discovery rather than premeditated design. When asked if she consciously thought about the play in terms of relevance to the Australian context, Davies said she found it more productive to find a level of 'personal connection' with the play.[48] Nor, as one reviewer reported, was the play 'about' gender:

> Davies does not think that Shakespeare is making any grand statement about gender roles in *As You Like It*, although she acknowledges 'I might be the only person who doesn't'. Instead she sees it as thriller that shifts to an examination of social issues once the setting moves to Arden. 'Everything becomes more complex in the Forest and the characters come to appreciate other people's perspective'.[49]

Alice McConnell's performance as Rosalind for the Bell Shakespeare Company adhered closely to Davies' principles of complexity and unfixed meaning and resembled Anita Hegh's performance in its sense of depth and edgy intensity. In rehearsal, McConnell evinced strong commitment to avoiding stale routine by making new discoveries and keeping fresh the impulses that shaped her performance. While many actors describe catching themselves in a self-analytical state during performance, McConnell seemed to give her whole consciousness to each moment, only to emerge afterwards with an evaluative sense of wonder or self-censure about what had taken place.[50]

One of the most salient features of McConnell's rehearsal approach was her sense of detail. While other actors in the Bell *As You Like It* cast were repeatedly cautioned by Davies to slow down, McConnell would voluntarily 'rewind' segments and attempt them repeatedly until she found, to her own satisfaction, the imaginative, emotional and physical links she required to achieve authenticity. What McConnell sought in this process were sources of associated impulse to impel her from one moment to the next. McConnell explained that for her a source could be 'something as small as the angle of my chin at a particular moment'.[51] The ways in which McConnell articulated, problematised, and engaged in her work strongly reflected the principles that shaped her training by Davies at the Victorian College of the Arts.

In rehearsal and in performance, McConnell's investment in the moment-by-moment authenticity of her work often lent her acting an intensely compelling quicksilver-like quality. Watching the actor, it became evident that she never resorted to easy solutions to define Rosalind. Rather, she wrestled to forge an organic connection with each word, phrase, and action of the character. When confidently in command of the flow of this process, McConnell as Rosalind was agile and energised, mercurial in her transformations and mesmerising to behold. Conversely, when she encountered obstacles to fluency – as actors do on occasion – she seemed overburdened, physically and mentally fatigued. The rewards of McConnell's commitment to authenticity – finding rather than making Rosalind – were obvious as was the debt she seemed to pay for being so meticulously diligent. While Mailman's Rosalind seemed robust, indomitable, and irrepressibly blithe, McConnell's Rosalind, like Sigrid Thornton's Laura in the popular ABC Television series *Sea Change*, was endearingly tense and neurotic albeit very resourceful in adverse circumstances.

The aspect of the role about which McConnell articulated a distinct sense of difficulty was 'finding Ganymede'.[52] McConnell was cognisant of the multi-layered quality of the role, pointing out that 'Rosalind is herself playing out the role of a man for much of the play'.[53] Unlike Anita Hegh and Deborah Mailman, who seemed immediately more at ease once 'disguised' as Ganymede, McConnell seemed to struggle with the secondary identity. Rather than seeking a fixed answer to her riddle of 'finding Ganymede', however, McConnell allowed that flexibility would be crucial to the growth of the role:

> You have to be prepared to let the role develop, so that it evolves into something quite different at the end of the season from where we're starting.[54]

Most actors would report development of their role through a long season but McConnell's point bore special emphasis. It exemplified in practice Lindy Davies' core principle for the actor: the possibility of genuine transformation through 'active receptivity' to environment, and to personal impulse:

> The only thing that interests me about acting is acting as a state of revelation...The only way that that can happen is if actors do two things. One is to remain in a state of active receptivity and allow themselves to be affected by the language and what's actually happening to them. The other is if they have a commitment to advance meaning and advance the dramatic rhythm and shape of the piece.[55]

In keeping with Davies's emphasis on transformation, McConnell made some significant alterations to her performance throughout the season.

One of her more radical decisions was to remove the hat that was part of her Ganymede disguise, freeing her shoulder-length blonde hair. This iconoclastic move was typical of the ways in which McConnell's performance disrupted the category of 'male disguise' and apparently disturbed a number of reviewers. Ken Longworth for the *Newcastle Herald* asserted that 'No attempt seems to have been made to make Rosalind a convincing boy'.[56] Another reviewer made a similar observation in a more circumspect manner:

> [McConnell's] Rosalind-as-Ganymede is less than convincing, but nor is it meant to be. Orlando and the Duke claim rather lamely, when she is revealed as herself, that they'd noticed a resemblance.[57]

Bill Perrett points out that the play itself draws attention to its own contrivance, raising the question of what might actually be gained by an unconvincing Ganymede.

These instances of criticism echo an insistent and popular preoccupation with the veracity of Rosalind's disguise. This preoccupation is signaled further in the hackneyed archaisms deployed by reviewers to describe the plot: Rosalind 'dons breeches'.[58] When referring to productions which evoke the Elizabethan social context, or which took place in the eighteenth and nineteenth centuries such a phrase retains some sense. But in the twenty-first century, what does it mean for Rosalind to suit herself 'in all points like a man'? Women in Anglo-European cultures have been wearing trousers for nearly a century and use of such phrases in the present reflects a certain intellectual complacency. Relying on the cultural cliché that still has a dominant person 'wearing the pants in the household' it hints at a containing ideology that implies two things: first, that the crux of the drama is Rosalind convincing Orlando that she is a boy, and secondly, that gender is 'worn' as an easily read binary.

Alice McConnell's Rosalind transgressed the requirement for a plausible and clearly determined version of masculine disguise. McConnell's shortcomings were derided with predictable resort to the putative authority of the 'real' Rosalind:

> This play has always been loved for its heroine, the brave, original Rosalind, who dons breeches and woos her man with wonderful wit and passion. Alice McConnell certainly looks the part: tall and fair and charming. But she lacks the dash and brio to make her the mistress of her fate. Her body language is irritatingly obsequious and fussy and, as the lover, Ganymede, she carries, for no obvious reason, a cloth wrapped staff, that she constantly thrusts at the other characters like a weapon.[59]

'NECESSARY TALLNESS'

Figure 4.5 Alice McConnell (Rosalind), *As You Like It*, Bell Shakespeare, 2003.
Photograph ©Heidrun Lohr
Courtesy of Bell Shakespeare and Heidrun Lohr.

Thomson's dissatisfaction relates to the obviousness of McConnell's devices, her clumsy apparatus of masculinity. However, there is no reason why Rosalind should be fluently adept in her disguise. McConnell, like many a Rosalind, struck poses (see figure 4.5). Playing consciously with the idiom of acting, she prepared herself for her first public encounter as Ganymede by placing one foot up on a block and thumping her staff to the floor. The gestural hyperbole of bracing herself for a performance of 'masculinity' was deliberately silly and provoked audience laughter. Elizabeth Grosz has identified this deployment of stereotypical traits in order to subvert the gender stereotype. With respect to femininity Grosz states that

> [t]he practices of femininity can readily function, in certain contexts…as modes of guerilla subversion of patriarchal codes, although the line between compliance and subversion is always a fine one.[60]

McConnell's clumsy 'masculinity' could likewise be seen as a mode of 'guerilla subversion of patriarchal codes' because it highlighted how unsophisticated a façade of 'masculinity' was required to convince Orlando.

McConnell seemed in her self-conscious performativity to harness her own uncertainty – constantly trying out expressions and mannerisms in her assay of masculine disguise. Her experimental approach to gender disguise, as at least one reviewer suggested, continued to be great source of fun:

> Manning's Orlando is a square jawed, physically effective man of action in the usual mode, while McConnell's Rosalind has more subtlety and range, with some nicely acted fun in the crossdressing.[61]

Stephen Dunne's critique in effect suggests a complementarity between Manning's conventional and McConnell's less stable representation of gender identity.

In his first encounter with Ganymede, Orlando appeared weary and indifferent, clearly anticipating an insignificant and passing encounter. As Rosalind pressed on with her pronouncements on 'Time' he became intrigued. However, when she circled him in a predatorial manner, enumerating his lack of 'marks of love', Orlando seemed more disconcerted by, than attracted to, her. This fractiousness between the two characters was further sharpened by Rosalind's accusation that Orlando was 'rather point device in [his] accoutrements, as loving [himself] than seeming the lover of any other', at which impertinence he seemed more exasperated than, as is often the case, amused. With or without her hat on, it was plain to see why Orlando did not link this cantankerous, aggressive, and awkward Ganymede with the effusive gentlewoman he had fallen in love with a few scenes earlier. His compliance with her scheme of curing him seemed more an idly welcomed diversion from his listlessness than an insatiable, erotic curiosity.

McConnell's expressed lack of self-assurance became, by turn, Rosalind's amusingly strange fits and starts. Arguably McConnell's struggle to 'find Ganymede' made her no less Rosalind than Hegh's and Mailman's discovery of Rosalind in Ganymede. McConnell kept the role alive through a certain tension between identities, Hegh and Mailman through the freedom they found in disguise.

Despite this major difference, the publicity and rhetoric that attended McConnell's appearance as Rosalind bore striking resemblance to that of each of the previously described Rosalinds. Among the identified tropes were those of a simple Australian childhood, promise of talent, overseas experience, and a popular identity outside the Shakespeare role. Perhaps most notable of all is the degree to which McConnell herself is complicit in the mythologising:

> She grew up in Ourimbah, which sounds like the Arden of the Central Coast.
> 'It was a huge farm, a beautiful old homestead in a valley surrounded by citrus', she said. 'A very simple country family: Dad worked the land and Mum worked the home'.[62]

Rose's article, titled 'Man enough for the role' goes on to give a potted profile of McConnell's life experience. Having begun by reminding his readers of McConnell's television celebrity status in the ABC drama *MDA* (Medical Defence Australia), Rose goes on to recount McConnell's winning of a scholarship to study in England at age nineteen, her training at the Victorian College of the Arts in Australia, and her having 'skipped straight into the leading role' of Bell's *As You Like It*. In this way Rose, like Jenyns' commentators, procures all McConnell's credentials for a popular, Australian-wrought and down-to-earth Rosalind.

Rosalind measures up

Rosalind is not an easily summed-up entity. She has the potential both to reinforce and to dispel essentialist notions of gender. Moreover, her ineluctable and multi-layered performativity disturbs assumptions about the sources of authority in theatrical performance. Rosalind therefore baffles the casual modes of understanding through which theatre, particularly Shakespearean theatre, is often approached.

Examining the legacy of critical reception that has attended Australian performances of Rosalind alerts us to the ways in which popular discourse exerts a force to contain Rosalind's perplexing proclivities. While the modern Rosalinds discussed in this chapter demonstrated far more contrasts than continuities, a common yardstick seemed to have been applied to them all. This measure used for Rosalind has little to do with the 'real' Rosalind but rather consists of a set of normalising narratives and preoccupations used to contain the anarchic potentialities of the role. The earliest case in point is the first Australian female star, Essie Jenyns and many tropes fixed by commentary around her identity can be seen to recur with more recent Rosalinds.

Investigating individual performances of the role however, offers resistance to these straitening and straightening narratives. Rosalind's 'body' is more than a hypothetical site on which popular and theoretical discourse is inscribed, because Rosalind's body is also Rosalind's embodiment by the living actor. In being so, it is revitalised by meaningful particularity, idiosyncrasy, and made newly rich by the living, if ephemeral, contingencies amongst which it performs. As much as narratives of receptions strive to construe Rosalind in terms of continuities and fixed conceptions of gender and theatre, Rosalind's body retains the capacity to resist. This is not least of all because Rosalind herself is an actor. Manifestly, her dextrous role-playing provokes her audiences, both onstage and off, to play out their expectations and prejudices too.

PART III

A MIDSUMMER NIGHT'S DREAM

5

'I Pyramus am not Pyramus': 'true performing' and the magic-within-the-magic of *A Midsummer Night's Dream*

BOTTOM	What is Pyramus? A lover or a tyrant?
QUINCE	A lover, that kills himself most gallant for love.
BOTTOM	That will ask some tears in the true performing of it. If I do it, let the audience look to their eyes. I will move stones.

A Midsummer Night's Dream, act 1, scene 2, lines 17–20

BOTTOM	I have a device to make all well. Write me a prologue, and let the prologue seem to say that we do no harm with our swords, and that Pyramus is not killed indeed; and for the more better assurance, tell them that I, Pyramus, am not Pyramus, but Bottom the weaver.

A Midsummer Night's Dream, act 1, scene 3, lines 15–20

This pair of quotations reflects Nick Bottom's contradictory aspirations as an actor. He wants to move tears through the 'true performing' of tragedy and yet to distance his audience with assurances that what they see is not real. In his solutions to the challenges of theatre, Bottom unwittingly prefigures the vast spectrum of practices that have animated the stage history of *A Midsummer Night's Dream*. His suggestion of opening the casement so that real moonlight can fall on the stage smacks of pictorial realism. His conviction in his performance's capacity to elicit empathetic engagement adumbrates Stanislavskian naturalism. His antidote to the perturbing effects of stage violence is a 'device' of Brecht-like anti-illusion: a prologue to inform the audience that he and the lion are not what they seem, but workers – Bottom the weaver and Snug the joiner – representing characters.[1] What both thrills and unnerves Bottom and the mechanicals are the protean possibilities of theatrical imagining: its magic. In response, Bottom problematises dramatic practice in a way that, for all its ludicrousness, resonates with successive attempts to access, generate, and re-formulate the magic of *A Midsummer Night's Dream* through history.

In this chapter I identify two kinds of magic in *A Midsummer Night's Dream*. The first is the magic that is practiced by the magical characters and that constitutes the magic plot. A deeper and more yielding enquiry, however, is concerned with the magic that unsettles the mechanicals – the transformative possibilities of theatre. This is the magic within the magic in a play that is pre-occupied with figurative and literal theatres, with dramatic illusion, transformation, and histrionic practice. The way each production understands this magic of theatre yields a picture of its cultural and theoretical underpinnings. Magic, in any culture, is a point of convergence and exchange. It is a point at which ideas of power, beauty, and morality intersect. As such, notions of magic are peculiarly susceptible to cultural inflexion. I relate the general trajectory of the play's stage life and, in that light, observe the specific uses to which Australian productions have put the magic of *A Midsummer Night's Dream*.

'I PYRAMUS AM NOT PYRAMUS'

The stage life of *A Midsummer Night's Dream*

If cultural history is seen as a figurative stage, Shakespeare's play seems to retain a capacity to ironise the conventions, fads, artistic codes, and aesthetic sensibilities that have been played out upon that stage. The metadramatic irony in the stage history of *A Midsummer Night's Dream* inheres in its peculiar proneness to technical innovations. This penchant for the spectacular is critiqued from within by the clumsy efforts of the mechanicals in their staging of 'Pyramus and Thisbe'.

Up until the end of the nineteenth century the prevailing attitude was that theatre since Shakespeare's time had undergone a gradual evolution. The 'modern' mode of staging Shakespeare's plays on elaborate scenic stages was seen as 'a sign of the gradual perfection of a medium which Shakespeare's own age scarcely envisaged'.[2] Like *As You Like It*, *A Midsummer Night's Dream* was deemed in need of help and appears to have undergone a period of relative unpopularity following the Restoration. After a 1662 performance, Samuel Pepys famously described it as 'the most insipid, ridiculous play that ever I saw in my life'.[3] The play was then rescued by 'modern staging' to the point which saw it launched into popularity by the late nineteenth century. Patricia Tatspaugh characterises the rescue operation in this way:

> Restoration tastes...preferred adaptations that imposed order on Shakespeare's sprawling plots and that employed advances in stage machinery to create spectator-pleasing spectacle.[4]

Consequently, as early as fifty years after Shakespeare's death, the magic of *A Midsummer Night's Dream* had begun to shift its centre. No longer was it a magic amended by the audience's imagination. No longer was it a dream – an event that largely takes place in the mind of the dreamer. Rather, the play had become a platform for the performance of newfound staging technologies.

This use of the play as a vehicle for extravagant visual spectacle dominated until the early twentieth century when film realism eclipsed anything that could be accomplished on stage in that vein. Even so, the twenty-first-century offers further examples of attempts to the rescue the play through stage spectacle. I will return to this point later in discussing the work of director Benedict Andrews. Up until the twentieth century, staging of the play also frequently included elaborate songs and dances[5] and time-consuming visual set pieces which necessitated omissions from the play-text. Elision of lines from the script was common, especially those, as both Tatspaugh and Irene Dash have pointed out, that clashed with the moral sensibilities and codes of social propriety of the period.[6]

A Midsummer Night's Dream, with its fantastical characters and their mythical analogues, served as the perfect pretext for elaborate entertainments that reinforced rather than challenged the socio-cultural status quo. The 'moving clouds, moonlight, and fog' of Samuel Phelps's 1853 production at Sadler's Wells; and the mechanical birds and alleged real rabbits that populated Herbert Beerbohm Tree's 1900 production at Her Majesty's,[7] kept audiences distracted from more disturbing aspects of the play: Egeus' tyranny with which Theseus is complicit, Puck's sinister incantations about night, and Oberon's cruelty to Titania.

This renovation of the play entailed concomitant patterns in reception. In the nineteenth and early twentieth century *A Midsummer Night's Dream* developed an aura of sentimental fairytale.[8] This can be traced to a number of causes. Along with the emendations of the play's cruelties, insubordination, and eroticism, casts usually included children.[9] The Romantic period witnessed a marked increase in recognition and idealisation of the state of childhood and, as Darlene Ciraulo has identified, '*A Midsummer Night's Dream* is an important play for Romantic writers who saw in it a reflection of the creative process that takes place in the early childhood imagination'.[10] Charles and Mary Lamb's *Tales from Shakespeare* (1807) directly promoted the play's status as a collectively cherished story suitable for children.

However, the notion of Shakespeare's *A Midsummer Night's Dream* as innocuous entertainment for children underwent a drastic challenge in the mid- and late- twentieth century. Peter Brook's *Dream* for the Royal Shakespeare Company in 1970 is famous for having used Shakespeare's play to give expression to a period of aesthetic upheaval, innovation, and experimentalism in European theatre. Brook took up some of the revolutionary ideas about the play proffered by Jan Kott in his famous *Shakespeare Our Contemporary*. Kott's essay 'Titania and the Ass's Head' suggests that the Renaissance sensibility from which the play sprang was much darker than most contemporary productions ever acknowledged. The rigorous intellectualism, new efforts at historicism, regard for the script as a whole, and radical experimental aesthetics of Brook's approach have left their mark on the Shakespeare landscape on an international scale.

Patterns related to these general trends in the *Dream*'s stage history can be seen in the Australian context. In this chapter I see conceptions of the play's magic as a touchstone for identifying features of Australian *Dream*s and the kinds of exchange which mark their participation in the ongoing dialogue between the play and its performance history.[11]

A Midsummer Night's Dream in Australia

In the early twentieth century Australia echoed the contemporary European predilection for elaborate scenic stagings of Shakespeare and *A Midsummer Night's Dream* was no exception. Oscar Asche, the actor-manager who had worked for Beerbohm Tree in London, offered Shakespearean spectacles to match public appetite for pictorial realism in Australia. Asche's *A Midsummer Night's Dream* played in Melbourne at the Theatre Royal in 1913. Asche himself commended the theatre's unique capability to accommodate his 'Titania's Bower' complete with a 'fern-clad gorge, up and down which the little fairies, represented by little children of eight and ten years of age, flitted like so many hued butterflies and moths'.[12]

A slightly less elaborate offering was Allan Wilkie's outdoor production performed at Government House Gardens in Perth in 1918. Despite the avant-garde stylistic decision of performing the play in the open-air, Bill Dunstone points out that this production's politics were still identifiably conservative; affirming rather than challenging Australia's identity as a colonial outpost of Britain. Dunstone identifies the way in which '[t]he production's utopian character masked its imperial politics and seems to have blunted its self-reflexive edge'. Wilkie, who played Bottom, apparently made no attempt to suggest parallels between the command performance of 'Pyramus and Thisbe' and his own company's appearance in 'a comedy of clowns attempting the histrionic' before royalty-at-a-remove in a Perth garden.[13] Dunstone notes the paradoxical combination of aesthetic novelty with political conservatism; a paradox which, as Chapter 6 suggests, resonates with patterns of production practice in more recent times.

Wilkie's open-air *A Midsummer Night's Dream* was followed closely by many more open-air productions of Shakespeare in Perth. Rose Gaby has attributed this development to the suitableness of the warm, dry climate to outdoor events and suggests that later national trends in outdoor Shakespeare as leisure activity owe a debt to Perth's evolution of the form.[14] In the open-air repertoire of Shakespeare performances, *A Midsummer Night's Dream* was from the start, and has remained, a staple.

Along with inaugurating a culture of outdoor 'Shakespeare leisure', the other use to which *A Midsummer Night's Dream* has been put in Australia, and to which it has been seen as ideally predisposed, is education. Allan Wilkie's traditionalist slant entailed a mission of enlightenment. He asserted the belief that

> ...however inadequately [the plays] might be performed, the mere representation of the language of Shakespeare improved the people who listened, and made them better citizens of the empire.[15]

This ethos, combined with Wilkie's morally conservative sensibility and assiduous 'purifying' of the text, made him the perfect candidate for state-subsidised educational touring activity. He even convinced the Australian government authorities to grant his company free rail travel.[16] Wilkie's ambitious touring project, which comprised travelling vast distances and adapting to a range of venues, also necessitated a new economy in set features. Throughout the course of his career, he procured sumptuous costumes from London for use against a simple heavy curtain, to which he later added changeable scenic back-drops. Eventually he developed innovative lighting techniques that simplified set requirements.[17] Wilkie's encounter with the specific challenges of touring Australia, with its range of terrain, climates, and far-flung communities, offers an informative prefiguring of the educational work of the Bell Shakespeare Company.[18]

From the decade 1988 to 1998 *A Midsummer Night's Dream* was Australia's most popular play, given no fewer than twenty-six separate professional productions.[19] This remarkable popularity has by no means been typical of the play's stage history in Australia. As Golder and Madelaine point out, in the early- and mid- nineteenth century, *A Midsummer Night's Dream* was thoroughly eclipsed in popularity by the tragedies and by *The Taming of the Shrew*, the *Merry Wives of Windsor* and *The Merchant of Venice*.[20] How might this be explained? One clue is offered in the changing organisational structures and ideological approaches of theatre companies. *A Midsummer Night's Dream* is, by virtue of its ensemble nature, much less of a star vehicle than the tragedies or comedies such as *As You Like It* which figure prominent lead roles. While an actor might be remembered for her Rosalind or his Hamlet, it is less likely that Titania or Puck would be seen as defining a performance career. The play would, therefore, lack appeal for the ambitious nineteenth-century actor-manager or for the touring international star. The very features that made the play less appealing in the nineteenth century could, moreover, be seen as contributing to its popularity throughout the twentieth when, in the wake of the Berliner Ensemble, ideas of the actor as a worker gained currency. Accordingly, *A Midsummer Night's Dream* was the perfect vehicle for an experimental, self-consciously performative ensemble production such as Peter Brook's of 1970.

Peter Brook's *Midsummer Night's Dream* for the Royal Shakespeare Company which toured Australia in 1973 offers an apt point of departure for study of more recent Australian productions of the play. Hailed by Katharine Brisbane as 'a great original interpretation',[21] Brook's production was seen by many as liberating the play from the sentimental accretions of Victorian stage tradition. Brook replaced skipping, gossamer-winged child-fairies with adult trapeze artists and tumblers. Sally Jacobs' minimalist, white-box set was described as a 'deliberately antiseptic design' (*The Age*, 13 June 1973). While praising the production's exuberance, H. G. Kippax made the interesting speculation that the production had 'coarsened' and 'slackened' since its much-acclaimed season in Britain three years earlier:

> This, I suspect, is partly the result of success – too much encouragement to hunt laughs. It is also partly deliberate. At Stratford, I am told, Mendelssohn's wedding march came softly as an ironic 'quotation' as the septet [*sic*] of lovers prepared to take their vows near the end. Now it blares forth as the ass-headed Bottom, with a suggestion of an enormous phallus, is borne off to Titania's bower. Irony has yielded to the belly-laugh and the send-up.[22]

'I PYRAMUS AM NOT PYRAMUS'

Kippax's criticism is informative as an instance of Australian reception which theorises the processes which shape a touring production over its life-span. The other conjecture at which Kippax might have arrived is that the company either assumed or perceived that Australian audiences rewarded broader, bawdier, forms of humour. Undoubtedly Brook's production left its mark on the Australian theatre landscape and the tour is still a reference point for many artists of his own and later generations.

Jim Sharman, when asked to comment on his 1982/3 production for Adelaide's Lighthouse Theatre Company, expressed a debt to Brook's production:

> I'd always wanted to produce *Dream* – ever since I saw Peter Brook's production in the early 70s, and it's taken all the time since then to feel I could approach it freshly. Of course, you really can't – a director comes to such a play with accumulated influences. It's the sort of play that's entered into theatrical mythology.[23]

Sharman's ensemble included Geoffrey Rush as Theseus/Oberon, Gillian Jones as Hippolyta/Titania, and John Wood as Bottom who, like all the other mechanicals, doubled as a fairy by sprouting mechanical wings. Utilising a cast of only thirteen, the production was praised for its economy as well as the kinds of resonance it made available between the 'two worlds' of the play through role-doubling. Praise for the production certainly echoed praise for Brook's, lauding it a double triumph 'liberating *A Midsummer Night's Dream* from conventional notions of faery dreaming [and]…liberating and purifying the text'.[24] Descriptions of the production design (Sue Blane) suggest a clear intention to locate the world of the play in a recognisably theatrical domain:

> ...all the world's a dream on a pearl grey stage that is goldenly melting into a star-studded void. The grand stairway that dominates the stage climbs up and lurches right with all the improbable theatricality of an old MGM musical.[25]

The 'magic of theatre' was hereby given a conspicuous place in the production's aesthetic.

Richard Wherrett's 1989 production for the STC was notable for distinguishing itself from both the 'faery dreaming' of the early twentieth century and from Brook's radically minimalist aesthetics. Unlike Sharman's production, which was described as located 'out of any definable time or place except the bizarre dreaming that can occur in any of our heads',[26] Wherrett's offered a concrete location. Attuned to the sensibilities of the city in which it was performed Wherrett's was an urban dream, set largely in a 1980s dance club called the Wood. The production abounded with recognisable local and contemporary cultural references and Brian Thomson's set seemed to achieve an adroit blend of 1980s brashness and decadence with counter-culture punk:

> This is indeed a feast for the eyes. On one side a vast circular bed of violet tulle, mismatched on the other with a quaint grassy knoll. Up behind is the globe, with the southern hemisphere conspicuously inverted. Inside it throbs the dance party club lit by an idly turning mirror ball. Two golden arcs, one a slide, the other a ramp, complete the moonlit scene...[27]

The dualities encoded in the design also pervaded the characterisation that explored 'the notion of people leading double lives: conservative by day, uninhibited by night'.[28] Once again the role doubling permitted this nuance intended by Wherrett:

> ...for me Oberon is the same person as Theseus. He changes his name and he changes his clothes and he goes out and parties all night.[29]

The magic of the Wherrett's dream world, therefore, comprised a distinctly late-twentieth-century-Sydney form of carnivalesque inversion. Not surprisingly, in this version of topsy-turvy, recreational drugs had a role to play in the enchantments.

Like Wherrett's drugged and decadent *Dream*, Simon Phillips' 1992 production offered a precisely identifiable period setting but, in contrast, a period of austerity. Phillips directed *A Midsummer Night's Dream* for the State Theatre Company of South Australia in repertoire with *'Tis Pity She's a Whore*. Both productions were set during World War II and Phillips purposely allowed the darkness of the latter play to infect *A Midsummer Night's Dream*. He explained that he saw in *A Midsummer Night's Dream* 'a glistening, glittering, forbidden, dangerous but exciting kind of release for people when the world itself was in chaos'[30] and claimed that the play itself was imbued with a sense of war, or war just over. The magic of this production inhered in its characters' need for escape from the oppressive 'real world' in which they existed.

Taking an utterly new direction again, Noel Tovey directed an all-Indigenous cast in a production for the Olympic Arts Festival in 1997. Tovey identified resonance in the relationship between *A Midsummer Night's Dream* and the Dreaming:

> In Aboriginal culture, all the ritual stories are about Dreamtime, a time when humans and animals were the same thing. So it's not really strange to our culture to have a man turned into an ass.[31]

The production opened with the courtly set wearing Elizabethan garments made in plain white calico.[32] The neck ruffs, doublets and farthingales suggested a Tudor aesthetic set in productive tension with bare feet on a red-earth floor.[33] The fairy world departed from this semi-Elizabethan dress code. Puck, played by Laurence Clifford, wore a muddy coloured head-to-foot body suit of tassels which, combined with his humorously camp characterisation, implied the spirit of pantomime (see figure 5.1).

Figure 5.1 Laurence Clifford (Puck),
A Midsummer Night's Dream, STC, Sydney, 1997.
Photograph ©Tracey Schramm
Courtesy of STC and Tracy Schramm.

Tessa Leahy as Titania and Glenn Shea as Oberon each wore a body-suit with a serpent streaking across the chest to the shoulder and a billowing cape. Amongst the other fairies were kangaroo and lyrebird sprites. Digital images projected onto the backdrop featured Australian landscapes and a winding Rainbow Serpent. The music and sound effects, composed by Sarah de Jong, combined Tudor court sounds of the virginal and percussion with didgeridoo and clicking sticks, effecting a surprisingly seamless and new concoction. The intermingling of cultural categories accomplished by the production's aesthetics meant that its magic seemed just beyond cultural classification; various, hybrid, and alive. However, the hybridity of the production met with censure from several reviewers, whose pleas for more 'authentic' and more identifiably distinct cultural products revealed, as Emma Cox has thoughtfully pointed out, essentialist notions of cultural identity.[34]

Even this brief survey suggests that, since Brook's production, there has been a strongly articulated emphasis upon reinventing the magic of *A Midsummer Night's Dream* for a recognisably Australian and contemporary context. The following case studies continue investigation of the uses made of the magic in Australian productions of *A Midsummer Night's Dream*.

'Dealing with the sky': the Australian Shakespeare Company

Glenn Elston's outdoor Shakespeare productions for the Australian Shakespeare Company began in 1988 with *A Midsummer Night's Dream* performed in Melbourne's Royal Botanic Gardens. Classified by some as 'rough theatre' lacking in vocal subtlety,[35] Elston's productions are lighthearted in tenor, invite audience participation, involve physical stunts and laser lighting effects, and draw dependably large audiences every summer. They generate a socio-cultural space which differs from that of indoor theatre and even from most open-air theatre. Geoffrey Milne has speculated that, as a consequence, Elston's productions draw audience members who would never usually attend theatre.[36]

The 'Shakespeare in the park' event has accrued a raft of well-rehearsed audience customs which involve arriving early, reserving a space, and consuming a picnic. With reference to the second season of Elston's *Dream* in Sydney, one reviewer stated,

> Spread out on lawns facing the lake between magnificent trees, the audience knows both what to expect and how to enjoy itself. Anticipation gives way to a sense of reunion.[37]

This confidence and sense of ease leads to a distinct and natural demographic stratification of the audience.[38] Older audience members typically sit on chairs at the back of the roped-off space, younger ones lounge on rugs on the grass, and children often sit close to the front of the stage. This pattern of autonomous grouping and socio-economic stratification, suggesting a parallel with the Globe Theatre, appears to permit each group the opportunity to perform its own identity for the others. The way the audience organises itself has obvious implications for the actors. Rather than seeing uniformly blended rows of faces, the actors see at a glance who has chosen the margins, who has chosen the centre, who is lying down, who is in a chair; and can shape their interaction with audience members accordingly.

The Australian Shakespeare Company performers cultivate a distinct two-way connection with audience members. This dynamic is facilitated by a playful and open responsiveness to unforeseen contingencies and evinces something of the Company's view of 'the magic of theatre'. Doug Anderson described this mutually indulgent relationship in the following way:

> If there is a tendency to illustrate and accentuate with florid, traditional mannerisms, it doesn't jar with the context – a

context which seems to encompass whatever it needs, confident the audience will accept and grant licence. And they do.[39]

The outdoor context makes Elston's productions vulnerable to uncontrolled variables such as weather, wildlife, and technical hitches. Instead of blocking out these interruptions and accidents, the actors exhibit an energetic ability to incorporate unexpected events, even to transform them into meaningful moments within the world of the play. In this way, the real world of the Botanic Gardens is magically transformed to fit the needs of the fictional Athens or Wood. The world becomes a stage and the stage becomes the world.

Most commonly, the marriage of fictional moment with accident produces a comic effect. For instance, during a 1993 performance Hermia (Jane Longhurst) and Lysander's (Guy Pearce) escape to the forest was dogged by the persistent drone of a low-flying plane. Rather than ignoring it, Pearce looked up at the plane – by now the focus of audience attention – and said to Hermia, 'your father's out looking for us!' In this way, what might have been a distraction ended by drawing the audience back into the world of the play and back together.

Permeability of the partition between the world and the play can also promote deeper kinds of artistic serendipity. In days prior to a 2005 Melbourne performance, a storm had struck Melbourne's Botanic Gardens and left a devastation of strewn leaves and branches. This chaos fused quickly in the imagination with the 'forgeries of Oberon's jealousy'. Moreover, just as Titania (Christie Sistrunk) spoke of the 'contagious fogs…falling on the land' (act 2, scene 1), a breeze caught the mist from the smoke machine and swept it over the audience in furls and claws.

At each performance occasion, the living backdrop of the outdoor venue offered up chance events that were adeptly transformed to become part of the drama. This kind of magic is not achieved by all outdoor Shakespeare productions. Most simply use the outdoor setting as a flat, if appealing, backdrop.[40] Through their integration of their living context into the imaginative life of the play, the Australian Shakespeare Company brought about a distinct kind of magic transformation.

This robust and playful approach to the work of dramatic transformation not only framed each performance, but also pervaded the fairy magic within the play. Just as the cast were evidently working against the odds to make the play a success, Puck and the lower fairies were maladroit magicians whose agency was flawed. In the 2005 Melbourne performance, the very first piece of fairy magic was deliberately inept. At the beginning of act 2 a fairy, played by Kate Fryer, entered and 'flung' coloured lights one by one onto three tall conifers. She had an instant of smug self-satisfaction at her 'trick' before the lights faded out one by one, demanding that she perform her trick again. Puck, played by Daniel McBurnie, was also prone to magical mishaps and, in one of his back-flipping routines, actually lost his outfit. This brought a spontaneous smile to Oberon (James Stafford's) face and fitted perfectly with this Puck's clumsy magic mischief. The audience seemed forever awaiting the next enchanting blunder.

Arguably, Elston's productions restore a populist appeal to theatre in Australia. Certainly Elston's *Dreams* are statistically popular and, what is more, draw the same people year after year. How might we explain this unusual serial attendance of the same play? I suggest that what audience members perceive as its quality of magic is the production's ability to expose and embrace the risks and chances implicit in out-door, live theatre. Phil Sumner, an actor with the company for several seasons, commented on the energising potential of uncontrolled variables in performance:

> It's formal theatre in a way but it's exciting because you can't control the environment… I love it. It's physically and vocally challenging and you can be epic and operatic because you're not dealing with a theatre building – you're dealing with the world: the sky. No stops on you.[41]

In modern Australian culture, as Richard Fotheringham has pointed out, there seems an intractable division between sport and theatre:

> the superior importance of sport in modern culture has led to a system of preferred values that venerates sport as an activity which is spontaneous, expresses ideas and ideals through action, conceals effort and pain, is structured but unpredictable, and which has unplanned resolutions but with results that can be objectively and empirically measured. In contrast, theatre is supposed to be artificial, verbal rather than active, given to exaggerating effort and suffering, predictable, and with contrived, pre-planned conclusions, and judged by non-empirical (and therefore rather dubious) standards of 'taste' and 'technique'.[42]

Elston's *Dreams* baffle this entrenched division – their spontaneity and dynamism coming as a novelty to the modern audience accustomed to forms of art in which all 'effects' are highly managed. In this respect Elston's *A Midsummer Night's Dreams* cultivated something of the open-ended excitement of a sporting contest. Perhaps this, and the mode of outdoor relaxation, can explain the spell Elston's *Dreams* seem to have cast over Australian audiences in recent decades.

'Physical magic': the Bell Shakespeare Company

The Bell Shakespeare Company's 2004 production of the *Dream* directed by Anna Volska, shared many characteristics of Elston's popular theatre mode. It was characterised by fluency of action, clarity of meaning and beguiling athleticism.[43] While Bell Shakespeare's 'main-stage' productions tour a few of Australia's major cities and perform chiefly in State theatre venues, the 2004 *Dream* was a regional touring production with an itinerary of nearly thirty far-flung venues from Mount Isa in western Queensland to Kalgoorlie in Western Australia. Volska explained that this made special demands upon the troupe of nine, including regular after-show engagements, many schools audiences and long hours of travelling.[44] Such a schedule also enforces constraints on set-design and technical requirements: the set and lighting rig needed to be highly flexible to suit a range of venues and needed to be able to be taken down or put up within three hours.

When asked to what degree the stylistic decisions were shaped by these constraints, however, Volska did not speak in terms of limitation but in terms of imaginative resourcefulness required of the audience:

> the less set you need, the less you're tied down, the more people's imaginations can wander and...really go into the words....I think Shakespeare's words provide the visuals for you and if you're not provided with them then your mind delights to work all the harder.[45]

The approach this production took to the magic in the play and to the 'magic of theatre' was indelibly shaped by this belief in resourcefulness. One reviewer claimed that the production 'trusts the text and trusts the cast, and is richly repaid by both'.[46] Certainly there was a pervasive confidence in the spirit of this production combined with warmth towards the audience. The craft and artistic ingenuity was not self-conscious and distracting but deft.

In Sydney, the Bell production premiered at the Riverside theatre in Parramatta – a large venue seating over seven-hundred with a proscenium-arch stage. The set, designed by Jennie Tate, consisted of a circular curtain rail suspended from the flies. From this fell diaphanous white layers of curtain. At the commencement these curtains formed a transparent cylindrical tent with a wide opening facing the audience. Behind the tent, and running the whole length and breadth of the cyclorama was an opulent purple curtain. The initial impression, efficiently conveyed, was anticipation of a regal wedding. To augment this, the action began with a long white gown being lowered from the flies. Michelle Doake as Hippolyta, with the assistance of an attendant, tried it on prior to Theseus' (Luciano Martucci) entrance. This short opening sequence of bridal costume-fitting was also a subtle reference to theatrical role-playing and was particularly apt in a production in which every actor played at least two roles. The pairing of drama and dream-state was also effected in the opening scene with Egeus (Tony Poli), Hermia (Georgia Adamson), Demetrius (Timothy Walter), and Lysander (Simon Bossell) lying on the floor as if asleep and rising up respectively to enter the action as they spoke.

In this way the first few minutes of the performance developed a rich metaphorical vocabulary for dramatic transformation as ritual, as role-play, and as dream. Like the play, the texture of Volska's stage-world reflected awareness of many layers and types of reality. As the play progressed, the actors also seemed adept at manoeuvering between different modes of performativity.

Helena (Kate Box), perhaps the character least associated with magic in the play, was a character in whom the complex notion of mediated reality as magic was concentrated. In Lysander and Hermia's act 1 account to Helena of their intended flight, her soppy sense of wonderment and vicarious longing was instantly familiar as a response to a television soap or to reality TV. Reinforcing this, the lovers had the self-conscious, tag-team confessional mode of talk-show guests or reality TV participants. Helena's longing seemed, as a consequence, as much a longing to partake of the magic of a public/secret love-match, as it was to find love herself. This echoed the contemporary cultural common-place that the more mediated a life is – by Facebook, by Twitter, by being on television – the more intensely real it becomes.

This feature merits consideration for several reasons. First, the mediated-life dynamic is germane to a play that treats competing kinds of reality and narratives told, untellable, and performed for audiences within audiences. Second, by locating a contemporary analogue for the play's self-conscious performativity, whether inadvertently or intentionally, the Bell production engaged its audience's interest and understanding. Thirdly, because Shakespeare's play problematises simplistic consumption of performed narratives, it has the potential to activate the critical faculties of audience members in relation to this and other kinds of 'performed' lives.

This notion of Helena's longing for the reality that only an audience can confer was advanced in the scene where Lysander and Demetrius, having forsaken Hermia, pursue Helena (act 3, scene 2). Helena, thinking Hermia is confederate in the men's prank against her, makes a long speech about their early days of friendship. This speech can be difficult to manage on stage. Do the men, who have been fighting one another, stop and listen to Helena's complaint? Or do they continue their fray in the background potentially upstaging Helena? Why does Helena speak at such length?

Within the dynamic already established, the Bell production made humorous sense of this scene. Self-consciously forming herself and Hermia into tableau, Helena poured out her idealising narrative of their shared childhood in a manner worthy of any talk-show guest with a grievance. Appropriately, Lysander and Demetrius forsook their skirmish and became an instant audience.

'I PYRAMUS AM NOT PYRAMUS'

Lysander leant jauntily, crooking his elbow on Demetrius' shoulder, and the two were lost in the vicarious emotional ebbs and flows of Helena's tale as if arrested by a television screen in a shop window. In this moment, ironically, Helena won the 'reality' of which she dreamt. She had her five minutes of fame but also began to suspect a distorting, mediating influence at play. Helena, like Bottom, aspired to be noticed in this production. However, when magic intervened to elevate each to a place of extravagant public attention and affection, they questioned the veracity of the experience.

Despite the critique of mediated fame that this production opened up, its means for doing so were very simple. When asked about the kind of magic she envisioned for this production, Anna Volska said that she placed emphasis on 'physical magic'.[47] The actors themselves generated the magic, whether in the form of acrobatic feats or by sleight of hand. Richard Gyoerffy, who played Puck, is an accomplished magician and acrobat. His back-flipping and tumbling not only contributed an awe-inspiring spectacle to the performance but also facilitated great fluency and energy in scene transitions. Puck's supernatural abilities were given a palpable life in Gyoerffy's unnatural dexterity.

The physical magic alluded to by Volska was not only in the form of tricks and stunts. It also took the form of evocative physicality and casting economy. The same actors who played the young lovers and the mechanicals, also played the fairies who took the form of half-human half-animal creatures. Their whirrs and clicks and scuttling, tumbling entrances in dim light denoted a new location; a forest, or more precisely, an Australian bush-clearing. They were uniform in appearance, dressed in baggy grey knee-length suits which implied simultaneously small nocturnal marsupials and mythical creatures. Instead of having one fairy address Puck, two fairies rolled and scrambled over each other and spoke alternate lines.

A MIDSUMMER NIGHT'S DREAM

In the first confrontation of Titania and Oberon the fairies built up the statures of the Fairy King and Queen by functioning as eerily living trains to their figures (see figure 5.2). Their responses to Titania and Oberon's feuding dialogue took the form of physical shapes that magnified the visual effect of the feud. While not being the dark or macabre creatures of Jan Kott's vision, these fairies were disconcerting. They belonged to Australian native bush lore rather than to European tradition, and they recalled cunning, tricksy creatures from Indigenous Dreamtime stories and children's books such as Mem Fox's *Possum Magic*, Dorothy Wall's *Blinky Bill*, and May Gibbs' *Snugglepot and Cuddlepie*. In this way the fairies tapped the idiom of fairytale but re-located it within a recognisably Australian tradition.

Figure 5.2 From left: Georgia Adamson, Michelle Doake (Titania), Kate Box, Timothy Walter, *A Midsummer Night's Dream*, Bell Shakespeare, 2004.
Photograph ©Heidrun Lohr
Courtesy of Bell Shakespeare and Heidrun Lohr.

The magic personae in the Bell production were decisively benevolent if cantankerous. Puck and Oberon's immense rapport with the audience gave a playful nuance to the magic spells and in turn shaped how the 'magic of theatre' was conceived. Despite the tendency of the proscenium arch stage to suit fourth-wall naturalism, Oberon and Puck often punctured the wall, addressing the audience directly and inviting collaboration in their magic. This was particularly evident in Oberon's use of Shakespearean comedy's open-hiding conceit.

Eavesdropping scenes are a recognised trope of Shakespearean comedy and usually ask for a balanced share of suspended disbelief and outright confederacy from the audience. In *Much Ado About Nothing* Beatrice and Benedick attempt to conceal themselves physically, even though we as the audience know that their friends are aware of their respective presences. In *Twelfth Night*, Andrew, Toby and Fabian get into the box-tree and, as inept as their concealment seems, Malvolio does not detect it. *A Midsummer Night's Dream* pushes this open-hiding conceit a step further. Oberon makes no pretence of hiding at all but directly seeks cover in the imaginative indulgence of the audience alone. In the Bell production, Luciano Martucci exploited the collusive delight of this moment. When Helena pursued Demetrius onstage in his presence, he said directly to the audience 'I am invisible, / And I will overhear their conference' (act 2, scene 1, lines 186–7). Using a wry tone, Martucci acknowledged the slightly ludicrous nature of the device before passing the sleeve of his kimono across his face. The ironic, confiding mode used by Martucci allowed him to command allegiance within the fictional world of the play but also to operate on the metatheatrical plane, prompting a sense of camaraderie with the theatre audience.

Magic in the Bell production was characterised by evocative clarity of communication and by the establishment of multiple levels of exchange between the actors and the audience. The metatheatrical dynamic of public narrative in the play found a contemporary analogue in mediated fame. The aesthetics of the fairy world were resonant of the Australian bush and, despite the fourth-wall dynamic implied by the proscenium arch space, Puck and Oberon established a spirited confederacy with the audience in acknowledging the playful contrivances which constitute a theatrical event. This dynamic is especially apposite in performance of *A Midsummer Night's Dream*, for as James L. Calderwood puts it, it is a play whose

> existence and significance are created by a collective imaginative act...the play and the audience imaginatively unite and mutually transform each other in the act of knowledge. The theatrical experience made possible by the play thus mirrors the fictional experience mirrored in the play.[48]

'Difficult pleasure': Company B

If the treatment of magic by the Volska and Elston productions exhibited an emphasis on popular and broadly accessible modes of entertainment, the 2004 Company B production implied a pointed counter-intention. Benedict Andrews' production received almost ubiquitous critical acclaim for doing something new and unexpected with Shakespeare's comedy. In response, I find myself swimming against the tide of popular opinion to identify in Andrews' production forms of stylistic and ideological anachronism which dilute the meta-theatrical complexity of the play. The point I made about the Elston and Bell produtions is that they tapped the intrinsic meta-theatricality of Shakespeare to open up spaces of play for local cultural idiom. My leading thought about Benedict Andrews' *Dream* for Company B is that it achieved the obverse.

Benedict Andrews has become recognised in Australia for his affinity with German expressionist modes of theatre. Citing Barrie

Kosky amongst his influences, Andrews stated that for him 'difficult pleasure is entertainment'.[49] *A Midsummer Night's Dream* was Andrews' Shakespeare directing debut and considered by many an uncharacteristic choice for him. The seeming clash of Andrews' artistic profile with the play was used for publicity: 'A director with a penchant for works about life's dark side has taken on Shakespeare's sunniest play'.[50] Having come from directing Sarah Kane's *Cleansed* in Berlin, Andrews expressed a deliberate desire to do the very different plays alongside each other, seeing them both as 'plays about love'.[51] He further advanced the notion of his bold experimentalism by expressing indifference to the play's production history.[52]

Figure 5.3 Helen Buday (Titania), Jacek Koman (Bottom), *A Midsummer Night's Dream*, Company B, Belvoir Street Theatre, Sydney, 2004.
Photograph ©Heidrun Lohr
Courtesy of Company B and Heidrun Lohr.

Despite the promise of something new, the Company B production echoed past productions in its assent to Jan Kott's vision of the play. In a well-honoured tradition the program quoted Kott: 'Titania and the Ass's Head' from Kott's 1965 work *Shakespeare Our*

Contemporary and, more accurately than most, the fairy-world of Andrews' vision recreated Kott's: 'Titania's court consisting of old men and women, toothless and shaking, their mouths wet with saliva, who sniggeringly procure a monster for their mistress'.[53]

In his commitments to a Kottian vision and expressionistic style, Andrews' production performed a muting effect upon both forms of the play's magic. The characters, rather than actively driving the plot, became elaborate spectacles of abjection; the fantastical was translated from supernatural kinds of power possessed by characters, to dark, subconscious appetites under which they laboured. The rulers of the fairly realm exercised a dubious and diluted kind of dominion. Oberon (Socratis Otto), his bare torso wreathed with a razor-wire tattoo, seemed bitter and damaged, hauling himself along the ground like a lizard. Titania's (Helen Buday) minions were lumbering masked old men in tutus and her union with Bottom was a public spectacle of bestiality and bondage.

Likewise, Andrews' production flattened out the magic within the magic of the *Dream*. Rather than giving play to the self-reflexive energies of the play – its dynamic realisation of theatres, its direct appeal to audience, its polyphony – Andrews offered an esoteric one-way spectacle.[54] This was particularly remarkable given the innate dynamics of upstairs Belvoir. Flanked on three sides by audience, the Belvoir stage invites two way exchange and recognition of the communal nature of theatre. Nevertheless, Andrews' *Midsummer Night's Dream*, with the exception of the mechanicals' scenes discussed in Chapter 6, drew on codes of voyeurism which functioned to distance the audience members, positioning them as detached observers rather than an integrated, living dimension of the theatrical moment.

The magic of Andrews' voyeuristic theatre spectacle was the extraordinary license to look granted by two factors. The first was the obscurity of a darkened theatre. The second factor was an expressionistic mode of acting that involved vacillating naturalistic and stylised vocabularies of gesture, uneven patterns of verse speaking and inexplicable stunts. This contributed opacity to the performance which militated against the sympathetic involvement associated with naturalism. However, it also fell short of achieving naturalism's opposite – Brecht's Verfremdungseffekt – in which anti-illusion and anti-naturalism are intended to block the obscuring emotion of empathy and provoke, instead, disinterested reasoning and judgment. The simultaneous cultivation of a voyeuristic license to look in Andrews' production displaced the exigency for reasoning engagement. In a voyeuristic theatre of spectacle, unlike in Brecht's Epic theatre, the spectator is rewarded for relaxing both faculties of judgment and feeling.

At the outset, most of the actors lay on the softly lit blue carpet singing the Velvet Underground's 'Pale Blue Eyes'. Eventually the gauze curtains dividing the stage from the audience were drawn and Luke Carroll as Philostrate in track pants and a formal, black jacket gently 'woke' some of the characters. At first the characters rose only to kneeling and much of the first scene was performed in this posture: Egeus (Tony Phelan) swiveled around appealing to Theseus in an agitated manner and Hermia (Billie Rose Prichard) remained kneeling in submission. Egeus' condemnation of Hermia was sinister and violent. Standing behind her, he tore the neck of her dress open to show the 'love token' necklace she wore. Hermia, rather than defensively fixing her clothes, spent the whole scene kneeling like a martyr with her upper chest exposed and her hands dangling by her side. Eventually Theseus, in advising Hermia of her potential fate, knelt behind her and refastened her dress.

Hermia's response to her dire abuse continued the vein of rigid anti-naturalism. Directly after the departure of the other characters, Lysander approached the still kneeling Hermia and held out a piece of gum. This she ate sullenly from the palm of his hand with her hands still dangling by her sides. Her action, like many to follow, was vaguely erotic, vaguely playful, and vaguely ritualistic. Apparently the purpose of the gum was to create another surprising effect cum heavy-handed metaphor: on vowing to 'keep promise' the couple kissed and the gum was strung out between their mouths.

This highly symbolic and stylised mode of acting jarred with the subsequent resort to naturalism. Helena, having lain on the floor throughout the preceding sequence, arrived in the lovers' presence by simply waking up. Helena and Hermia's duet about swaying the motion of Demetrius' heart (act 1, scene 1, lines 181–201) was played by the actors as children; lying side-by-side on their stomachs and swinging their feet in the air. This relaxed, natural mode of companionship seemed forced after the previous image of Egeus shuffling on his knees and Hermia submitting to humiliation like a sacrificial lamb. To conclude the sequence, Hermia, as if observing a compulsive ritual, made her departure by leaping each of the orange chairs that lined the curtained perimeter of the stage.

This stylistic vacillation between non-naturalistic and naturalistic gestural vocabularies was reinforced in the speaking of dramatic verse. Rarely were verse passages invested with a sense of living exigency. Rather, the words had an air of mechanical recitation at times subjected to inexplicable contortions. For instance, Oberon, in explaining to Puck the origins of the 'love in idleness' flower (act 2, scene 1, lines 155–74), spoke lines with a pedantically leaden stress pattern, while clambering over Puck, pressing his palms to Puck's eyes and staring blankly into the footlights. This contrivance flattened out the individual performer's vivacity and the magic, or at least mercurial possibilities, of poetic utterance.

Some of the actors slipped out of this rigidly codified mode into engaging naturalism at times. When Helen Buday entered as Titania she was the first character to speak verse in a purposeful, integrated way. Her compassionate grief about the trouble wrought upon the human, fairy, and natural worlds – the 'forgeries' of Oberon's jealousy – carried force. She spoke as if to change things within the world of the play, rather than simply in conformity with an established stylistic convention. Such moments of purposeful speech alternating with highly self-conscious chanting and recitation created the unevenness observed by reviewer Stephen Dunne:

> It's bitsy because it's uneven – in performance terms, with some actors more attuned to the work and the direction than others…Andrews is rescuing a play that doesn't need rescuing, and the play's textual strengths and emotions are made remote and uneven by uneven acting and flashy 'look-at-me' directorial invention.[55]

If *A Midsummer Night's Dream* has achieved status as a well-known and collectively loved form of escapism, Andrews' voyeuristic/expressionist slant made it newly strange. The production struck the note of the play's weirdness, particularly its deviant sexual appetites and cruelty, in an unforgettable way, revealing humanity deformed rather than transmuted by desire. In striking this single note, however, the complex harmonic of the whole was lost. In this manifestation of director's theatre, the intellectual project was the thing – played, as it were, on what was (mis)understood as the flat platform of the play. Such an intellectual project is a bad fit for *A Midsummer Night's Dream* – a play that is sprung with its own sophisticated mechanisms of estrangement. Kott's commentary and Brook's subsequent production were couched as attempts to resuscitate these embedded complexities after a long period of stifling behind the Victorian picture stage. In contrast, the frame imposed by Andrews' approach re-instated a dynamic which smothered the self-reflexive energies of the play, turning a vitally challenging and multi-voiced work into a titillating spectacle.

As much as Company B's production sought to defy the moral 'niceness' historically associated with *A Midsummer Night's Dream*, it bore uncanny resemblance to the Victorian appetite for sensationalist theatre. Andrews' approach was accepted as sophisticated postmodern pastiche: enthrallment to eclecticism and stylistic possibilities rather than a cohesive and communicable vision of the play. However, in the light of the play's stage legacy I cannot help but observe that this work replicates much earlier productions in its attempt to renovate or, as Dunne puts it, to rescue Shakespeare.

Unlike the renovators of the nineteenth century, Andrews left most of the text intact. He articulated recognition of the potential force of the poetry in performance, calling the play 'a gorgeously light, beautiful, naïve, playful thing with breathtaking poetry', adding 'It's like breathing to hear this play'.[56] Andrews even expressed a positive commitment to the play's aurality:

> It's incredibly exhilarating to see the way the language works like body explosions, thought explosions, imagination explosions...the poet Ted Hughes calls it a flinging open of the door of the left side of the brain, when a kind of animal comes out. It's just great stuff to plug into. Words that become incredibly present through the body of the actor and through the act of staging.[57]

Yet, despite being attuned to the play's dominant aesthetic currency of sound, Andrews' dual commitment to voyeurism and expressionistic modes of acting left little scope for the innate power of the language to do its work. In a manner comparable to Beerbohm Tree and Charles Kean, Andrews strove to elicit astonishment and in doing so heightened the spectacle but diluted the affective complexity of the play.

The disjunction between Andrews' articulated emphasis upon the language of the play and his production's obscuring of its poetic force, highlights a discernible tension within contemporary Australian theatrical practice. On the one hand, there is a well-grounded confidence and excitement about the potential for Shakespeare's play to speak to the immediate context. (After all, *A Midsummer Night's Dream* is, surely by now, part of Australia's own cultural history.) On the other hand, there is an anxious drive to exculpate the play, and perhaps Australian theatrical activity, from the charge of easy pleasure by importing models from Europe. This is possibly a new incarnation of Australian cultural cringe, one that simply looks further east on the European continent for the stamp of respectably rigorous and contemporary ideological approaches to theatre.

The magic characters and events of *A Midsummer Night's Dream* are rife with unresolved tensions between light and dark. These tensions have their play in the genuinely unpredictable space between the performance and the audience. *A Midsummer Night's Dream* is not a two-dimensional realist drama which prescribes simplistic empathy. On the contrary, the essential magic of *A Midsummer Night's Dream* is its metatheatricality: it invites recognition of its own status as art and acknowledges its own dependence on the living bodies of actors and of audience members. As such it is a play whose meaning is radically permeable to the particularity of place, time, and the personalities by whom and before whom it is performed.

In contrast to Andrews' production, Elston's and Volska's cultivated a lively and living interaction between the imaginative world of the play and its specific Australian performance context. In Elston's *Dream* this comprised a robust responsiveness to the vicissitudes of the live outdoor event and a fairy world correspondingly prone to humorous mishaps. In Volska's production this comprised deployment of Australian fairy lore and a cheeky undercutting of theatrical contrivance to collude with the audience. Both productions in some measure recalled the histrionic practice of the mechanicals – opportunistic, inviting risks and courting serendipitous coincidences. Rather than being imposed from the director down, magic in these productions was generated from Bottom up.

6

Power and play: staging authority and subversion in *A Midsummer Night's Dream*

To what extent does authority depend upon the effective performance of authority? *A Midsummer Night's Dream* is a play that, in performance, confronts us repeatedly with this question. It is a play which gives prominence to seemingly rigid hierarchies of gender and social class: wives are expected to submit to husbands, the conquered to conquerer, daughters to fathers, the young to the old, the minion to the ruler, and the actor to the actor manager. Yet this last instance – the instance of theatre – is one that hints at the fragility of the whole edifice and at the manner in which it can be dismantled.

Peter Quince's authority over the mechanicals is one of many instances in the play where assumed authority is splintered from authority-in-fact. Ostensibly, Quince is allocated a role of authority: in act 1, scene 2, he holds the book and calls the names, addressing the 'whole company' as no other member of the company does. While seeming to submit to this arrangement, Nick Bottom corrodes it from the outset. He repeatedly addresses Quince in an obsequious manner as 'good Peter Quince', and after every interruption seems to return focus to Quince's project. Yet Bottom's very insistence on Quince's 'authority' undercuts the performance of that authority. If it were authority-in-fact, it would hardly need to be handed back to Quince over six times in the course of the short scene. Bottom's excessive designation of Quince's authority, together with his own compelling performativity, equates to Bottom's authority in performance. That this paradox of authority takes place amongst a company of actors serves as a metatheatrical realisation of the mercurial quality of authority in performance and of the many variables that shape it.[1]

Peter Quince is not alone in his failed performance of authority. The play opens with such a failed performance. Theseus makes a histrionic and very egocentric gesture of public authority – he claims the moon 'lingers' *his* desires and his remedy for impatience involves further imperious inventions:

> Go, Philostrate,
> Stir up the Athenian youth to merriments.
> Awake the pert and nimble spirit of mirth.
> Turn melancholy forth to funerals –
> The pale companion is not for our pomp (act 1, scene 1, lines 11–15).

He then assays to mend the past with poetic remedy:

> Hippolyta, I wooed thee with my sword,
> And won thy love doing thee injuries.
> But I will wed thee in another key –
> With pomp, with triumph and with reveling (act 1, scene 1, lines 16–19).

Theseus' supposed authority, extended through rhetorical ingenuity, knows no bounds. It stretches from earth to heaven, and from the past to the future. It can even govern, by proxy, the personified entities mirth and melancholy. It is an aesthetically striking and agile performance of authority but is Theseus' authority, authority-in-fact? The play offers several possibilities for its subversion. Not immediately evident to a reader, however, these possibilities rely on staging to give them particular subversive force.

First, rather than prompting an exchange of affection, Theseus is left alone in his claim of love reciprocated. 'I...won thy love doing thee injuries', he says to Hippolyta, but her silence as the wounded party haunts the surety of his statement. In performance meaning must be made of her silence: whether submissive, stoic, indifferent, resentful, or frankly hostile.[2]

Secondly, Theseus' command to 'Stir up the Athenian youth to merriment' and to 'Send melancholy forth to funerals', is followed directly by the arrival of one of his subjects 'full of vexation with complaint against his child' (act 1, scene 2, lines 22–3). The dramatic irony of this juxtaposition – joltingly evident in performance through tonal shift – is that Theseus' commands are immediately contradicted.[3] His sanguine projections are met with their exact opposite. Instead of playing the self-fashioned spur to mirth, he is cornered into becoming the pedantic enforcer of law.

The idea of Theseus' 'failure' is not new, but precisely what kind of failure is it? Laura Levine has argued that it is a failure endemic to theatre: Theseus' project is one of transforming his own sexual violence through theatre ('pomp', 'triumph', and 'reveling'), and that, in this project, he fails. Moreover, Levine suggests that

> beneath the play's apparent resolution of discord lies a view of theatricality itself as the producer of insistent and unmanageable sexual desire, a desire that is inherently animalistic.

In Levine's view, theatre fails as a transformative remedy in *A Midsummer Night's Dream* because it is – as its early modern detractors claimed – a kind of violation of both the intellect and the imagination.[4] For Levine, this kind of theatre is a form of cultural production which, like Theseus' court and patriarchal society in general, necessitates the violation of female bonds and of the female body.[5]

However, Levine's otherwise rigorous analysis stops short of overturning the notion of the play-text as anything other than an authoritative and autogenous form of cultural production. I hasten to point out that what Levine detects as 'the play's view of theatricality' is only one of many competing variables in the way it makes meaning as a cultural product. Levine addresses static historical conceptions of theatre, but not the uniquely volatile *experience* of theatre and the multiple dimensions through which meaning is made and challenged within it. As the Quince example makes plain, there is a built-in volatility to authority in theatre. For, implicit in theatre's unpredictable arousal of and dependence on desire is its equally 'unmanageable' generativity. New, and potentially subversive, meanings are born every time a play unites with a new context and, importantly, with a new set of performing bodies. This generative view of theatrical meaning is one which seems to elude Levine and baffle Quince, but which a focused survey of Australian productions of the play serves to illuminate.

In discussing the play's 'meanings' it is important to reiterate the centrality of staging to my approach. As W. B. Worthen has pointed out, there are two domains in which scripted drama makes meaning today:

> In the West today scripted drama is identified at once through the institutions that conceive its meanings in terms of its textual form, and through the institutional practices that transform the text into something else – *stage behaviour* – and that lend that behaviour significance, *force* in theatrical performance.[6]

It is with the latter kind of meaning, 'significance', or 'force' that I am chiefly concerned. Chapter 2 introduced the notion that 'force' and 'authority' in dramatic performance are inseparable from the force of the particular actor's performance. It follows then that, once again, the most fruitful kind of inquiry into authority and subversion of authority will attend to particular instances of their staging.

Authority and subversion are crucial studies in theatre because, in the constitution of the theatrical event, power never resides purely in the text. Regardless of how flatly power seems to be presented by the text, a mere wave of the actor's hand or wink of her eye retains power to ironise, to subvert and to re-orientate the assumed politics of a scene, even of an entire play. This is further enriched by the fact that the text itself appears to acknowledge and revel in the mercurial force of the performative moment. In Hippolyta's silence, in Helena's verbosity, in Titania's enigmatic overthrow, in Bottom's vision – in short, in the spaces between the words and the bodies who speak them – Shakespeare's play lays down as its foundation a protean instability of power structures.

Helena: gender and power

It has often been observed that Helen and Hermia are as indistinguishable as Lysander and Demetrius: ironic humour thereby adhering in the insistence of the characters in choosing particular partners.[7] However, like the men's ironically ineffectual arguments for their difference, Helena's repeated claims of sameness (act 1, scene 1, line 227; act 3, scene 2, lines 204–15) to Hermia are revealed to be ill-founded. Helena is importantly different from Hermia and in staging the play it is at the point of their difference, and not in their sameness, that there lies a potential hub of subversive energy.

Unlike Hermia, Helena is a socially and romantically marginalised figure in *A Midsummer Night's Dream*. Her marginal status can be coded in performance as empowering or disempowering. A vital feature of the performance context that distinguishes it from a reading of the play or of a literary fictional narrative, is the ironic power that can be wielded by an ostensibly disempowered figure. While a written narrative can allow a character to fade in significance through lack of mention, abjection on stage is a more complex phenomenon. A character who stands, whether literally or figuratively, at the margins of events on stage draws the eye of the audience as much as, if not more than, characters who are imbedded in the action of the scene. If the marginal character is conspicuously silent or, moreover, confides compellingly in the audience, her performative force can be multiplied again, even as she bemoans her outcast state.

Operating within dominantly patriarchal societies, it is chiefly Shakespeare's female characters who retain the potential to activate this paradox of power. Viola in *Twelfth Night* offers the perfect example of a character who is ostensibly disempowered from the very outset of the drama, but who can use her social-misfit status to mobilise the sympathy of the audience. Viola is in every sense a monster in the margins: in the margins of Illyrian structures of authority and in the margins of the stage.

At the outset of *A Midsummer Night's Dream* Helena is, somewhat like Viola, stranded. Hippolyta, Hermia, and Titania are dramatised in dilemmas of constraint or coercion by oppressive patriarchal structures of authority. In contrast, Helena is abandoned, spurned, and socially and relationally wracked. As a consequence of being excluded from the determining influences of social hierarchy (albeit against her wishes) and of her relationship with the audience, Helena is a character left peculiarly free to be determined by the force of the particular actor who plays the role, and by choices made by the director about the kind of world in which she exists. It is certainly the case that the degree of agency that Helena's outsider status permits her varies to an extraordinary degree from one production to the next. Below I examine some choices made about Helena in the casting, performance and direction of the play in Australia and discuss the implications of these choices for staging authority and subversion.

In Noel Tovey's 1997 all-Indigenous production of *A Midsummer Night's Dream* for the STC, the rigid authority structures of Duke Theseus' Athens were evident from the outset. There was a ceremonial stiffness about the speech patterns and movement in the initial scenes that implied a sense of oppressively imposed order. Many of the actors, particularly Gary Cooper who played Lysander, spoke with a formal, English-inflected accent. In this light, the pale Tudor garments worn by the characters offered an echo of Julie Dowling's *The Paper Dress*: a painting which depicts a young Aboriginal girl in a stiff, frilly paper prototype of a dress – a practice garment, with all that this implies. The characters' Aboriginality, not to mention vitality, seemed subsumed by the blank and oppressive machinery of British theatrical and cultural traditions.

If Tovey's selection of Shakespeare as the vehicle for proving the merit of Aboriginal talent implied (in some reviewers' opinions) too much reverence for Shakespeare, then the use of Elizabethan garments could be seen as reinforcing the problematic Eurocentricity of the endeavour. If not for Tovey, then for many non-Indigenous Australian commentators, these choices proved a source of chagrin. Emma Cox encapsulates the dilemma:

> Tovey's desire to demonstrate the skill of Aboriginal actors via Shakespeare has problematic implications, inasmuch as it confirms Shakespeare's Euro-imperialist guise as a conferrer of cultural value and artistic merit.[8]

Cox also cites Aboriginal actor and director Wesley Enoch who adumbrates the risks involved in such a project:

>...indigenous performance that subscribes to dominant discourses of theatrical worth – in particular the conception of Shakespeare as a touchstone of cultural value – can perpetuate systems of Eurocentric enculturation.[9]

This critical perspective, articulated chiefly by Anglo-European critics of the production, could be seen as a kind of cultural paternalism. Its correctness certainly constitutes an important structure of authority in the Australian context. What this authority resists is of course another perceived form of authority: the unquestioning adulation of Shakespeare and, through his work, the legitimation of British cultural imperialism.

Once again, however, this is a theoretical stance that fails to take into account the subversive presence of the particular actor's body. It formulates an ideological construct without taking into account the participant, and potentially subversive, corporeality of the actors. Deborah Mailman's particular vitality in performance undercuts this theoretical overlay serving as an instance of how important the body of the actor is in the process of making theatrical meaning.

If the opening of the production implied a kind of enthrallment to European cultural traditions, the clearest signal that this enthrallment would not be lasting was introduced by Deborah Mailman's Helena. Mailman undermined and exploited structures of cultural authority from within: from within sixteenth-century English drama and even from within an Elizabethan bodice and farthingale. Mailman's costume seemed not to inhibit, but rather to augment and impel her physical energy. It did not prevent her wrangling playfully with Demetrius or wrestling with Hermia. Mailman's angry departure from the suddenly besotted Lysander (act 2, scene 2, line 140) was particularly effective: she spun and stormed away, her swaying white skirts accentuating her decisive movement down the dark corridor as Lysander looked on in amazement.

At ease in her attire, Mailman was even more the master of the language of the play. She utilised the stage space, the costume, and the language with confidence, as part of her own stock of creative resources. In particular, her easy use of her own Australian accent permitted her to exploit the full expressive range of Helena's speech. The first laughter from the audience came on her riposte to Hermia's comment about Demetrius:

HERMIA:	I frown upon him, yet he loves me still.
HELENA:	O that your frowns would teach my smiles such skill! (act 1, scene 1, lines 194–5)

Mailman spoke this line with dry Australian sarcasm, almost as an aside: 'O that ya frowns'd teach my smiles such skill!' and this reflected potential to elicit a response from the audience on many levels. First, there was the ostensible meaning of the line which wryly shows up the smug self-reference of Hermia's complaint. Secondly, the humour in this specific instance inhered in the delicious irreverence of Mailman's treatment of the line. It is part of a long rally of rhyming couplets and, therefore, part of a highly stylised rhetorical exchange. Yet, despite the rigid patterning of the language Mailman, through her tone and facial expression, made it her own. She spoke the sense of the verse and spoke with a pointedness of purpose that exceeded anything that had been said on the stage until that moment. In this way Helena deftly performed an Aboriginal, and an Australian, rebellion against the structures of cultural authority within and around the play; but one for which the play itself offers the potential.

The other very important form of authority that Mailman's Helena defied was that intrinsic to the play – patriarchal domination.

Helena's 'freedom' from the mesh of filial obligations is accompanied by a distinct kind of vulnerability. There is no one to whom her duty is dramatised but there is also no-one to protect her or to grieve for her harm. As Levine has made abundantly clear, *A Midsummer Night's Dream* seethes with coercion and violence, particularly sexual violence perpetrated by men upon women. Helena is the victim of one of the play's most direct threats of sexual violence. Demetrius threatens both to rape her and to leave her 'to the mercy of wild beasts':[10]

> You do impeach your modesty too much,
> To leave the city and commit yourself
> Into the hands of one who loves you not;
> To trust to the opportunity of night,
> And the ill counsel of a desert place,
> With the rich worth of your virginity (act 2, scene 1, lines 214–19).

This threat reveals a Demetrius maliciously at odds with any kind of comic resolution. However, as is the case with all threats of physical violence, it depends entirely on performance for its precise nuance and force. In Tovey's production, on account of Mailman's strength, stature, and physical energy, the threat held little veracity. Incontestably, Helena's speeches in this scene point towards a disturbing tendency of self-abasement. However, in performing this self-abasement with such force of hyperbole, Helena has the paradoxical potential to command the scene. Mailman did precisely this: her verbose and resourceful rhetoric of 'self-abasement' combined with her physical command, amounted to a performance that overturned the ostensible power dynamics of the scene. A stiffly formal Demetrius, played by Tony Briggs, seemed feeble and put upon, oppressed by Helena's superior vitality and conviction. His threats were thereby delivered as desperate but ineffectual bids for power over her.

The authority-in-fact wielded by Helena throughout the scene was perfectly encapsulated in her response to his flight: 'Run where you will...' taunted Helena, as she, laughing, grabbed and tickled him so that he was forced to struggle against her embrace to go anywhere, '...the story shall be changed / Apollo flies, and Daphne holds the chase, / The dove pursues the griffin, the mild hind / Makes speed to catch the tiger' (act 2, scene 1, lines 230–3). In this way, Mailman convincingly changed the story, reinventing the trope of romantic pursuit on her feet, defying the authority of the Petrarchan model and its implicit violence.

What becomes clear in looking at Deborah Mailman's performance as Helena is that humour has a mutinous function in relation to the kinds of authority which structure Theseus' court. In the opening scene Hermia is persecuted, coerced, threatened; the victim of what begins to look like a tragic scenario. Her best friend enters, but instead of commiserating with and comforting Hermia, Helena calls her 'happy fair', sensibly belittles the scale of her plight, and rails with humorous hyperbole against her own unhappy lot:

> HERMIA: God speed fair Helena! Whither away?
> HELENA: Call you me fair? That fair again unsay.
> Demetrius loves your fair – O happy fair!
> Your eyes are lodestars and your tongue's
> sweet air...(act 1, scene 1, lines 180–4)

Presumably Helena stumbles upon Hermia and Lysander – the last people in the world she would wish to encounter – in the ecstasy of their vow-making, and makes to leave when she is called back ('Whither away?'). Helena's transparent self-pity and frustration with Hermia disrupts Hermia's tragic trajectory and therefore offers a potential turning point in the tone of the play in performance. It is often the case that Helena with her love complaint and wry humour breaks the tension that accrues in the earlier scenes.

In Noel Tovey's *A Midsummer Night's Dream* Helena's entrance fittingly offered the first taste of spirited subversion of the existing order. Similarly in the Bell Shakespeare's 2004 production, it was Kate Box's entrance as Helena that introduced a new spirit of comedic subversion to the performance. Prior to Helena's entrance, the actors seemed rigidly positioned along the front of the stage, performing flat and formal kinds of exchange. Box, appearing behind and between Hermia and Lysander, initiated the first triangular dynamic and the first possibility of self-reflexive performativity. She was wry and sarcastic from the very outset, softening to a genuine plea when she begged Hermia: 'teach me how you look, and with what art you sway the motion of Demetrius' heart' (act 1, scene 2, lines192–3). Her desire to emulate Hermia, and at the same time her striking difference of stature, was accentuated by the actors' almost identical apparel. Helena's biting wit throughout the successive rally ('I frown on him and yet he loves me still…') elicited loud laughter from the audience.

Another way in which Box's Helena undercut the grand dimensions of Hermia's romantic tragedy was through the manner in which she attended the lovers' plans for escape. As discussed in chapter 5, Helena listened to Hermia and Lysander's florid, tag-team account of their intended flight as if she were watching a daytime soap. In doing so, Box was the audience to a play-within-the-play – establishing a dynamic that proliferates throughout the *A Midsummer Night's Dream* – and demonstrated the power of the framing, 'onstage audience' to undercut, ironise, and transform the power and authority of the inner performance.

Although Helena's entrance seems to be a defining moment, a comic subversive change of mood, the play offers earlier instances of mutinous humour. Despite the oppressive weight of the law and a father's tyranny, it is not inevitable that the tenor of the opening scene be consistently solemn. In the Australian Shakespeare Company's outdoor productions, a humorous and convivial mood is established from the outset in accord with the relaxed picnic style of the event.

At the beginning of performances of the 2005 production (Melbourne Botanic Gardens), two of the actors, one of whom was later to play Helena (Kathryn Tohill) came before the audience carrying flares. They explained in clunky rhyming couplets the arrangements for the evening including directions to the toilets and banning photographs, mobile phone calls and littering. There were gales of laughter from the audience. This pragmatic introduction to the evening of entertainment can be seen to be subversive of cultural authority. First, rhyming couplets about mobile phones offer an amusing anachronism that draws audience members' attention to their temporal particularity. Moreover, the playful pairing of verse with candid warnings and instructions in broad Australian accents (along with distorted word-endings to complete rhymes) signals at once a utilitarian frankness and a sacrilege of high culture that most Australians find gratifying. It also de-mystifies the stage and the performers, placing emphasis on the need for the audience's imaginative as well as practical co-operation.

Having established this spirit of subversive playfulness as a frame for the event, the Australian Shakespeare Company often proceeds to play self-consciously with the play. Of all the productions I have seen, it was the Australian Shakespeare Company production of 1993 (Sydney Botanic Gardens) that made the most humorous sense of Lysander's early insubordination. After

Theseus had given his solemn sentence on the family dispute, Demetrius turned to Hermia and Lysander, to add some sanctimonious advice:

> DEMETRIUS: Relent sweet Hermia: and Lysander, yield
> Thy crazed title to my certain right.

Lysander (Guy Pierce) responded with derisive wit:

> LYSANDER: You have her father's love Demetrius;
> Let me have Hermia's: do you marry him.
> (act 1, scene 1, lines 91–4)

Lysander's solution is brazenly insubordinate. Its preposterousness cuts across the serious tone of the previous exchanges. It highlights Demetrius' sycophancy and avarice and it threatens the whole order through which patriarchal authority is perpetuated: the exchange of women.[11] Surprisingly, this line is often entirely lost in performance. However, the Australian Shakespeare Company production, having established a mood of cheeky subversion of cultural authority from the outset, produced a Lysander whose rebellion was triumphant. The audience erupted in laughter and some members even cheered his line, creating the mood of a live contest.

Company B's 2004 production of *A Midsummer Night's Dream* made much of the violence and coercion implicit in the play. How did this affect the staging of authority and subversion? Striking in this production was not only the kind and degree of cruelty perpetrated upon characters but their ritualistic modes of submission to cruelty. Helena, played by Rita Kalnejais, was doubly disempowered: first by the exclusion and cruelty she suffered within the world of the play, and secondly by the choices made about how Helena performed her own self-abasement. This performance of submission to domination was entirely in keeping with the voyeuristic aesthetic of the production. Moreover the anti-naturalism of Kalnejais' performance made her Helena remote, cryptic, and inexplicable; more an object of curiosity and pity than of empathy to the audience. Helena, whose marginal status and whose loquacious wit can win her agency and subversive force, was in this production systematically mortified.

An examination of the staging of authority and subversion in Company B's production suggests that, while its aesthetics were radical and inventive, its social and gender politics were intractably conservative. The serious, because plausible, cruelties which litter the play lost their particular force as a consequence of being enlisted and elaborated for shocking effect. They became extravagant spectacles of cruelty insulated by a smugly sophisticated frame. Spectacles of female submission to cruelty and self-abasement were at the heart of the entertainment. For example, as mentioned in Chapter 5, Hermia seemed in a submissive trance in act 1 when her father tore open the collar of her dress to publicly deride the necklace given her by Lysander.

A similar spectacle of male sexual domination was achieved in the scene where Helena pursues Demetrius. His words 'Tempt not too much the hatred of my spirit; / for I am sick when I do look on you' (act 1, scene 2, lines 211–12) were spoken with unequivocally vicious intent. Helena's response was to begin removing her schoolgirl clothes in a child-like way. When reasoning that Demetrius' company was as good as having 'all the world to look on her' Helena childishly lifted up her skirt. Demetrius' threat-proper was then to grab her and push her to the ground, grinding and groping her as he said '…do not believe but I shall do thee mischief in the wood'. The kind of mischief he intended was further clarified as, sitting astride her, he used one hand to roughly pin her throat. Before departing, he spat at her and she, leaving her clothes where they lay, pursued him.

A comparison of the choices made in this staging of the scene with those that shaped Deborah Mailman's performance, reveals the range of meanings the scene can be made to yield in performance. Mailman used Helena's eloquence and her own physical energy to enfeeble Demetrius, turning his threats of violence into the peevish subject of a joke shared with the audience. The two antithetical renderings were further advanced in the scene when both Demetrius and Lysander turned their affections on Helena. In keeping with the previous dynamic of submission, Kalnejais' Helena was plainly gratified. She allowed many of their advances and at one point, lifted aloft by the men, she used their adoration as a platform from which to launch her criticisms of Hermia. Deborah Mailman's Helena revealed a decidedly different response to the men's sudden affection. In keeping with Helena's words she showed herself keenly sensible of, and indignant at, the mockery. Unlike Kalnejais's Helena, who seemed happy to receive attention of any kind, Mailman's Helena did not accept what she perceived as their derision as any kind of substitute for affection and respect. On the contrary, she pushed Demetrius to the ground, held him there with her foot on his chest and slapped away his hands. There was no equivocation whatsoever in Mailman's Helena's rejection and censure of this false admiration.

The staging of the scene's physical conflict continued in keeping with each production's implicit politics. The Company B production took the more common solution of having the men protect Helena against Hermia's attacks in line with her request 'I pray you gentlemen…Let her not hurt me…Let her not strike me' (act 3, scene 2, lines 299–305). The STC production, however, had Helena and Hermia descend into their own private brawl on Helena's line: 'I told him of your [flight] unto this wood' (act 3, scene 2, line 310).[12] The men, involved in their own tussle, did not intervene. Consequently, for an extended period of time there were two writhing centres of conflict. These battles subsided, to humorous effect, not through any arbitration but through both parties succumbing to exhaustion.

The choices made by the STC production, therefore, harnessed the self-conscious performativity of Helena's rhetoric, Mailman's physical force, and the presence of an empathetic audience to mutiny against orthodox structures of courtship and, by extension, against the kinds of violence they legitimate. Kalnejais, in contrast, played out an abjection that fitted the needs of the voyeuristic spectacle of which her performance was part.

An examination of the choices made in the casting, performance and reception of Helena functions as an acid test of the gender politics informing each production. It becomes evident in the Company B production, that the dual informing ideological frames of Brechtian Epic theatre and voyeurism clash in their philosophical objectives and are, in some sense, at cross-purposes. While Epic theatre invites detached intellectual discernment, voyeurism invites the gaze. In theatre, voyeurism offers, thereby, a liberation from moral reasoning or accountability but, paradoxically, entails entrapment – a codifying of the kind of engagement that can take place between the audience and the performer. The difference between Epic theatre and voyeuristic spectacle is the difference between a provocation to revise assumptions, and titillation as an end in itself. In *A Midsummer Night's Dream* Andrews supplied placebo radicalism but no substantial subversion or revision of the political status quo.

Framing Titania and the Weaver: cultural authority and its subversion

Australian artist Arthur Boyd's etching *A Midsummer Night's Dream I* is harrowing and grotesque. Its subject is the act 3, scene one union of the 'transformed' ass-headed weaver, Bottom, with the fairy queen, Titania. The work presents an indecipherable turmoil of grasping limbs and flailing hooves. The faces of the characters are nearly impossible to descry: Titania's head is thrown back and Bottom's face is darkly crowned with demonic curling horns rather than donkey's ears. The image is strikingly subversive of the modes in which Shakespeare's play has been performed and received throughout most of its history. As visual art, Boyd's work is able to perform a unique distilling of the cruelty and dire sexual violence of the encounter. The work freezes and frames a momentary Australian imagining, a fantastical and isolated vision. Jan Kott's famous essay, and its ubiquitous use in theatre programs, suggest that such visions have a legacy of appeal in interpretative approaches to the play. However, such static fantasies can never fully account for the dynamic matrix of embodied voices in a time-bound relationship with an audience offered by theatrical performance. The following discussion treats choices made about Titania's encounter with the weaver on Australian stages and reflects upon what they imply in terms of authority and subversion.

Of all the numerous critiques of the encounter of Titania and Bottom, Louis A. Montrose's gives the most astute observation of its staging of authority as an Elizabethan fantasy:

> Titania treats Bottom as if he were both her child and her lover. And she herself is ambivalently nurturing and threatening, imperious and enthralled. She dotes upon Bottom, and indulges him in all those desires to be fed, scratched, and coddled that make Bottom's dream into a parodic fantasy of narcissism and dependency. The sinister side of Titania's possessiveness is manifested in her binding up of Bottom's tongue, and her intimidating command, 'Out of this wood do not desire to go:/Thou shalt remain here, whether thou wilt or no' (act 3, scene 2, lines 145–6). But if Titania manipulates Bottom, an artisan and an amateur actor, she herself is manipulated by Oberon, a 'King of shadows' (act 2, scene 2, line 347) and the play's internal dramatist. A fantasy of male

dependency on a woman is expressed and contained within a fantasy of male control over woman; the social reality of the player's dependence on a Queen is inscribed with the imaginative reality of the dramatist's control over a Queen... Shakespeare's public play-text embod[ies] a culture specific dialectic between personal and public images of gender and power; both are characteristically *Elizabethan* cultural forms.[13]

Montrose reflects on the original currency of the Titania and Bottom story as an 'imaginary reality' during a period in which the ultimate (and anomalous) political reality was a female sovereign. Montrose's insight is informative in terms of its awareness of the dialectical relationship between authority as it is performed on stage and political authority as it conditions psychical and imaginative possibilities in a particular cultural context.

Applying Montrose's insight to more contemporary contexts raises the question of how the Titania and Bottom relationship is shaped by and shapes later contexts in which the play is performed. Jan Kott's 1965 essay 'Titania and the Ass's Head',[14] is worthy of note because it reflects a distinct period of cultural revolution, namely the sexual revolution; and because of its reach. The essay still wields pervasive force over productions of the play in twenty-first century Australia. Kott repudiates the accretions of Victorian theatrical tradition: 'tunic-clad lovers' and 'marble stairs' in favour of the belief that 'The *Dream* is the most erotic of Shakespeare's plays' and that '[i]n no other tragedy or comedy of his, except *Troilus and Cressida*, is the eroticism expressed so brutally'.[15] For this conjecture Kott procures generous, if disjointed, textual evidence. Where Kott's account reveals its cultural vintage and opportunistically selective treatment of the events of the play, is in assumptions about the actions and intentions of the female characters. Identifying Goya's 'Caprichos' as sharing a sensibility with Shakespeare's play, Kott opines that

> [o]f all the characters in the play Titania enters to the fullest, the dark sphere of sex where there is no more beauty and ugliness; there is only infatuation and liberation.[16]

Kott stages a sensational elaboration of this notion that draws detectably upon psychoanalytic theory of dream:

> The slender, tender and lyrical Titania longs for animal love. Puck and Oberon call the transformed Bottom a monster. The frail and sweet Titania drags the monster to bed, almost by force. This is the lover she wanted and dreamed of; only she never wanted to admit it, even to herself. Sleep frees her of her inhibitions. The monstrous ass is being raped by the poetic Titania...[17]

The maliciousness of Oberon's plot to humiliate Titania is thereby diffused with the explanation that she is in fact fulfilling her own repressed desire. The psychoanalytic reading is, to appropriate Montrose's exquisite term, Kott's 'shaping fantasy' and has had an influence on the tenor of the play as a cultural producer for many decades.

Kott's reading, because of its cultural iconoclasm and supposed emphasis upon rawer sensibilities of the Elizabethan period, has become a source of authority which successive productions of the play re-instate. By the very nature of the psychoanalytic 'shaping fantasy' Kott knits around the play, however, it also reinforces the patriarchal and misogynist status quo. It sets up a comfortingly conventional and rigid order of gender relations for which the play itself may or may not give grounds. One result of Kott's shocking, if not so revolutionary, reading is that a production can be at once in thrall to Kott's radical aesthetics (Kott's aesthetic focus is hinted by the preoccupation with visual arts) yet still reproduce deeply traditional figurations of gender and power. While Montrose recognises the overlapping fantasies that comprise the Bottom and Titania union, together with their varying discourses of gender and power, Kott centralises and literalises one fantasy; Titania's, and fails to identify his own framing fantasy of the psychoanalytic, misogynistic and distinctively voyeuristic gaze.

Kott's approach to Shakespeare, despite being subject to academic criticism at the time of publication,[18] became enshrined in theatre culture through its adoption by Peter Brook. Brook's landmark *King Lear* for the Royal Shakespeare Company (1962–64) and later film version (1971) was directly inspired by Kott's work. Kott's argument for Shakespeare's contemporaneity – its innate Beckettian absurdism – as realised in theatre by Brook's productions, exercised a tenacious hold over the sensibilities of theatre artists throughout the sixties and seventies. Moreover, the Kott/Brook/Shakespeare plait seems still, in theatre practice, to occupy the puzzling status of perpetual epiphany. The ubiquity of reference to it in rehearsal rooms, by directors as they discuss their work, and in theatre programs, attests to this status. Academic criticism continues, if sporadically, to take Kott to task for his 'reading' of the Shakespeare play. David Bevington, for example, counters Kott's sexual darkness by suggesting that the union of Titania and Bottom is more allegorical than physical – an image of the yoking of the carnal and ethereal in human love and therefore 'touchingly innocent'.[19] Bevington still, however, echoes Kott's bias in accusing Titania of infidelity.

The Kott legacy is distinctive as a pseudo-academic discourse sustained by its popularity in the sphere of theatre. My interest lies not simply in providing an alternative 'reading' to Kott's, but in pointing out its incongruity with the agile and multi-dimensional operations of Shakespearean metatheatre. Returning to the more local context, I argue that the way in which the Titania and Bottom fantasy is framed for its audience by a production offers insight into the informing politics of the production. Kott frames one kind of static picture, one that simultaneously blames Titania and removes her self-determination. If a production frames the event similarly – promoting the notion of Titania's sub-conscious complicity in a degrading match with Bottom – it partly vindicates the enjoyment of the audience in such a misogynistic and debasing spectacle. This is a frequent staging choice. As Irene Dash has identified, despite the fact that Titania has been blinded by Oberon's magic spell:

> few productions…dramatise the evil inherent in this kind of magic. Rather they concentrate on Bottom, and, salaciously, the humour of Titania's plight.[20]

This approach was epitomised by the 2004 Company B production. The treatment of the scenes between Bottom and Titania were exploited for their sadistic potential with an emphasis (that resembled Kott's) on visual spectacle that invoked contemporary tropes of bestiality and bondage. Titania, rather than resorting to a bower with her beloved, resorted to an arena. Bottom was led to her accompanied by a throbbing soundtrack while one of Titania's masked minions flailed ribbon whips in the background. After interval the spectacle of bestiality was given further play in the form of flickering shadow puppets from within the now curtained ring. This sequence made Titania just one puppet in an elaborate visual tableau of orgiastic decadence. The distinct primacy of visual effect and elaborate paraphernalia of the bondage conceit displaced the force of Titania's seductive verbal rhetoric and so supplanted her stage-managerial role in the scene.

In both the Bell and Elston productions, delight was also taken in what Dash calls the 'salacious humour of Titania's predicament'. Yet, the predicament and the humour were subtly different. As a plot event Oberon's trick is intended to debase Titania. Yet Titania's performance of seduction can turn his vindictive intention against itself by seducing the audience as well. In both the Bell and Elston productions this was the case. The force of Titania's rhetorical conceit, rather than the uber-motif of aesthetic design, held sway. In these productions Titania's performance of desire was decisive and persuasive. Importantly, in both the Bell and Elston productions Titania had Bottom led away to her 'bower'; a concealed onstage space and an imaginary off-stage space respectively. She retreated from the audience to her own territory with her chosen love object rather than remaining in the public arena to become an object of their derision.

This conceit of Titania's retreat, which the play-text supports – 'Come, wait upon him, lead him to my bower.' (act 3, scene 2, line 178) – serves an important function in the figurations of gender and power in performance. Orchestrating her own physical departure, Titania remains indisputably in control of the stage, if not of the plot, and if the actor herself embodies Titania's forceful appeal, she preserves a seductive power over the audience's curiosity. Despite in some sense being mortified by Oberon, she is not made to perform her own degradation before the audience.

The way in which this encounter is framed for the audience, therefore, has ramifications for the degree to which it participates in Titania's humiliation and for the amount of force she herself retains as a character. In the world of the Company B production, the spectacle of bondage by which Titania was framed also bound the spectators in a posture of abjection towards the play. Choosing to return to their seats after interval constituted a condoning of the sadistic spectacle. In the power economy of Andrews' production, short of going home, there was limited scope for a self-determining and original response from the audience. The audience was rigidly cast in its role as voyeurs from the outset, like Titania in Kott's fantasy, at once blameful and disempowered.

The radical contingency of meaning in performance offers some alternatives to framing Titania's actions as the result of her own salacious perversity. As a number of recent productions have made plain, Titania can retain her agency and audience sympathy, and, thereby, subvert Oberon's machinations from within. Montrose points out that there are more layers to the encounter between Bottom and Titania than reading it as plain narrative of one character's wish fulfillment will ever reveal. In investigating the multi-faceted and multivalent nature of the encounter, a crucial point to bear in mind is that Bottom is an actor. Everything he participates in, therefore, has a double significance: it is significant on the plane of the play's narrative but it is also of metatheatrical import.

Since Bottom's own words permit him to be anything from a self-deluded egotist to a figure of charismatic masculine appeal, the exact nature of the liaison is defined chiefly by how it, and the characters who participate in it, are played. It is important to note that the absurdity of the match, as Puck sees it, is not in Bottom's innate repulsiveness but in his social status as 'the shallowest thickskin' (act 3, scene 2, line 13) of 'a crew of patches, rude mechanicals/That work for bread upon Athenian stalls' (act 3, scene 2, lines 9–10). Puck's disdain encodes a distinct class bias which, as I will elaborate under the next heading, can take on very different inflections depending on the context of performance. The audience may not concur with Puck who sees Bottom's monstrosity as, at least partly, his social and artistic presumption. 'My mistress with a monster is in love' is not simply, if at all, a statement of his repellent appearance. Bottom is also monstrous because he is an actor: a character-compound, a hybrid (to evoke the Elizabethan sense of the term) and an interloper in worlds other than his own. Bottom, as an actor, partakes of the same monstrosity as Viola: he subverts the rigidly containing definitions of his designated place in society.[21] He is a thick-skinned artisan and yet, as an actor, he assays sublime tragic heroism. Bottom's encounter with Titania might be seen as allegorising artistic ambition: he is a mortal artisan who tangles with a queen of fairies.

Despite being poetically available in Shakespeare's text, it is unlikely that such an understanding of Bottom's monstrosity would have garnered great support in the highly stratified social context of Elizabethan England. However, with the growth of egalitarian sentiment in the twentieth century, and the performance of Shakespeare's plays in countries that define themselves in resistance to the English class system, Bottom has undergone another transformation.

In the 1999 film *A Midsummer Night's Dream*, directed by Michael Hoffman, Kevin Kline as Bottom 'starred' as a deeply reflective, at times self-effacing artist. In this instance, Oberon succeeded only in procuring for his wife a genuinely desirable lover and moreover, through his own orchestration of the pairing, exonerated her from blame. When the audience identifies imaginatively with Titania's and Bottom's desire for each other, rather than viewing it as a spectacle of degradation, the power of the performance is weighted subversively against Oberon and his misused authority; the joke is on Oberon.

If Bottom's monstrosity is embodied as the enigmatic force of the actor who plays him, it is possible to suggest that Titania actively and consciously pursues him, and that Oberon's spell is merely exculpation. Titania, therefore, moves from a position of blame and disempowerment to subversive yet exonerated self-determination. This dynamic energised Richard Wherrett's 1989 production for the STC[22] and it made Oberon's coup a questionable triumph. Luciano Martucci's portrayal of Bottom as affable, young, and sexy had the audience as well as Titania on his side. Martucci played a Bottom who was so far from fulfilling Oberon's vindictive incantation that Titania would 'wake when some vile thing [was] near', that Oberon's spell was foiled and entailed its own punishment.

This approach embraces the redemptive valence of carnivalesque inversion and the potential redress it provides, through performativity, of oppressive structures of authority. Oberon's supposed omnipotence does him little good. He is usurped and cuckolded (not by a lion, bear, wolf, or boar) but by a mortal with the mask or temporary disguise of an ass, in other words, by a player. The courtly and patriarchal order is turned thoroughly on its head through theatre. The canny design of the play, while subverting Oberon's authority in one respect, makes it the subversive engine of the play in another. Oberon's magical intervention is, ironically, the catalyst for overturning Egeus' will and Theseus' command.

Unquestionably in the context of Elizabethan England, Titania and Bottom's union had a complex function as fantasy in addressing the anomalous and potentially disturbing circumstance of a female sovereign. The focus of my argument, however, has been upon the fantasies and fears addressed by the monstrous marriage in contemporary contexts. Manifestly, in performance, Bottom's transformation and Titania's love for him can either reinforce the oppressive gender and class hierarchies which dominate the opening of the play or, conversely, make indelible breaches in them. To better understand the subversive possibilities of the Titania and Bottom story it makes sense to look more closely at the cultural currency of the mechanicals in the contemporary context.

The Mechanicals: power and social rank

Australian culture has a uniquely configured relationship with the 'mechanicals' of *A Midsummer Night's Dream*. The roots of this are evident in the play by Tony Taylor and Keith Robinson called *The Popular Mechanicals*. Premiering at Belvoir Street in Sydney in 1987 *The Popular Mechanicals* took the mechanicals from *A Midsummer Night's Dream* and expanded their offstage story, hence the witty subtitle, 'a play without the play'. The play was seen as a brilliant confusing of accustomed 'high' and 'low' culture categories. It retained large portions of Shakespeare's play but blended them with vaudevillian song, dance, and puppetry set pieces, Elizabethan bawdry, and contemporary references. The play provoked identification in the Australian context by its irreverence. It centralised the margins, and hence challenged the ostensible hierarchies both within the play and in Australia's relationship to Shakespeare. Furthermore it satirised theatrical activity – both amateur and professional – and in doing so echoed the self-reflexivity of Shakespeare's play. The Popular Mechanicals were clowns of the kind with which Australian popular culture has a natural affinity – ambitious, contradictory, unwitting bearers of wisdom:

> In a way, because they are clowns, they automatically have an innocence and naivety. They drink raspberry cordial. They also have grand emotions. They're either depressed or over-excited, there's nothing in between.[23]

In Australian culture there is a ready-made place for a character such as Bottom and in many Australian productions of *A Midsummer Night's Dream*, Bottom occupies a similar place to other fiercely loved Australian clowns in the cultural strata. Rather than being seen as an object of derision for his misplaced aspiration to cultural sophistication, in the Australian context, Bottom is actually likely to be seen as more genuine than the other characters, possessed of real charisma and 'hard-boiled' wisdom. While far from representing the current experience of most modern Australians (particularly theatre-goers), 'sweet bully Bottom' the worker calls up a collective reverence for the image of the blue-collar sage.

The world of *A Midsummer Night's Dream* is characterised by distinctly stratified social classes. Because conceptions and experiences of social class are deeply culture specific, the precise power implications of the play's social stratification rely for animation on the culture in which the play is performed. Audiences in different socio-economic and cultural contexts bring different assumptions about social class to the play and may, therefore, identify more overtly with one of the play's social echelons than with another.

This intersection of the play's social structures with the social structures which shape the audience's own experience is further inflected by choices made in production. Decisions made in direction and design serve an important function in tilting sympathy towards one or another of the social sets figured in the play, or in blurring the boundaries between the groups altogether. Whether articulated or not, these kinds of directorial decisions encase ideological approaches to the structures of power within the play. Below I turn attention to how a number of productions construed social class and reflect on how this intersected with the contemporary Australian cultural context to produce meaning.

Peter Brook's 1970 production of *Dream* (which toured Australia in 1973) serves, once again, as a useful point of departure. Brook deliberately challenged the default patterns of reception, particularly audience sympathy, in relation to the mechanicals. Identifying the fact that traditionally the play-within-the-play had been seen as a 'knock about farce climax of the play', Brook pointed out that the mechanicals are usually laughed at rather than identified with. His production eschewed this interpretation and saw the scene as a pivotal challenge that could give way to a whole new approach to *A Midsummer Night's Dream*:

> [T]he play within the play was perhaps the start of the whole production. Because, traditionally, it's considered that the actors acting badly is a funny joke. And this is something that has rarely been questioned. The play within the play has been treated as something very silly. The traditional business is the actors forgetting their lines, and getting lines wrong, and doing things that no actor would possibly do…In *A Midsummer Night's Dream*, there are no grounds for taking a condescending nineteenth-century upper-class view that

peasants who try to do a play, must be comic. That is a pure nineteenth-century snobbish view of the world, in which servants are always comic characters. If you just naively read what was written, you see that a group of underclass, small artisans are trying to do a play, and then you actually see the play they do.[24]

In his production Brook sought consciously to renovate this status of the mechanicals, focusing on the complex and subtle implications of their artistic endeavour within the play:

The play they present is a mixture, done with love and respect by these men trying to act. To me, what the whole of *A Midsummer Night's Dream* is about, amongst other things, is acting – and illusion.

[But it is also about role playing?]

Yes, about role playing and love. And one sees where the two go together: Men with no skill, but with a capacity for a certain form of love, can reach, in their own way, a truth which goes beyond illusion. Because in direct terms, an audience sees for itself how you can be laughing at a clumsy actor. Yet, the next second, when Thisbe does her ridiculous lament over a character called Pyramus, whom you're not taking seriously, a simple feeling comes through because of the boy's identity with the role. Therefore, what he actually believes in comes true. You certainly realise that Thisbe's suicide – ridiculous though it is – is also serious. And you're forced in that moment to wonder about the whole nature of what you believe and what you don't believe. And even then, you're forced to wonder: Are you believing in an actor? Whom are you believing in? Are you believing in yourself?[25]

Brook saw the players as a kind of touchstone for the truth that can be conveyed beyond the success or failure of illusion in theatre. Metatheatre was at the conceptual core of Brook's approach because it activates the human capacity to experience contradictory emotional responses simultaneously. If an audience member is transfixed or begins to cry while laughing, something real is happening despite the fact that it is a reality ignited by an ostensibly ridiculous fiction.[26] Furthermore, awareness, or what we might more precisely term meta-cognitive awareness, of this contradiction constitutes an expansion of the individual audience member's consciousness, and for Brook this kind of epiphany was at the hub of the play's force.

There is strong evidence of an Australian cultural sanctioning of art which uses clown-like figures to provoke contradictory emotional responses at the same time. The highly theatrical 1994 film *Muriel's Wedding* is an outstanding example of an Australian sensibility which can blend derision of a clown-like character with sudden pathos and fierce identification. *Strictly Ballroom* (1992) and *The Castle* (1997) are other Australian films that blur the boundaries between broad farcical derision and passionate identification with working-class 'battler' characters. It is arguable that Australians are more prone than many cultures to mock, love, and identify with the same character. The proclivity to extol the working-class clown as representative artist is also part of Australia's international popular profile; the obvious icon of the Australian artist/artisan being Paul Hogan, whose years prior to Hollywood fame were spent as a construction worker and rigger on the Sydney Harbour Bridge.

It is revealing to compare Brook's diligently articulated British project of rescuing the dignity of the mechanicals with choices made by Australian productions. For the way that the play engages with features of the Australian cultural context seems almost to bring Brook's project full circle. While in reaction to English nineteenth-century snobbery Brook pleads the innate dignity of the actor/artisan, Australian audiences are likely to side with the actor/artisans from the outset and to see the courtly set as the cultural 'other'. The roots of this tendency can be traced to the Australian attachment to the idea of the 'underdog'.

In the Australian context it is possible to detect a pattern in which audiences forge a distinctive sympathy with the mechanicals. At a simple level this can be accounted for by the common characterisation of the mechanicals as distinctly Australian workers or labourers. In most productions, the mechanicals appear to be Australian in a way that other characters, with their Old-World hierarchies, are not. The mechanicals are often attired in labourers' clothes, specifically: navy blue Bonds vests, King Gee stubbies shorts and Blundstone boots. These items of clothing have their original use in the context of labouring work but Bonds shirts and Blundstone boots have also, because of their affordability, in recent decades become the ubiquitous attire of university students and artists. It is also common for the mechanicals to wear football colours either by way of scarves or jerseys. This adds another layer of identification with the prominent Australian love of sport. Thus, in many productions, the mechanicals provide a matrix of associations with Australian culture yielding an unproblematic combination of worker and creative identities. It is hardly surprising that it is the mechanicals with whom Australian audiences quickly identify and who contribute enormously to the sense of ownership of the play by the audience. Augmenting this is the fondly held notion of resistance to cultural and class pretension and a willingness to afford the clown respect as a sage, an artist and a representative Australian identity.

Ross Williams, who has performed in at least ten productions with the Australian Shakespeare Company, played the essential Australian Bottom. He was a comedian whose utter rapport with the audience equated to real force in performance and won him

A MIDSUMMER NIGHT'S DREAM

near-heroic status by the end of the play. In Elston's production the audience laughed at the characters whom it loved and Bottom and Puck were the beloved clowns. Williams had made the role his own and, evidently, Elston had given him special carte blanche to improvise, to play, and to upstage other characters. Because of his gifted extemporising and his ease in the role he seemed closer and more real to the audience than the other characters. While the courtly set, and the higher fairies, were comically preoccupied with their own dilemmas, Bottom (and Puck) were preoccupied, first and foremost, with getting the audience's attention. As a self-consciously performative character, Bottom has the clown's prerogative for this divided consciousness and in Williams' case it permitted a special kind of access to the audience's sympathy.

Figure 6.2 Ross Willliams (Bottom), Terri Brabon (Titania), *A Midsummer Night's Dream*, Australian Shakespeare Company, 2007.
©Australian Shakespeare Company

Further establishing his common ground with the audience, Williams regularly integrated references to contemporary popular culture. The most outstanding instance of this was after Puck had 'transformed him' (act 3, scene 1) and his fellow players fled.

Williams swaggered casually along the front of the stage as if with a microphone singing his 'number': 'The ousel cock so black of hue, / With orange tawny bill…' (act 3, scene 1, line 110) to a Frank Sinatra melody, brilliantly mimicking the singer's gravelly voice and mannerisms. Titania awoke and contributed to the conceit; supplying 'cuckoo, cuckoo', from behind him in the manner of a coy backing chorus. Bottom's performance was met with enthusiastic applause from the audience to which he responded in a smug American accent 'Thank you. You've been beautiful'. Having effectively styled himself as the popular entertainer Bottom seemed glad rather than dismayed to be deserted so that he could soak up the limelight alone. He became the commanding presence on stage to which even Titania was temporarily a support player.

In keeping with the sensibility of the Elston production the finale was a comic extravaganza. Like much of the play it was played as high farce, littered with contemporary references, visual gags and mishaps, and without a hint of pathos. However, it would be erroneous to assume that the play-within-the-play was simply a snobbish derision of the mechanicals in the tradition alluded to by Brook. The production was one in which there were multiple plays within plays and each forged a new fellowship between the performance and the audience. Hence, by the end of the play, the mechanicals had developed a robust rapport with their audience. Their antics were fully condoned through laughter and applause, and thereby served as a reflection of where the audience had allowed itself to be taken. The audience was deeply and, it would seem, happily implicated in the nonsense. Moreover, the aristocrats who can serve as an acerbic filter to the play-within-the-play, were inconspicuous through placement in the audience.[27] Their commentary was of negligible force in the face of the act that clearly had centre stage.

If, as I have suggested, the various social strata in *A Midsummer Night's Dream* have a capacity to critique the power structures within each other, the most obvious way in which this critique can come to the fore in performance is through role doubling. Role doubling permits the same actor to move as different characters on several social planes and this can facilitate ironic undercutting of the ways power is distributed within those planes. The most usual role double is that of Hippolyta with Titania and Theseus with Oberon. This doubling, popular at least since Brook used it, inevitably produces a distinct emphasis upon the psychoanalytic concept of 'dream',

> ...it creates a sense that the fairy action of the play is related to and a reflection of the action in the outer Athenian frame; that Oberon and Titania are the dream personae of Theseus and Hippolyta through which the Athenian couple can enact their secret desires and work out their buried resentments. This reading of the play as having conscious and subconscious levels, and as exploring the release in the dream-world of emotions which are repressed in waking life, clearly accords with Freudian methods of interpretation.[28]

Arguably this reading imposes too neat a paradigm upon the complexities of the play and relegates the 'fairy action' to serving only as an explanatory myth for the often inexplicable behaviour of its participants. It is equally valid to posit that the fairy realm complicates and magnifies, as much as resolves, the problems of the human realm. Titania's jealousy about Oberon's love for Hippolyta – a real force in the dramatic narrative – is difficult to account for if Titania is simply Hippolyta's dreaming self. Titania and Oberon's wars certainly draw upon sources of conflict adumbrated in the faintly drawn relationship between Theseus and Hipployta. Yet, there is so much more to the 'fairy action' that we may be justified in suggesting by the end of the play, that the human realm is simply a weak echo of the more richly developed and artistically complex 'fairy reality'. This was certainly the inference to be made from Anna Volska's production for the Bell Shakespeare Company.

Leaving aside this most common role doubling, with its all too obvious psychoanalytic interpretation, leaves room to interrogate other kinds of doubling that take place in productions of the play. The most provocative in terms of challenging structures of power within the play is doubling the fairy minions with the mechanicals. Minions though they are, Cobweb, Mustardseed, Moth, and Peaseblossom are equipped with magical agency and are attendants at the court of the fairy queen. They belong firmly in the night-time world of enchantment and are in this sense more powerful than any of the human characters. If the actors who play the mechanicals double as the fairies, their power and the significance of their 'work' as players is metaphorically enriched.

In Anna Volska's 2004 production, for the Bell Shakespeare Company, the four actors who played the lovers also played fairy minions and the mechanicals. Moreover, the actor who played Egeus played Peter Quince and a fairy. The actor who played Bottom also played a fairy. Actors playing Theseus and Hippolyta doubled as Oberon and Titania respectively, and the actor who played Puck played Philostrate. The small cast size was necessitated by the financial exigencies of the touring program. Nevertheless, it is fruitful to reflect upon how this intensive role doubling and tripling affected the meaning of the play.

The most obvious thing to note is that the cast members themselves were required to effect the most agile feats of dramatic transformation. The actors made each of their roles so effectively distinct that the stage seemed peopled by twenty actors rather than simply the cast of nine. The actors' plasticity in performance was aided by costumes which disguised salient characteristics of their features. For example, Georgia Adamson and Kate Box who played Hermia and Helena in costumes that accentuated their height difference, appeared as Flute in baggy overalls and Starveling in a long loose tailor's gown respectively. As members of the fairy train, all actors wore uniformly baggy animal disguises and moved in ways that even disguised their differences of height.

The fact that it was reasonably difficult to identify the actors across their various roles suppressed, to a degree, the impulse to make comparisons between the structures of authority in each realm. In two respects, however, meaning was born of the doubling. First, the mischievous allegiance between Oberon and Puck was preserved during later scenes between Theseus and Philostrate. Clearly the chief contenders for the audience's attention and confederacy, Luciano Martucci and Richard Gyoerffy sustained a charming sense of inside knowledge across all of their roles and a talent for including the audience in their enjoyment. Philostrate's admission of having 'heard' Pyramus and Thisbe rehearsed came as an obvious reference to his own performance as Puck and was offered as a conspiratorial hint to the audience.[29] In this way the formal rigidity of Theseus' human court was infected by fairy, and hence theatrical, magic.

Secondly, the mechanicals, having played a successfully humorous version of 'Pyramus and Thisbe', effected an onstage transformation to their initial identities as Hermia, Helena, Lysander, and Demetrius. They retreated upstage and assisted each other to disrobe from their playing costumes and re-dress as the young lovers. This took place while, downstage, Theseus spoke his final, lyrical passage reflecting on the overlapping cycles of play and rest, waking and dreaming:

> The iron tongue of midnight hath told twelve.
> Lovers to bed; 'tis almost fairy time.
> I fear we shall outsleep the coming morn
> As much we this night have overwatched.
> This palpable-gross play hath well beguiled
> The heavy gait of night. Sweet friends, to bed.

> A fortnight hold we this solemnity
> In nightly revels and new jollity. (act 5, scene 2, lines 346–53)

The serendipity of this staging choice was that Theseus' speech, rather than addressing only the close-knit courtly set, seemed to address the whole theatrical moment. 'Lovers to bed' could not be understood as spoken exclusively to the lovers, because, at that precise moment they did not exist strictly as the lovers, but as actors in a vulnerable moment of transition. If we allow that his address was not aimed at actors as particular characters but more inclusively, at the actors as actors and, by extension, at all participants in the theatrical event; then the 'palpable-gross play' that 'hath well beguiled / The heavy gait of night' referred not only to 'Pyramus and Thisbe' but also to *A Midsummer Night's Dream*. The nebulous 'Sweet friends, to bed' affirmed the community of the theatrical venture in closure, a community that pointedly included the audience.

Volska's production implied that the mischief and shape-shifting possibility of the fairy realm, once ignited, exploded the mundane hierarchies of the human court. This is because by act 3, all of the humans had changed into fairies and would change many more times before the play was over. Their mutability, combined with the imaginative collaboration of the audience established a pattern of metamorphosis whose vital energies perpetually destabilised the rigid determination of social structure. All participants in the theatrical event were sustained in constantly changing relation to one another. The lovers became the fairies, and then the workers, and then the players and then themselves as actors, and then the lovers once again. Theseus' later appearances were inflected with Oberon's charisma and Philostrate revelled in hinting that we had met him before in another guise. The social stratification of the play was dismantled by the constant revelation that all were actors first, and rather magically, lovers, mechanicals and fairies as the situation required. All were primarily hard-working artisans of the stage.

The mechanicals in Benedict Andrew's production for Company B exercised an important role in undermining the stylistic principles upon which the production itself seemed based. In this sense they, evidently the most disempowered characters within the world of the play, wielded extraordinary power in the theatre.[30] One of the ways in which they engaged attention was through their individual distinctiveness. Often the mechanicals are a gang, a group of people confident of their collective identity and sharing similar statures, costumes, accents, and mannerisms. In the Belvoir production, this was not the case. Each of the characters was distinctive in stature and Starveling (Ralph Cotterill) and Snug (Ian Watkin), in particular, conveyed a remarkable sense of isolation.

The actors who played these roles used a style of acting that was less affected and more direct than that of most of the other actors in the production. This rendered their plights the most recognisably human, transparent, and therefore poignant. In their scenes as 'players', the mechanicals utterly lacked stylistic sophistication, and this deficiency, as well as their touching awareness of it, was brought to the audience's attention in their very first appearance. Following Hermia's highly stylised chair-jumping exit and Helena's elaborately gesticulated rendering of her soliloquy, the mechanicals entered for their first scene. Several sat remote from one another, waiting and looking nervous, on their widely spaced chairs. Starveling took up his knitting. Snout wheeled on a gas cylinder heater and began pulling cords to light it. There was a purpose to these actions that established the moment as an island in the busy stream of stylised effects. It provoked a genuine curiosity as to what would follow.

Jacek Koman as Bottom began trying to warm his hands at the heater but then evolved his hand warming action into the beginning of a routine that involved elaborate kicks, claps, and sidesteps. One by one, the other mechanicals joined in, clumsily imitating Bottom's actions. The whole scenario parodied the unspoken protocols and anxieties of the rehearsal room. Bottom's 'warm-up' ritual, as ludicrous as it seemed, wielded power over the other members of the group. Nobody wanted to be left out of the artistic drift and their need to be included was as touchingly transparent as their lack of personal conviction about what they took part in.

It is common-place in productions of *A Midsummer Night's Dream* to make, during the mechanicals' first appearance, some reference to contemporary conceptions of artistic pretentiousness. For example, Bottom will often observe bizarre rituals of 'getting into character' prior to his Hercules speech (act 1, scene 2, lines 19–31). The supreme irony of the theatrical in-joke in this case was that it drew attention to the arcane performance practices of the very production in which it took place. The superbly convincing art*less*ness of Snug, Starveling, Snout and Flute, showed up the self-conscious layers of artistic effect built into the production as a whole. In this way the stylistic simplicity that characterised the mechanicals' performances undercut the intense sophistication of the production as a whole, prompting one reviewer to comment:

> It's the smaller roles, and smaller moments, that really shine – Anthony Phelan's prissy Peter Quince, Ian Watkin's Snug and Mustardseed, and Ralph Cotterill's rather lovely Robin Starveling. Indeed Starveling's recourse to surreptitious knitting may be the production's warmest and most human moment.[31]

As in the Bell production, the actors who played the mechanicals doubled as the fairies, but to very different effect. While the Bell production disguised the doubling, the Belvoir production drew attention to it. The actors cast as the mechanicals – Ralph Cotterill as Robin Starveling, John Leary as Francis Flute, Nathan Page as Tom Snout, Anthony Phelan as Quince and Ian Watkin as Snug – each had a distinct physique, obvious in their costumes as mechanicals and made even more obvious in their costuming as fairy minions. The fairy costumes consisted of a range of short and ragged tutus and frightening masks reminiscent of those used for burn-victims (with the strange exception that some had animal ears). All their outfits were bandage or skin coloured.

There were many inferences to be garnered from the powerful and incongruous visual effect of this costume choice. One was a sense of damage, continuing the vein of Oberon's scarring. Simultaneously, there was the implication of a freak-show spectacle recalling the 'gimp' in the 1994 film *Pulp Fiction*. Most insistent, however, was the oppressive sense of sadness. The performers themselves seemed vulnerable and subjected to a kind of sartorial mortification with most of their skin showing but their faces, except for their eyes, were hidden. Where Titania's attendants often have a beguiling agility to their movements, these attendants were transparently the mechanicals in strange attire: identically stolid, meekly submissive, and awkwardly distinctive in their various statures. Whether participating in Bottom's warm-up, flailing whips as part of a bondage ritual, or performing 'Pyramus and Thisbe', the mechanicals seemed resignedly in the service of other people's bizarre ideas.

The play-within-the-play was, as it often is, a raucous success. Jacek Koman, who is known for his performances as tragic protagonists, brought his experience to bear upon the role of Bottom, parodying actorly intensity to great comic effect. John Leary, as Flute, was also hilarious, exhibiting a desire to execute the role of Thisbe with a point-by-point precision. Against this, Snug and Starveling's meek and serious submissiveness was at times piercingly sad, achieving exactly the quality of poignant ambiguity commended by Peter Brook. With utter commitment and gravity, Ralph Cotterill's Starveling, dressed in striped pajamas, awaited his moment. Finally he stepped out as Moonshine fumbling an unwieldy selection of props including a milk-crate, a lantern, a stick, and a mechanical dog on a low trolley whose feet were pinned to and moved with its wheels. While Moonshine had the silliest appearance of all the characters in 'Pyramus and Thisbe' he seemed the least aware of it. The ardent sincerity with which Starveling performed his role was intensified by the absurdity, creating a sense of pathos.

Moonshine took great pains to assemble his props before addressing the courtly audience:

> This lantern doth the hornèd moon present (act 5, scene 1, line 231).

The barrage of criticism that followed was related to how the moon should be represented on stage. During this barrage, Starveling let his arms, laden with their props, drop down by his sides. Often Moonshine uses the repetition of his statement as an increasingly irritated rebuttal of the courtly criticism. Cotterill's Starveling, however, seemed genuinely cowed. His final statement, rather than being defiant, was a last, transparent plea for respect:

> All that I have to say is to tell you that the lantern is the moon, I am the man i'th' moon, this thorn bush my thorn bush and this dog my dog (act 5, scene 1, lines 247–9)

as the actor drooped his head in despair. His departure was made poignantly ridiculous by the bobbling gait of the dog contraption.

Cotterill's performance seasoned the quality of the play-within-the-play with an unexpected and tender sadness. There was substance and plausibility to Starveling which made me concur with Brook that Starveling had come to perform with great love, perhaps carefully selecting his own props, and had been, in return, starved of basic respect. His humble light was snuffed. Still, he faithfully performed the bergamasque at the end, albeit with a sad and serious expression on his face. The audience was forced to a cross-roads of imaginative sympathy: whether to side with the courtly set and their sophisticated and derisive voyeurism, or to accept the unsettling burden of their implicit cruelty. Cotterill's forceful performance as Starveling, more than any other aspect of the production, compelled the audience into a genuine encounter with the dark side of humanity.

Figure 6.3 Ralph Cotterill (Starveling), Nathan Page (Snout), John Leary (Flute), Jacek Koman (Bottom), Ian Watkin (Snug), *A Midsummer Night's Dream*, Company B, Belvoir Street Theatre, Sydney, 2004.
Photograph ©Heidrun Lohr
Courtesy of Company B and Heidrun Lohr.

Afterword

> Beauty is momentary in the mind –
> The fitful tracing of a portal;
> But in the flesh it is immortal.
>
> Wallace Stevens,
> *Peter Quince at the Clavier*

This book opens with the assertion that moments of metatheatre in Shakespeare can make a play 'ours as we play it'. It then examines three of Shakespeare's plays in production in Australia in an effort to substantiate and examine the qualities of that ownership. What remains is to touch upon the ideas that led my inquiry and to point out its most salient discoveries and directions for future work.

My working model for Shakespeare as performance has been W. B. Worthen's theorising of that pivotal, if ineffable, element of theatre – 'force'. Refuting the citational model of acting, Worthen sees performativity at the very hub of force in Shakespearean performance. Taking up this notion, I see moments of metatheatre as special portals of performativity which, by generating different realities in different contexts, actually signal the multivalent performativity of the play.

The contribution this book makes to the larger field of Shakespeare scholarship is to offer sustained discussion of how meaning is made through particular performances of plays as situated in a culturally and temporally specific context. In other words, I look at how performances of Shakespeare's plays *perform* in Australian culture. But to make this my sole project would be, ironically, to evade the obvious imperative of situating myself within that discussion. In seeking models of thought and writing akin to my own, I have noticed that many excellent studies which purport to have 'Shakespeare in performance' as their subject, fall short on this count. They are concerned with the reception of performance or the ways in which a play, or plays, perform on the stage of culture at the expense of exploring the ephemeral, affective, singularity of the performance experience. Scholars of such work find a firm foothold in established discourses of cultural theory and avoid, perhaps wisely, integrating the more slippery material of their own experience as audience members. I have sought to do more. I have wrestled with the minutiae, the un-theorised and ephemeral, felt moments of performance and rehearsal. The fractious life of such fleeting and subjective impressions – their simultaneous indelibility and resistance to theorising – has been, throughout, a spur to continue.

This dimension of my work constitutes a kind of 'unauthorised' authorship because it over-spills the validating frames offered by theoretical discourse. Certainly, I discuss how the productions in question 'mean by Shakespeare', and use the sanctioned tools of critical and cultural theorising to ground my assertions. Yet, at another level, what I engage in through my very selectivity and privileging of my own personal impressions is my own idiosyncratic activity of 'meaning by Shakespeare'. I invent this notion of 'unauthorised authorship' because authority and resistance to authority provide a useful nexus, a key-note, for summing up how Shakespearean metatheatre operates as a 'space of play' on the Australian stage.

Authority in *Hamlet* is constituted by a range of visible and invisible social and political codes. One of these codes, which it can be demonstrated takes on particular form and pressure in

AFTERWORD

the Australian context, is that associated with playing the 'male role'. In each of the four productions discussed, Hamlet's 'madness' had utterly different qualities and manifestations. Even so, in each production, Hamlet's 'madness' bore direct relation to the pressure exerted upon him to perform the 'male role'. Australian conceptions of masculinity and social coercion ignite this junction, making it performative in the contemporary Australian context.

Role-playing is, we discover, an indispensable figurative term in modern societies for discussing, challenging, and/or reinforcing socio-political structures of authority. In *Hamlet* instances of literal role-playing demonstrate a capacity to perturb the social and political order (as in the case of Hamlet's The Mousetrap), but also to perturb the decorum of theatre. The First Player's Tale, as an impromptu performance, tests the force of the production of which it is part. Its content tests Hamlet's resolve, its force tests Polonius' aesthetic sensibilities, but if it fails to genuinely compel the theatre audience, the former tests are defunct. In the three productions discussed, the force of the First Player's impromptu was compelling because it was fashioned from conventions of performance readily available in the contemporary Australian context.

Authority in *As You Like It*, in the form of a tyrant's court, is that from which the protagonist escapes. The Forest of Arden, configured in the play as a linguistically woven landscape of the imagination, seems to offer liberation – a liberation akin to that of theatre. However, the history of *As You Like It* on stage reflects an accretion of expectations that posture as absolute authorities on the subject of what 'Shakespeare's Arden' really is. The three Australian productions under scrutiny resisted these entrenched traditions in inventive ways, re-calibrating Arden as an Australian and a theatrical 'space of play'.

If Arden has been colonised over time by forms of cultural authority, so has its most anarchic inhabitant. Rosalind, as a self-conscious actor and director within the play (and within the theatre) harbours the promise, or perhaps the threat, of performativity. In Rosalind and her roles we are confronted with the vital, shape-shifting power of embodied rhetoric to subvert the established order of gender relations. In reception discourses that attend performance of the role in Australia, however, there is an observable tendency to confine and stabilise Rosalind. These accounts draw their authority from the putative 'real' Rosalind over whom the collective imagination exercises consensual ownership. Curiously, in each case under consideration, this collective and proprietorial impulse also extended over the body of the actor who played Rosalind. Such generalising public narratives were nevertheless resisted by the distinctive way in which each actor embodied Rosalind's performativity.

Authority in *A Midsummer Night's Dream* is at times reinforced, at times challenged by magic. In the productions under investigation the nature of the play's magical events and characters is shown to be strongly inflected by the cultural context in which the play was performed. Moreover, the 'magic of theatre' was given particular nuances depending on how each production framed its own theatrical identity within the Australian context.

Authority in *A Midsummer Night's Dream* is a matrix. Ostensibly, the play itself presents a patriarchal order enforced with varying degrees of violence, and a rigid stratification of social classes. Around the play further structures of authority have accrued over time; patterns of cultural authority generated by the way in which the play and its characters have come to be understood in various contexts and theatrical traditions.

In investigating how *A Midsummer Night's Dream* makes meaning, the authority of performance is the source of authority most difficult to analyse because it is the least predictable in the way it operates. As Chapter 6 demonstrates, a performance of Helena can have the audience laughing with her at the absurdity of male domination through violence; a performance of Bottom can have the audience applauding Titania's good taste rather than scorning her degradation, and a performance of Starveling can have the audience reflecting upon their participation in an event which uses spectacles of cruelty as a keynote of the entertainment.

It would be naïve to suggest that any of these analyses constitutes an excavation of the deepest designs of the plays themselves. Nevertheless, it is more true than strange, that the imaginative plenitude of each of the plays invites and accommodates a living host of semantic possibilities. To examine these possibilities it is necessary to take into account not only the structures of authority that inform the play itself, but also those with which the play intersects when it is performed in a particular cultural context.

Theatrical meaning is a fleeting encounter with infinite ramifications. I shall conclude by reflecting upon two responses to this kind of encounter modelled in *A Midsummer Night's Dream*. Theseus seeks to cauterise it immediately through retreat to solitary and rational consciousness. 'I' he states, 'never may believe these antic fables nor these fairy toys', and he repudiates invention as bearing too haphazard and too shifting a relation to reality to be of any worth. Hippolyta, however, stakes her plea for the dream's importance on the fact that it was shared:

> But all the story of the night told over,
> And all their minds transfigured so together,
> More witnesseth than fancy's images,
> And grows to something of great constancy;
> But howsoever, strange and admirable
> (act 5, scene 1, lines 23–7).

For Hippolyta, the encounter, though transitory, and its meaning, though elusive, amount to something of cogent import because they were communal experiences: undeniable if not wholly explicable.

Dramatic force is both the theoretical and imaginative lynchpin of this book. Force in performance is difficult to comprehend, even more difficult to crystalise in an instance; yet, it is the one thing that all members of an audience apprehend together. Theatrical force transfigures minds together by leaving its imprint on the body – on the senses. It thereby offers something of great constancy, something worthy of record and reflection, despite the fitful and fleeting nature of the theatrical experience. In summing up then, I offer Hippolyta's defence of her curiosity for the lovers' story as the raison d'être for *Ours As We Play It*.

Acknowledgments

Many people have played a role in the making of this book. First and foremost I wish to thank Penny Gay, whose discriminating intelligence and generosity of spirit have been founding forces. From the English Department at the University of Sydney, I also thank Will Christie, Jenny Gribble, Margaret Rogerson, Liam Semler, and Elizabeth Webby for taking consistent interest in my project and offering valuable advice. As a postdoctoral research fellow within the 'Shakespeare Reloaded' project, I am grateful for funding from the Australian Research Council and for the support the project has offered me in completing this book. To Laura Ginters and Ian Maxwell from Performance Studies, I owe thanks for access to video archives and for the riches gleaned during my time as a student in the Department, and to the School of Letters, Arts and Media I am grateful for funding towards production costs. I would also like to thank the Philament team past and present whose ambition and diligence has been a light.

I thank Alan Brissenden from the University of Adelaide for encouragement and parcels of reviews in the early stages of the project. For assistance with accessing theatre archives I would like to thank Judy Seeff from the Sydney Theatre Company; Andrew Ousley at the Bell Shakespeare Company; Vanessa Allen and Sophie Gardner at the State Theatre Company of South Australia; Jane May and Stephen Asher at Belvoir Street Theatre; Joanna Leahy at the Performing Arts Museum in Melbourne; Margaret

Leask at the National Institute of Dramatic Art; Ebony Hack from the Australian Shakespeare Company; Gavin Clarke at the Royal National Theatre in London; and all of the staff at the Shakespeare Centre Library in Stratford-upon-Avon. For eloquent images I am indebted to photographers Philip Le Masurier (STC), Tracey Schramm (STC), Heidrun Lohr (Belvoir and Bell), Wendy McDougall (Pork Chop Productions), Shane Reid (STCSA), Julian Watt (Belvoir), to artist Evert Ploeg, and to the National Library of Australia. I also owe special thanks to Paul Livingston for kind permission to use his image on the cover of this book.

For welcoming me into the rehearsal room I am deeply grateful to the Bell Shakespeare Company and particularly to John Bell and the cast and crew of *Hamlet* (2003), and to Lindy Davies and the cast and crew of *As You Like It* (2003). For their generosity in setting aside time to talk with me, I thank Robert Alexander, John Bell, Adam Cook, Lindy Davies, David Freeman, Roy Luxford, Aubrey Mellor, Pip Miller, Alice McConnell, Catherine Moore, Simon Phillips, and Anna Volska.

For other very helpful conversations I'm grateful to Christie Carson, Rob Conkie, Veronica Kelly, Edel Lamb, Gordon McMullan, and Richard Madelaine.

I offer warm thanks to all of my students, both at the University of Sydney and the University of Newcastle who have taught me much.

Parts of Chapter 2 first appeared in *Sydney Studies in English* 31 (2005); parts of Chapter 3 in *Contemporary Theatre Review* vol. 19, no. 3 (2009); parts of Chapter 4 in the Proceedings of the 2006 Conference of the Australasian Drama Association (Sydney e-Scholarship Repository, 2009, http://hdl.handle.net/2123/2494); and parts of Chapter 5 in *Shakespeare in Stage: New Directions in Theatre History* published by CUP in 2010. To editors of these publications: Tony Miller, Liz Schafer, Ian Maxwell, Chris Dymkowski and Christie Carson I am grateful for much thoughtful input.

ACKNOWLEDGMENTS

At UWA Publishing I thank Terri-ann White for answering my many questions, Anne Ryden, for her detailed eye and spirit of collaboration, and Sylvia Defendi for her creative labours. At the University of Western Australia, via Brisbane and London, I have Brett Hirsch to thank for the UWAP suggestion. It was a good one.

Finally, I wish to thank my friends and family who little know how much their assumption that I would complete this book has helped to make it happen. I am grateful to Tash Staszak, and James Clendon for technical expertise of one kind or another, to Linda Flaherty who transcribed hours of recorded interviews, and to Jack whose unobtrusive company during the years of writing was indispensible. Finally, I thank Jasper and Caleb, whose arrivals have both hastened and deepened the process of writing, and my husband Justin, whose loving confidence and imperturbable good sense have seasoned every stage of the endeavour.

Kate Flaherty

NOTES

Introduction
1. Peter Brook quoted in M. Croyden, *Conversations with Peter Brook*, p. 11.
2. H. Gilbert and J. Tompkins, *Post-Colonial Drama: Theory, Practice, Politics*, p. 23.
3. In her notes to the scene in which Prospero threatens to curse Caliban (act 1, scene 2), Christine Dymkowski offers concrete examples of how productions have facilitated many different responses to Caliban, from pity, to distaste, to compassion. See William Shakespeare, *The Tempest*, (*Shakespeare in Production*), C. Dymkowski, ed., pp. 164–6.
4. J. C. Bulman, 'Introduction: Shakespeare and performance theory', p. 1.
5. W. B. Worthen, *Shakespeare and the Force of Modern Performance*, p. 24.
6. W. B. Worthen, 'Shakespearean performativity', p. 132.
7. R. Luxford, interview with the author, 18 April 2005.
8. ibid.
9. R. Alexander, interview with the author, 30 August 2004.
10. T. Hawkes, *Shakespeare in the Present*, p. 111. For an excellent account of 'presentism' in relation to its theoretical legacy, see also E. Fernie, 'Shakespeare and the prospect of presentism'.
11. See Douglas Lanier, 'Drowning the book: *Prospero's Books* and the textual Shakespeare', p. 203.
12. R. N. Watson, 'As you liken it: simile in the wilderness'.
13. G. McAuley, 'The emerging field of rehearsal studies', p. 8.
14. Examples of these categories are offered respectively to indicate the range of resources consulted: C. Rutter, *Clamorous Voices, Shakespeare's Women Today*; J. Gordon-Clark, 'The hard road to stardom: The early career of Essie Jenyns'; W. B. Worthen, *Shakespeare and the Force of Modern Performance*; C. Belsey, 'Disrupting sexual difference: Meaning and gender in the comedies'; J. Butler, *Excitable Speech*.

NOTES

15 B. Hodgdon, 'Looking for Mr Shakespeare after "the Revolution": Robert Lepage's intercultural dream machine', p. 69. (When using the term 'discursively saturated materiality', Hodgdon cites H. A. Giroux and S. I. Roger, 'Pedagogy and the critical practice of photography', in *Disturbing Pleasures: Learning Popular Culture*, H. Giroux, ed., Routledge, London and New York, 1994, p. 98.)
16 W. Shakespeare, *Hamlet, Prince of Denmark*, Robert Hapgood, ed., p. 108.
17 J. Golder and R. Madelaine, '"To dote thus upon such luggage": appropriating Shakespeare in Australia', p. 2.
18 M. D. Bristol, *Shakespeare's America, America's Shakespeare*.
19 H. Gilbert and J. Tompkins, *Post-Colonial Drama: Theory, Practice, Politics*.
20 M. Campbell, 'Introduction', p. 1.
21 ibid., p. 2.
22 A. Parker and E. K. Sedgwick, 'Introduction', p.5.
23 W. B. Worthen, *Shakespeare and the Force of Modern Performance*, p. 6.

Chapter 1

1 J. Golder and R. Madelaine, 'Elsinore at Belvoir St', p. 67.
2 R. W. Connell, *Masculinities*, pp. 22, 68.
3 J. Golder and R. Madelaine, 'Elsinore at Belvoir St.', p. 61.
4 ibid., p. 57.
5 ibid., quoting the *Telegraph Mirror, Bulletin*, and *SMH*, p. 57.
6 ibid.
7 ibid., quoting Katherine Brisbane interviewed by A. Bennie, *SMH*, 20 August 1994, p. 58.
8 A. Bennie, 'A tortured *Macbeth*; a glorious *Hamlet*'.
9 I am indebted to the Performance Studies Department of the University of Sydney, and particularly to Dr Laura Ginters and Russell Emerson, for their help in accessing archival video footage of rehearsals and performances of this production.
10 There is a remarkable persistence, in productions of *Hamlet* in this period, of the single, flexible and opulent piece of red furnishing. Compare Armfield's Persian rug and Sims' drape to the 'single blood orange-coloured carpet' used by Peter Brook in his 2000 *Hamlet* starring Adrian Lester for Bouffes du Nord in M. Croydon, *Conversations with Peter Brook*, p. 253.
11 Jeremy Sims interviewed by J. Adamson, 'Remixing the Bard'.
12 J. Adamson, 'Remixing the Bard'.
13 B. Hallet, 'Nothing rotten in the state of this spirited staging'.
14 ibid.

15 N. Munro-Wallis, 'Hamlet,' 612 ABC Brisbane,
16 B. Cochrane, 'QTC Hamlet: a curiously domestic tragedy'.
17 R. W. Connell, *Masculinities*, p. 68.
18 J. Golder and R. Madelaine, 'Elsinore at Belvoir St.', p. 67.
19 ibid., p. 57.
20 ibid., p. 66.
21 ibid., p. 67.
22 Linzi Murrie has argued that the masculinity of the Australian legend entails a resistance to the roles of husband, family provider, and father, which had so characterised the masculinities of the pre-industrial and rural contexts. Of the 'bushman' type, Murrie states: 'His independence, his inarticulateness, and his nomadic existence all position him outside of society at large, but not outside all society. Among his mates – where his independence is sacrificed to the obligations of group loyalty – his masculinity is given its legitimacy.' L. Murrie, 'The Australian legend', p. 68.
23 J. Golder and R. Madelaine, 'Elsinore at Belvoir St.', p. 68.
24 ibid., Armfield described these as 'the sources of her distraction', p. 67.
25 ibid., p. 60.
26 As the culture of this *Hamlet* suggests, it was pitched at a young audience. The performance under discussion took place during the day and was evidently attended by groups of senior school students for whom *Hamlet* was scheduled as a Higher School Certificate text.
27 J. Adamson, 'Remixing the Bard'.
28 Bell Shakespeare Company schools package (media release), 2003.
29 K. Flaherty, notes taken in rehearsal, *Hamlet*, 20 January 2003.
30 ibid., 22 January 2003.
31 A. Colby Sprague, *Shakespeare and the Actors: The Stage Business in His Plays (1660–1905)*, quoted by Robert Hapgood ed., in a textual note in W. Shakespeare, *Hamlet, Prince of Denmark*, p. 180.
32 R. Hapgood, *Hamlet, Prince of Denmark*, p. 183.
33 A. Cook, interview with the author, 21 July 2010.
34 ibid.
35 ibid.
36 Munro-Wallis, 'Hamlet,' 612 ABC Brisbane.
37 M. Bramwell, 'Boy wonder'.
38 A. Cook, interview with the author, 21 July 2010.
39 R. Berry, 'Hamlet and the audience', p. 25.
40 While *The Norton Shakespeare* uses 'nightly colour', I have used 'nighted colour' because it is the more common version of the phrase used in performance and was used in each of the productions discussed in this chapter.

NOTES

41 J. Adamson, 'Remixing the Bard'.
42 K. Flaherty, notes taken in rehearsal, *Hamlet*, 20 January 2003.
43 Statistics from the Australian War Memorial website http://www.awm.gov.au/encyclopedia/gallipoli/fatalities.asp, accessed 3 November 2011.
44 D. Coad identifies the irony of the tenacious 'legend of heterosexual hypermasculinity': 'As a simultaneous stereotype of nationality or Australianness, the sex/gender fantasy is queer because it excludes the Indigenous population of the country as well as the non-Anglo-Celtic. The stereotype is also sexist…Women are excluded from Australianness. The rapid urbanisation of Australia, even in colonial times, has meant that the idea of a nation of bushmen surrounded by their wife, children and dogs somewhere back o' Bourke, is a poetic fiction'. D. Coad, *Gender Trouble Down Under: Australian Masculinities*, pp. 13–14.
45 L. Murrie, 'The Australian legend', p. 68.
46 R. Berry, 'Hamlet and the audience', p. 28.
47 C. Stollery, 'Arriving at an actor's interpretation of Hamlet'.
48 E. Ashmead-Bartlett, 'Not found wanting' and 'A stand as worthy as Mons', *Hobart Mercury*, 12 May 1915.
49 M. Lake, 'What have you done for your country?', p. 21.
50 B. Hallett, 'Nothing rotten in the state of this spirited staging'.
51 The square-bracketed punctuation was specific to the Bell Shakespeare script and suggests a much more exclamatory tone of speech. David Garrick is also recorded to have added the exclamation after 'spirit' to avoid the implication – as actor Edwin Booth suggests – that spirits were a common sight. (See Hapgood's textual note in W. Shakespeare, *Hamlet, Prince of Denmark*, p. 122.) This agrees with Bell's emphasis upon the educated Hamlet who would scorn superstition and be astonished by the mere possibility of a spirit walking, let alone his father's and 'in arms'.
52 This interpretative possibility is also posited by Philip Edwards in a textual note: '[Hamlet] has become reckless because of what is in his mind. Horatio believes that Hamlet's dangerous behaviour arises from his *idea* of the Ghost, which has obliterated the reality that the Ghost is capable of tremendous harm', in W. Shakespeare, *Hamlet, Prince of Denmark*, p. 105.
53 K. Flaherty, notes taken in rehearsal, *Hamlet*, 21 January 2003.
54 J. Golder and R. Madelaine, 'Elsinore at Belvoir St.', p. 69.
55 ibid.
56 ibid., pp. 69–70.
57 ibid., p. 65.

58 A. Cook, interview with the author, 21 July 2010.
59 ibid.
60 P. Gay, 'Recent Australian *Shrews*', p. 36. While describing larrikinism as a culture of resistance, Gay notes that larrikinism 'was contaminated by that most insidious of imperialist institutions, patriarchy. Put simply, Australian 'larrikin' culture is and has been, since its first cheeky steps on Australian soil, overwhelmingly male and masculinist', p. 37. Gay goes on to explore the specific ramifications of this larrikinism for performances of Shakespeare's Katherine in the Australian context.
61 John Bell, quoted by Frank Harris, *Daily Telegraph*, 12 February 1979 in A. Kiernander, 'A post-colonial Shakespeare, 1963–2000', p. 246.
62 J. Rickard, 'Lovable larrikins and awful ockers', p. 79.
63 Bruce Smith, *Shakespeare and Masculinity*, pp. 2–3.

Chapter 2

1 Neil Armfield interviewed by Golder and Madelaine, 'Elsinore at Belvor St.', p. 60.
2 Howard Felperin claims that '…Hamlet's discourse on the art of theatre is the nearest thing we have to a statement of Shakespeare's own aims and principles as a dramatist', moreover that 'Hamlet's speech is predominantly a plea for the new doctrine of dramatic illusionism and falls into line with the special pleadings of such Elizabethan classicists as Sidney and Jonson.' H. Felperin, 'O'erdoing termageant: An approach to Shakespearean mimesis', pp. 372–3. Conversely, Pauline Kiernan, in her chapter on Shakespeare's repudiation of mimesis, offers the following synopsis of recent scholarship: 'It is a commonplace of *Hamlet* criticism that the Prince's advice to the Players is completely at odds with his creator's practice'. P. Kiernan, *Shakespeare's Theory of Drama*, p. 126. In support of this summary Kiernan cites R. W. Battenhouse, 'The significance of Hamlet's advice to the Players'; and R. Weimann, 'Mimesis in *Hamlet*'.
3 Numerous critics treat The Murder of Gonzago/The Mousetrap in *Hamlet*. For example, Judd D. Hubert investigates the recourse to theatrical devices as a means of testing truth in *Hamlet*, most notably Hamlet's use of The Mousetrap. J. D. Hubert, *Metatheatre: The Example of Shakespeare*, p. 103.
4 The most famous treatment of Hamlet's 'antic disposition' as a part of an actual psychological profile is that by Sigmund Freud. Freud uses Hamlet as an instance of how 'in every epoch of history those who have had something to say but could not say it without peril have eagerly assumed a fool's cap'. Freud then goes on to draw a metaphorical parallel between the function of the Prince as a 'madman'

and the function of dreams in '…concealing the true circumstances under a cloak of wit and unintelligibility'. S. Freud, *The Interpretation of Dreams*, p. 444. This view of Hamlet as a plausible and purposeful psychological unity is splintered by the postmodern recognition of a rift between signifier and signified. In this vein Robert Weimann observes that '[a]lthough motivated from within the needs of the self-contained play, Hamlet's madness constantly serves to subvert the representational logic of his own role in the play: in a strictly representational context, Hamlet's antic disposition arouses rather than allays suspicion…Madness as a "method" of mimesis dissolves important links between the representer and the represented, and can only partially sustain a logical or psychological motivation'. R. Weimann, 'Mimesis in *Hamlet*', p. 285.
5   In his biographical work Stephen Greenblatt explains Rozencrantz's account of the child players in the light of the relationship between Shakespeare's company – the Lord Chamberlain's Men – and the children's companies – the Children of Paul's and the Children of the Chapel at Blackfriars. See S. Greenblatt, *Will in the World*, p. 293.
6   The textual note accompanying Stephen Greenblatt's commentary on *Hamlet* in the Norton Edition outlines the various major theories concerning the three texts of *Hamlet*. Greenblatt, et. al., eds, *The Norton Shakespeare*, pp. 1666–7.
7   See L. Erne, *Shakespeare as Literary Dramatist*.
8   J. Gleckman, 'Shakespeare as poet or playwright?', p. 6.
9   W. B. Worthen, 'The weight of Antony' p. 298.
10 In her book *Shakespeare's Theory of Drama*, Pauline Kiernan investigates this dynamic comprehensively. The immediate comment is distilled from the following: 'When we are reminded that we are sitting in a theatre and have been, in the words of one contemporary spectator at *Julius Caesar*, "ravished" by events on stage, it merely reinforces the power of the fiction to coerce our belief – *in the fiction*.' Kiernan, *Shakespeare's Theory of Drama*, p.120.
11 R. Weimann, 'Mimesis in *Hamlet*', p. 285.
12 ibid., p. 288.
13 James C. Bulman traces 'the emergence of stage-centred criticism from traditional literary study' to J. L. Styan's *The Shakespeare Revolution*, Cambridge University Press, 1997. See J. Bulman 'Introduction: Shakespeare and performance theory', p. 1.
14 K. Flaherty, notes taken in rehearsal, 20 and 22 January 2003.
15 The text used for the Bell production omitted the five lines prior to Polonius' interjection.
16 K. Flaherty, notes taken in rehearsal, 24 January 2003.

17 T. Hawkes, 'Telmah', p. 312.
18 J. Golder and R. Madelaine, 'Elsinore at Belvoir St.'.
19 ibid., quoting *Weekend Australian*, 11–12 June 1994, p. 59.
20 ibid., quoting 'Director's note', *Hamlet* program, p. 59.
21 ibid., p. 56
22 ibid., p. 73.
23 ibid., p. 60.
24 A. Bennie, 'A tortured *Macbeth*; a Glorious *Hamlet*'.
25 J. Golder and R. Madelaine, 'Elsinore at Belvoir St.', p. 79.
26 W. B. Worthen, *Shakespeare and the Force of Modern Performance*, p. 24; and 'Shakespearean performativity', p. 132.

Chapter 3

1 P. Makeham, 'Framing the landscape; Prichard's *Pioneers* and Esson's *The Drovers*', p.121.
2 R. N. Watson, 'As you liken it: simile in the wilderness'.
3 For a discussion of why we 'embraced the legal fiction' that *terra nullius* was the pretext for dispossession of Australia's indigenous population see A. Fitzmaurice, 'The genealogy of terra nullius', p.1.
4 For a lucid and succinct account of Mabo see P. E. Butt and R. Eagleson, *Mabo: What the High Court said and what the government did*. See also M. Bachelard, *The Great Land Grab*, p. 8.
5 A. Kennedy, 'The Bard on skates'.
6 H. G. Kippax, 'Bubble and squeak'.
7 ibid.
8 A. Mellor, interview with the author, 18 August 2003.
9 R. Page, 'Stature to the pleasurable', p. 25.
10 R. Alexander, interview with the author, 30 August 2004.
11 H. G. Kippax, '*As You Like It* reveals new outback romance'.
12 B. Hoad, 'Wallowing in hindsight', p. 78.
13 H. G. Kippax, '*As You Like It*'.
14 J. Tompkins, *Unsettling Space: Contestations in Contemporary Australian Theatre*, p. 33.
15 J. McCallum, 'Postmodern Bard matched by brilliant performers'.
16 ibid.
17 B. Hoad, 'As you might expect it', pp. 77–8.
18 For a fuller explanation of the origins of the methektic model of space, its relationship to Australian landscapes, and its operation in theatre see J. Tompkins, *Unsettling Space*, pp. 10–13.
19 *How to do Things with Words* is the title of J. L. Austin's seminal work which treats illocutionary speech or speech which 'does things'. Austin excludes dramatic performance from this category as 'peculiarly

hollow' because of it is citational character. However, taking into account the critical legacy that has succeeded Austin's work, W. B. Worthen has recently argued that theatrical performance might in fact be seen as definitive of performativity in the sense that all utterance, whether on stage or in 'real-life', depends for force and meaning upon recognised regimes of behaviour and situation. See W. B. Worthen, *Shakespeare and the Force of Modern Performance*, pp. 4–9.

20 S. Phillips, interview with the author, 14 September 2004.
21 J. Jameson, 'Good time with the Bard in our backyard'.
22 Neil Armfield interviewed by J. Morgan, 'Where there's a Will…'
23 Deborah Mailman interviewed by J. Hampson, 'Black and white'.
24 Deborah Mailman interviewed by B. Holgate, 'Actors hurdle the colour bar'.
25 Neil Armfield interviewed by J. Morgan, 'Where there's a Will…'.
26 H. Gilbert and J. Lo, *Performance and Cosmopolitics*, p. 136.
27 Neil Armfield, interviewed by B. Holgate, 'Actors hurdle the colour bar'.
28 On 13 February 2008 Prime Minister Kevin Rudd apologised to the Aboriginal people 'for the laws and policies of successive Parliaments and governments that have inflicted profound grief, suffering and loss on these our fellow Australians…especially for the removal of Aboriginal and Torres Strait Islander children from their families, their communities and their country'.
29 B. Perret, 'As you like it'; H. Thomson, 'Bell's winter of discontent'; S. Dunne, 'Not enough to like in empty pantomime'.
30 K. Flaherty, notes taken in rehearsal, *As You Like It*, 7 July 2003.
31 ibid. This comment bears remarkable affinity with that made by director Gale Edwards: 'The most important thing a director can do is have an honest relationship with what she reads.' G. Edwards, address to the World Shakespeare Congress, 17 July 2006.
32 C. Moore, interview with the author, 31 October 2003.
33 R. Alexander, interview with the author, 30 August 2004.
34 K. Flaherty, notes taken in rehearsal, *As You Like It*, 7 July 2003.
35 B. Perret, 'As you like it'.
36 H. Thomson, 'Bell's winter of discontent'.
37 K. Longworth, 'Some like it not really'.
38 S. Dunne, 'Not enough to like in empty pantomime'.
39 'The first recorded performance of *As You Like It* was at the Theatre Royal, Drury Lane on 20 December 1740. The first concrete allusion to it in the theatre is its presence in a list now in the Public Records Office…made in January 1669, of 108 plays, twenty-one of them by Shakespeare, formerly acted at the Blackfriars Theatre by the King's

Men, and 'now allowed of' to Thomas Killigrew, Master of the Theatre Royal in Bridges Street; inclusion in such a list however, is no guarantee of performance. It is a tantalising thought, but one which must be seriously considered, that this play, immensely popular since 1740, may not have been performed at the time it was written.' A. Brissenden, 'Introduction' in W. Shakespeare, *As You Like It*, p. 50.
40 Lindy Davies, 'Director's note', Program for *As You Like It*, Bell Shakespeare, 2003.
41 S. Dunne, 'Not enough to like in empty pantomime'.
42 H. Thomson, 'Bell's winter of discontent'.
43 E. Schafer, 'Reconciliation Shakespeare? Aboriginal presence in Australian Shakespeare production', p. 63.
44 In this, Phillips' production might also be seen as activating the play's built-in self-reflexivity for, as Jonathan Hall has pointed out, 'Postmodern awareness of the mobility of signs, which subvert the very identities that they precariously construct, is in some ways a return to Renaissance modes of understanding rhetoric and wit'. J. Hall, *Anxious Pleasures: Shakespearean Comedy and the Nation State*, p. 265.

Chapter 4

1 Simon Phillips quoted by P. Cochrane, 'Out of the wood and into the forest'.
2 M. Hamer, 'Shakespeare's Rosalind and her public image', p. 109.
3 ibid.
4 'The Criterion Theatre'.
5 'The first recorded performance of *As You Like It* was at the Theatre Royal, Drury Lane on 20 December 1740. The first concrete allusion to it in the theatre is its presence in a list now in the Public Records Office...made in January 1669, of 108 plays, twenty-one of them by Shakespeare, formerly acted at the Blackfriars Theatre by the King's Men, and 'now allowed of' to Thomas Killigrew, Master of the Theatre Royal in Bridges Street; inclusion in such a list however, is no guarantee of performance. It is a tantalising thought, but one which must be seriously considered, that this play, immensely popular since 1740, may not have been performed at the time it was written.' A. Brissenden, 'Introduction' in W. Shakespeare, *As You Like It*, p. 50.
6 H. G. Kippax, 'Bubble and squeak'.
7 Page, 'Stature to the pleasurable', pp. 24, 25.
8 A review of Fiona Shaw's performance of the role for London's Old Vic in 1989 opines that '[w]ith her boyish haircut, solitary dangling earring and rakish demeanor, she seems less Vanessa Redgrave and more Vanessa Bell'. H. De Vries, 'Britain Boasts a New Stage

NOTES

Star'. More locally, a review of Simon Phillips' 1995/6 production for Sydney Theatre Company reflects that 'Vanessa Redgrave made her name as Rosalind at Stratford in 1961 in Michael Elliot's much admired Royal Shakespeare Company production'. Cochrane, 'Out of the woods, into the forest'.

9 *Birmingham Mail*, 11 January, 1962 quoted in P. Gay, *As She Likes It: Shakespeare's Unruly Women*, p. 54.
10 Both Penny Gay, who traces the production history of the play through the second half of the twentieth century, and Mary Hamer, who discusses the relationship between the role, the actors, and the public image of Rosalind, document remarkable shifts in what actors and directors have made of the character over time. See Gay, *As She Likes It*, pp. 48–85, and Hamer, 'Shakespeare's Rosalind and her public image'.
11 Brissenden, 'Introduction' in Shakespeare, *As You Like It*, p. 57 quoting G. Fletcher, *Studies of Shakespeare*, Longman, Brown, Green, and Longman's, London, 1847, p. 239.
12 C. Rutter, *Clamorous Voices, Shakespeare's Women Today*, p. 120.
13 See P. Taylor, '*As You Like It*, Directed by Declan Donnellan', *Shakespeare in the Theatre: An Anthology of Criticism*, p. 316.
14 P. Holland, *English Shakespeares, Shakespeare on the English Stage in the 1990s*, pp. 91, 92.
15 A. B. Dawson, 'Performance and participation: Desdemona, Foucault and the actor's body', p. 31.
16 Clarifying this potential, Lorraine Helms has helpfully drawn attention to the almost ineffable ways in which the body of the female actor can destabilise and subvert power relations implicit in the play and even those explicit in a particular production's program notes. See L. Helms, 'Playing the woman's part: Feminist criticism and Shakespearean performance', p. 206.
17 J. Gordon-Clark, 'The hard road to stardom', p. 85.
18 'If instead of being tied to Holloway's company with its reliance on a mixture of melodrama and a few Shakespearean plays, she had, for instance, joined the recently formed Brough Boucicault Company with their concentration on modern serious dramas and elegant comedies, she could have widened her repertoire. Such a move would have gained a different type of training, and perhaps she could have emerged as an actress equally capable of playing Shakespeare and modern dramatists such as Pinero and Henry Arthur Jones before moving on to Shaw and Ibsen…Marriage must have seemed the best option, thereby unshackling her from financial and social constraints which limited her rather than giving her independence as a woman earning her own living'. Gordon Clark, 'The hard road to stardom', p. 85.

19 G. M. Thompson, 'Miss Essie Jenyns', p. 88.
20 ibid., p. 83.
21 J. Gordon-Clark, 'The hard road to stardom', pp. 77, 78.
22 G. M. Thompson, 'Miss Essie Jenyns', p. 84.
23 ibid., pp. 83, 84.
24 ibid., p. 84.
25 ibid.
26 Simon Phillips interviewed by Cochrane, 'Out of the wood'.
27 My direct accounts of the STC production are distilled from my own attendance of a performance in 1996, and my viewing of the STC archival video (recorded 19 February 1996), courtesy of STC archives and archivist Judith Seef.
28 McCallum, 'Postmodern Bard matched by brilliant performers'.
29 S. Phillips, interview with the author, 14 September 2004.
30 C. Busby, 'I like it like that'.
31 The source of this comment is my observation of the Royal Shakespeare Company archival video of the 1985 Royal Shakespeare Company production held at the Shakespeare Centre Library and viewed on 19 April 2006.
32 S. Phillips, interview with the author, 14 September 2004.
33 C. Busby, 'I like it like that.'
34 D. Banks, 'Electric (Lucy) Bell'.
35 E. Tom, 'A man of many parts'.
36 S. Hawkins, 'Fool on the bill'; J. Morgan, 'Comics enter the character building stage.'
37 S. Phillips, interview with the author, 14 September 2004.
38 P. Morrison, 'Bard true to title'.
39 McCallum, 'Postmodern Bard matched by brilliant performers'.
40 A. Stone, 'As you like it'.
41 D. Anderson, 'The Bard, me and Company B – some enchanted evening'; C. Kablean, 'Silly Shakespeare'; J. McCallum, 'Bard bent for a purposeful laugh'; C. Rose, 'As you love it'.
42 J. Morgan, 'Where there's a Will…'.
43 J. Hampson, 'Black and white.
44 Schafer, 'Reconciliation Shakespeare?', p. 67.
45 A. Dennis, 'Mailman people's top banana'.
46 Deborah Mailman interviewed by B. Holgate, 'Actors hurdle the colour bar'.
47 J. Hampson, 'Black and white'.
48 Lindy Davies, conversation with the author, 19 August 2003.
49 R. Usher, 'Playing with gender roles'.
50 The source of my comments on rehearsals of the Bell *As You Like*

NOTES

It are my own recordings and notes taken as a rehearsal observer throughout July 2003. For this unique opportunity I am indebted to the Bell Shakespeare Company, Lindy Davies, and the *As You Like It* cast and crew.

51 A. McConnell, interview with the author, 2 August 2003.
52 A. McConnell, interview with the author, 18 August 2003.
53 R. Usher, 'Playing with gender roles'.
54 Alice McConnell interviewed by Usher, 'Playing with gender roles'.
55 Davies quoted in H. Strube, The autonomous actor: a case study of Lindy Davies, MA thesis, Queensland University of Technology, 1994.
56 K. Longworth, 'Some like it not really'.
57 B. Perret, 'As you like it'.
58 H. Thomson, 'Bell's winter of discontent'.
59 ibid.
60 E. Grosz, *Volatile Bodies*, p. 114.
61 Dunne, 'Not enough to like in empty pantomime'.
62 C. Rose, 'Man enough for the role'.

Chapter 5

1 Pauline Kiernan makes similar observations in *Shakespeare's Theory of Drama*, pp. 108–16.
2 R. Jackson, 'Actor managers and the spectacular', p. 124.
3 *The Diary of Samuel Pepys* quoted by P. Tatspaugh, 'Reading: *A Midsummer Night's Dream*', p. 540.
4 ibid., p. 541.
5 One reviewer of a 1903 production (*The Age*, 13 April 1903) at Melbourne's Princess Theatre went so far as to suggest that Mendelssohn's Overture was more capable of capturing the spirit of the play than the language itself: 'the keynote of the entertainment was struck by a sympathetic rendering on the part of an augmented orchestra, conducted by Mr A. Zelman jun., of Mendelssohn's lovely overture to the incidental music which he composed for this play. An echo of its sentiment, and instinct with its poetry, the composition attunes the minds of its auditors for what follows. It is full of suggestions of the mystic beauty of elfin life, of the subtle harmonies of nature, and of a world of thoughts and feelings which the imagination may explore, but which are voiceless by reason of the inadequacy of human language'.
6 P. Tatspaugh describes the political preoccupations of 'Britain's expanding empire' and 'the duty of women to their husbands and fathers' promulgated by nineteenth century stagings of the play. See Tatspaugh, 'Reading: *A Midsummer Night's Dream*', p. 542. Irene Dash

draws attention to textual elisions and directions which have diluted the discomfort of Hippolyta's silence, of Egeus' threats of brutality to Hermia, and of the cruelty perpetrated by Oberon upon Titania. See I. G. Dash, *Women's Worlds in Shakespeare's Plays*, pp. 74–8, 97.

7. See P. Tatspaugh, 'Reading: *A Midsummer Night's Dream*', pp. 541–2.
8. Helen Hackett suggests that the staging of the play as a 'light, playful, good humoured spectacle' had its origins in the 1692 staging of Elkanah Settle and Henry Purcell's opera the *Fairy Queen*. H. Hackett, *William Shakespeare: A Midsummer Night's Dream*, p. 47.
9. Famously, in Charles Kean's 1856 production at the Princess Theatre in London, the young Ellen Terry as Puck emerged on a mushroom from a trap. This set a trend for the casting of Puck as a child, and for this particular mode of entrance. See R. A. Foakes, 'Introduction' in W. Shakespeare, R. A. Foakes, ed., *A Midsummer Night's Dream*. See also Dash, *Women's Worlds*, p. 85.
10. Ciraulo further points out that while this is true of Charles Lamb's view, Mary Lamb's treatment of the play simultaneously evinces 'an anxiety about the role of fancy in young women's educational development'. D. Ciraulo, 'Fairy magic and the female imagination: Mary Lamb's '*A Midsummer Night's Dream*', p. 441.
11. W. B. Worthen takes up the notion of 'the ability of texts to stage a dialogue across history', particularly commending the insight brought to the subject by M. D. Bristol's *Big-Time Shakespeare*. See Worthen, 'Shakespearean Performativity', p. 121.
12. O. Asche, *Oscar Asche: His Life by Himself*, p. 143.
13. B. Dunstone, 'Dinkum Shakespeare? Perth, Empire and the Bard', p. 170.
14. R. Gaby, '"Here's a marvellous convenient place for our rehearsal": Shakespeare in Australian Space', p. 132.
15. Hobart *Mercury*, 11 January 1922, quoted in J. Golder, 'A cultural missionary on tour: Allan Wilkie's Shakespearean Company, 1920–30', p. 122.
16. A. Brissenden, 'Australian Shakespeare', p. 249.
17. J. Golder, 'A cultural missionary on tour', pp. 125–27.
18. Another important precursor to the large-scale touring activity of the Bell Company was the John Alden Company which operated from 1948 to 1953. See P. Gay, 'International glamour or home-grown talent? 1948–1964', pp. 185–90.
19. G. Milne, 'Shakespeare under the stars: a new populist tradition', p. 65.
20. J. Golder and R. Madelaine, '"To dote thus upon such luggage": appropriating Shakespeare in Australia', p. 15.
21. K. Brisbane, *The Advertiser*.

22 H. G. Kippax, 'A midsummer day's lark', *SMH*, 12 July 1973, in H. Heseltine, ed., *A Leader of His Craft: Theatre Reviews by H. G. Kippax*, p. 183.
23 M. Prerauer, '*Dream* becomes a reality',.
24 M. Harris, 'Sharman's risks pay off in *Dream*', p. 44.
25 P. Ward, 'All the world's a pearly stage'.
26 Harris, 'Sharman's risks pay off'.
27 B. Evans, 'Glitter outshines substance'.
28 P. Payne, 'Dream of the future'.
29 ibid., interview of Richard Wherrett.
30 S. Phillips, interview with the author, 14 September 2004.
31 *SMH*, 12 September, 1997.
32 The source of my comments on this production is the STC archival video (recorded 25 September 1997) viewed on 22 November 2005 courtesy of Sydney Theatre Company archives.
33 Set designed by Andrew Raymond and lit by Tony Youlden.
34 '...the keen receptive focus on Aboriginal/European opposition might only be partly the result of Tovey's stylistic choices; it may also reflect an essentialist understanding of cultural and racial difference'. E. Cox, 'Negotiating cultural narratives: all Aboriginal Shakespeare dreaming', p. 23.
35 G. Milne, 'Shakespeare under the stars', p. 68.
36 ibid., p. 69.
37 D. Anderson, 'The stuff that dreams are made of'.
38 I have attended three of Elston's *A Midsummer Night's Dream*s: two in Sydney in 1993 and 1994, and one in Melbourne in February 2005.
39 D. Anderson, 'The stuff that dreams are made of'.
40 Rose Gaby has drawn attention to the very different ways outdoor spaces are used in open-air Shakespeare productions. See Gaby, '"Here's a marvellous convenient place"'.
41 Phil Sumner interviewed by G. Burchall, 'A natural setting for drama'.
42 R. Fotheringham, *Sport in Australia*, p. 1.
43 I attended the production at Riverside theatre, Parramatta in February, 2004.
44 A. Volska, interview with the author, 9 September 2005.
45 ibid.
46 S. Dunne, 'Aussie wit and Will in perfect harmony'.
47 A. Volska, interview with the author, 9 September 2005.
48 J. L. Calderwood, *Shakespearean Metadrama*, p. 141.
49 C. Iaccarino, 'The whiz-kid who won't be making it easy'.
50 L. A. Low, 'Dreams of an explosive imagination'.
51 Iaccarino, 'The whiz-kid who won't be making it easy'.

52 'Andrews says he has limited interest in past productions'. Iaccarino, 'The whiz-kid who won't be making it easy'.
53 J. Kott, *Shakespeare our Contemporary*, p. 182.
54 I attended an evening performance in July 2004.
55 S. Dunne, 'Bit players the stars in a post-punk garden of dreams'.
56 Low, 'Dreams of an explosive imagination'.
57 ibid., interview of Andrews.

Chapter 6

1 Recent criticism has drawn attention to the way in which the *Dream* exposes authority's dependence on manufactured or mechanical shows of authority. See chapter 6 of Hall, *Anxious Pleasures: Shakespearean Comedy and the Nation State*. See also chapter 3 of P. Parker, *Shakespeare from the Margins: Language, Culture, Context*.
2 In his essay, Philip C. McGuire identifies the protean quality of Hippolyta's silence by analysing the treatment it received across four different productions. McGuire's hypothesis is that 'Hippolyta's silence is textually indeterminate. It is open in the sense that it is established by the words that constitute the playtext, but once established, it is capable of having meanings and effects that are not fixed by those words and that take on distinct form and shape only during performances of the play. We cannot probe her silence with any precision unless we attend to what has happened during performances'. P. C. McGuire, 'Hippolyta's silence and the poet's pen', p. 142.
3 Laura Levine, seeing Theseus' first address as an effort to transform violence through theatre, points out that in the question of Hermia, Theseus fails in his project immediately: 'Rather than transforming the sexual coercion that he begins the play by promising to get rid of, Theseus immediately repeats it. Rather than undoing an act of sexual violence, he reenacts one.' L. Levine, 'Rape, repetition, and the politics of closure in *A Midsummer Night's Dream*', p. 211.
4 ibid., p. 222.
5 ibid., pp. 213–14.
6 W. B. Worthen, *Shakespeare and the Force of Modern Performance*, p. 3.
7 'Commentators have long since noticed that the lovers in this love quartet are hardly distinguishable at all from one another. The girls differ only in height and in the colour of their hair...The lovers are exchangeable.' Kott, *Shakespeare Our Contemporary*, pp.175–76. Helen Hackett, also emphasising the arbitrariness of affection in the play, states that there are 'some superficial distinctions between the two women – Helena is taller and fairer, Hermia is more spirited – but even here there is no *logical* reason to prefer one over another. The

switches of affection among the four lovers are facilitated by a sense that the two men and the two women are effectively interchangeable'. Hackett, *William Shakespeare: A Midsummer Night's Dream*, p. 35.

8 E. Cox, 'Negotiating cultural narratives: all Aboriginal Shakespeare dreaming', p. 19.
9 ibid., quoting Wesley Enoch, p. 19.
10 As Levine points out, there is a persistent correlation in the play between these two forms of threat. See Levine, 'Rape, repetition, and the politics of closure'.
11 Jonathan Hall has pointed out that '[i]n the opening scene, the violence culminates in a joke whereby the audience is brought to laugh at the whole patriarchal principle of ownership'. See Hall, *Anxious Pleasures: Shakespearean Comedy and the Nation State*, p. 100.
12 The STC production replaced the word 'stealth' with 'flight'.
13 L. A. Montrose, '"Shaping fantasies": figurations of gender and power in Elizabethan culture', p. 107.
14 Kott, *Shakespeare Our Contemporary*, pp. 69–88.
15 ibid., p.175.
16 ibid., p.183.
17 ibid.
18 See J. D. Hainsworth, 'Shakespeare, son of Beckett?', p. 364.
19 D. Bevington, '"But we are spirits of another sort": the dark side of love in *A Midsummer Night's Dream*', p. 34.
20 I. G. Dash, *Women's Worlds in Shakespeare's Plays*, p. 97.
21 Viola, having apostrophised her own disguise as '…a wickedness / Wherein the pregnant enemy does much' goes on to bemoan her predicament: 'My master loves her dearly, / And I, poor monster, fond as much on him, / And she, mistaken, seems to dote on me' (*Twelfth Night* act 2, scene 2, lines 25–33). Viola's lament of her own circumstances cannot but draw attention to the other 'poor monster' – the Elizabethan boy player or more broadly players in general – in whose 'deceitful' practices contemporary detractors saw the devil at work.
22 See Chapter 5 for a fuller account of this production.
23 Keith Robinson interviewed by R. Hessey, 'Shakespeare gets a co-byline'.
24 Peter Brook in interview with Croyden, *Conversations with Peter Brook*, pp. 14, 15.
25 ibid., p. 15.
26 Michael Hoffman's 1999 film (starring Kevin Kline) followed Brook's emphasis. Using quick transitions between the play-within-the-play and the emotions registered by the courtly audience (thus modeling

a response for the film audience), the film engineered a surprising moment of empathetic engagement when Thisbe killed herself.

27 Speculating on its original performance context, Michael Shurgot offers a comprehensive discussion of the different effects achieved through different placings of the 'inner-play' and onstage audience in *A Midsummer Night's Dream*. See M. W. Shurgot, *Stages of Play: Shakespeare's Theatrical Energies in Elizabethan Performance*, pp. 68–76.

28 Hackett, *William Shakespeare: A Midsummer Night's Dream*, pp. 55, 56.

29 The Bell production made the common choice to preserve the Quarto's exclusion of Egeus from the final scenes. (Folio gives all of Philostrate's speeches to Egeus). See footnote in Greenblatt, et. al., eds, *The Norton Shakespeare*, p. 851.

30 The propensity of the mechanicals to undermine the ostensible structures of power within *A Midsummer Night's Dream* and around the theatrical event has been remarked by P. Parker: '…their insistence on laying bare the mechanics of theatrical illusion (on exposing the means of its construction rather than producing the seamless or naturalised) calls attention both within and beyond the play to other illusions and spectacles, including the theatrics of power itself.' P. Parker, *Shakespeare From the Margins*, p. 106.

31 S. Dunne, 'Bit players the stars in post-punk garden of dreams'.

Bibliography

Adamson, J., 'Remixing the Bard', *SMH*, 6 July 2001.
The Age, 13 April 1903, 'Princess Theatre'.
Anderson, D., 'The Bard, me and Company B – some enchanted evening', *SMH*, 28 May 1999.
—— 'The stuff that dreams are made of', *SMH*, 17 January 1994.
Asche, O., *Oscar Asche: His Life by Himself*, Hurst and Blackett, London, 1929.
Ashmead-Bartlett, E., 'Not found wanting' and 'A stand as worthy as Mons', *Hobart Mercury*, 12 May 1915, reprinted at http://www.anzacsite.gov.au/1landing/bartlett.html, accessed 17 August 2010.
Austin, J. L., How to do things with words: The William James lectures delivered at Harvard University in 1955, J. O. Urmson, ed., Clarendon, Oxford, 1962.
Bachelard, M., *The Great Land Grab*, Hyland House, Melbourne, 1997.
Banks, D., 'Electric (Lucy) Bell', *The Sydney Weekly*, 23–29 January 1996.
Battenhouse, R. W., 'The significance of Hamlet's advice to the Players' in *The Drama of the Renaissance: Essays for Leicester Bradner*, Elmer M. Blistein, ed., Brown University Press, Providence, RI, 1970, pp. 3–26.
Bell Shakespeare Company schools package (media release), 2003.
Belsey, C., 'Disrupting sexual difference: meaning and gender in the comedies' in *Alternative Shakespeares*, 2nd edn., John Drakakis, ed., Routledge, London and New York, 1988 (1985), pp. 170–94.
Bennie, A., 'A tortured *Macbeth;* a glorious *Hamlet*', *SMH*, 27 June 1994.
Berry, R., 'Hamlet and the audience, the dynamics of a relationship' in *Shakespeare and the Sense of Performance: Essays in the Tradition of Performance Criticism in Honor of Bernard Beckerman*, M. Thompson and R. Thompson, eds, U of Delaware P and Associated University Presses, Newark and London, 1989, pp. 24-28.
Bevington, D., '"But we are spirits of another sort": the dark side of love in *A Midsummer Night's Dream*' in *New Casebooks: A Midsummer Night's Dream*, R. Dutton, ed., St. Martin's, New York, 1996, pp. 24–37.
Bramwell, M., 'Boy wonder', *The Adelaide Review*, 13 April 2007.

Brisbane, K., *The Advertiser*, 9 June 1973.
Brissenden, A., 'Australian Shakespeare', *Shakespeare Performed: Essays in Honor of R. A. Foakes*, Grace Ioppolo, ed., U of Delaware P and Associated University Presses, Newark and London, 2000, pp. 240–59.
Bristol, M. D., *Shakespeare's America, America's Shakespeare*, Routledge, London and New York, 1990.
Bulman, J. C., 'Introduction: Shakespeare and performance theory' in *Shakespeare, Theory, and Performance*, J. C. Bulman, ed., Routledge, London and New York, 1996, pp. 1–11.
Busby, C., 'I like it like that', *Beat*, 31 January–6 February 1996.
Butler, J., *Excitable Speech*, Routledge, New York and London, 1997.
Butt, P. E., and R. Eagleson, *Mabo: What the High Court said and what the Government did*, 2nd edn, Federation Press, Sydney, 1996.
Calderwood, J. L., *Shakespearean Metadrama*, U of Minnesota P, Minneapolis, 1971.
Campbell, M., 'Introduction' in *Shakespeare's Books: Contemporary Cultural Politics and the Persistence of Empire*, P. Mead and M. Campbell, eds, Department of English, University of Melbourne, Parkville, Victoria, 1993, pp. 1-5.
Ciraulo, D., 'Fairy magic and the female imagination: Mary Lamb's *A Midsummer Night's Dream*', *Philological Quarterly*, vol. 78, no. 4, 1999, pp. 439–53.
Coad, D., *Gender Trouble Down Under: Australian Masculinities*, Presses Universitaires de Valenciennes, Paris, 2002.
Cochrane, B., 'QTC *Hamlet*: a curiously domestic tragedy', *MC Reviews Culture and the Media*, 7 May 2007, http://reviews.mediaculture.org.au/modules, accessed 14 July 2010.
Cochrane, P., 'Out of the wood and into the forest', *SMH*, 19 December 1995.
Colby Sprague, A., *Shakespeare and the Actors: The Stage Business in His Plays (1660–1905)*, Harvard UP, Cambridge, Mass., 1944.
Connell, R. W., *Masculinities*, 2nd edn, Allen and Unwin, Sydney, 2005.
Cox, E., 'Negotiating cultural narratives: all Aboriginal Shakespeare dreaming', *Southerly*, vol. 64, no. 3, 2004, pp. 15–27.
Croyden, M., *Conversations with Peter Brook, 1970–2000*, Faber and Faber, New York, 2003.
'The Criterion Theatre', *Sydney Morning Herald*, 28 November 1887
Dash, I. G., *Women's Worlds in Shakespeare's Plays*, U of Delaware Press and Associated University Presses, Newark and London, 1997.
Davies, L., 'Director's note,' Program for *As You Like It*, Bell Shakespeare, 2003.
Dawson, A. B., 'Performance and participation: Desdemona, Foucault and the actor's body', *Shakespeare, Theory, and Performance*, J. C. Bulman, ed., Routledge, London and New York, 1996.

De Vries, H., 'Britain boasts a new stage star', *San Francisco Chronicle*, 14 January 1990.

Dennis, A., 'Mailman people's top banana', *SMH*, 30 April 1999.

Dunne, S., 'Not enough to like in empty pantomime', *SMH*, 29 September 2003.

——'Bit players the stars in a post-punk garden of dreams', *SMH*, 23 July 2004.

——'Aussie wit and Will in perfect harmony', *SMH*, 8 June 2004.

Dusntone, B., 'Dinkum Shakespeare? Perth, Empire and the Bard' in *O Brave New World*, Golder and Madelaine, eds, pp. 163–79, 170.

Erne, L., *Shakespeare as Literary Dramatist*, Cambridge UP, Cambridge and New York, 2003.

Evans, B., 'Glitter outshines substance', *SMH*, 11 December 1989.

Felperin, H., 'O'erdoing termagant: an approach to Shakespearean mimesis', *Yale Review*, vol. 63, no. 1, 1974, pp. 372–3.

Fernie, E., 'Shakespeare and the prospect of presentism', *Shakespeare Survey*, no. 58, 2005, pp. 169–84.

Fitzmaurice, A., 'The genealogy of terra nullius', *Australian Historical Studies*, no. 38, April, 2007, pp. 1–15.

Fletcher, G., *Studies of Shakespeare*, Longman, Brown, Green, and Longman's, London, 1847.

Fotheringham, R., *Sport in Australia*, Cambridge UP, Cambridge, 1992.

Freud, S., *The Interpretation of Dreams*, trans. James Strachey, Allen and Unwin, London, 1953.

Gaby, R., '"Here's a marvellous convenient place for our rehearsal": Shakespeare in Australian space', *Australasian Drama Studies*, no. 46, 2005, pp. 124–38.

Gay, P., 'Recent Australian *Shrews*: the "larrikin element"' in *Transforming Shakespeare: Contemporary Women's Re-Visions in Literature and Performance*, Marianne Novey, ed., St. Martin's, New York, 1999, pp. 35–50.

——*As She Likes It: Shakespeare's Unruly Women*, Routledge, London and New York, 1994.

——'International glamour or home-grown talent? 1948–1964' in *O Brave New World*, J. Golder and R. Madelaine, eds, pp. 180–99.

Gilbert, H. and J. Lo, *Performance and Cosmopolitics: Cross-Cultural Transactions in Australia*, Palgrave Macmillan, Houndmills, Basingstoke, Hampshire, 2007.

Gilbert, H. and J. Tompkins, *Post-Colonial Drama: Theory, Practice, Politics*, Routledge, London, 1996.

Gleckman, J., 'Shakespeare as poet or playwright?: the Player's speech in *Hamlet*', *Early Modern Literary Studies*, vol. 11, no. 3, 2006.

Golder, J. and R. Madelaine, '"To dote thus upon such luggage": appropriating Shakespeare in Australia' in *O Brave New World: Two Centuries* of *Shakespeare on the Australian Stage*, J. Golder and R. Madelaine, eds, Currency Press, Sydney, 2001, pp. 1–16.

——'Elsinore at Belvoir St.: Neil Armfield talks about Hamlet', *Australasian Drama Studies*, April 1995, pp. 54–80.

Golder, J., 'A cultural missionary on tour: Allan Wilkie's Shakespearean Company, 1920–30' in *O Brave New World*, J. Golder and R. Madelaine, eds, pp. 121–42.

Gordon-Clark, J., 'The hard road to stardom: the early career of Essie Jenyns', *Australasian Drama Studies*, no. 40, 2002, pp. 74–89.

Greenblatt, S., W. Cohen, J. E. Howard and K. E. Maus, eds, *The Norton Shakespeare*, W. W. Norton & Company, New York and London, 1997.

Greenblatt, S., *Will in the World: How Shakespeare became Shakespeare*, Norton, New York, 2004.

Grosz, E., *Volatile Bodies*, Allen and Unwin, Sydney, 1994.

Hackett, H., *William Shakespeare: A Midsummer Night's Dream*, Writers and their Work, Northcote House, Plymouth, 1997.

Hainsworth, J. D., 'Shakespeare, son of Beckett?', *Modern Language Quarterly*, no. 25, 1964, p. 364.

Hall, J., *Anxious Pleasures: Shakespearean Comedy and the Nation State*, Fairleigh Dickinson U P and Associated University Presses, Madison, Teaneck, and London, 1995.

Hallet, B., 'Nothing rotten in the state of this spirited staging', *SMH*, 7 March 2003.

Hamer, M., 'Shakespeare's Rosalind and her public image', *Theatre Research International*, vol. 11, no. 2, summer, 1986, pp. 105–18.

Hampson, J., 'Black and white', *Sun Herald*, Time Out, 2 May 1999.

Harris, M., 'Sharman's risks pay off in *Dream*', *Bulletin*, June 1982.

Hawkes, T., *Shakespeare in the Present*, Accents on Shakespeare, Routledge, London and New York, 2002.

——'Telmah', in *Shakespeare and the Question of Theory*, P. Parker and G. Hartman (eds), Methuen, New York and London, 1985, pp. 309–30.

Hawkins, S., 'Fool on the bill', *Daily Telegraph*, 12 January 1996.

Helms, L., 'Playing the woman's part: feminist criticism and Shakespearean performance' in *Performing Feminisms*, S. E. Case, ed., Johns Hopkins UP, Baltimore and London, 1990, pp. 196–206.

Hessey, R., 'Shakespeare gets a co-byline', *SMH*, 19 November 1987.

Hoad, B., 'Wallowing in hindsight', *Bulletin*, 9 August 1983, p. 78.

——'As you might expect it', *Bulletin*, 13 February 1996, pp. 77–8.

Hodgdon, B., 'Looking for Mr Shakespeare after "the Revolution": Robert Lepage's intercultural dream machine' in *Shakespeare, Theory and Performance*, J. C. Bulman ed., Routledge, London and New York, 1996, pp. 68–91.

Holgate, B., 'Actors hurdle the colour bar', *The Australian*, 21 May 1999.

Holland, P., *English Shakespeares, Shakespeare on the English Stage in the 1990s*, CUP, Cambridge, 1997.
http://www.adelaidereview.com.au/archives, accessed 14 July 2010.
Hubert, J. D., *Metatheatre: The Example of Shakespeare*, U of Nebraska P, Lincoln and London, 1991.
Iaccarino, C., 'The whiz-kid who won't be making it easy', *Sun Herald*, 18 July 2004.
Jackson, R., 'Actor managers and the spectacular' in *Shakespeare: An Illustrated Stage History*, J. Bate and R. Jackson, eds, Oxford University Press, 1996.
Jameson, J., 'Good time with the Bard in our backyard', *The Daily Telegraph*, 28 May 1999.
Kablean, C., 'Silly Shakespeare', *Sunday Telegraph*, 30 May 1999.
Kennedy, A., 'The Bard on skates', *The Sun*, 26 January 1971.
Kiernan, P., *Shakespeare's Theory of Drama*, Cambridge UP, 1996.
Kiernander, A., 'A post-colonial Shakespeare, 1963–2000' in *O Brave New World*, J. Golder and R. Madelaine, eds, Currency Press, Sydney 2001, pp. 236–55.
Kippax, H. G., 'Bubble and squeak', *SMH*, 25 January 1971.
—— '*As You Like It* reveals new outback romance', *SMH*, 25 July 1983.
—— 'A midsummer day's lark', *SMH*, 12 July 1973, in H. Heseltine, ed., *A Leader of His Craft: Theatre Reviews by H. G. Kippax*, Currency Press, Sydney, 2004, p. 183.
Kott, J., *Shakespeare our Contemporary*, Methuen, London, 1965.
Lake, M., 'What have you done for your country?' in M. Lake and H. Reynolds, eds, *What's Wrong with Anzac?*, University of New South Wales Press, Sydney, 2010, pp. 1–23.
Lanier, D., 'Drowning the book: *Prospero's Books* and the textual Shakespeare', in *Shakespeare, Theory and Performance*, J. C. Bulman, ed., Routledge, London, 1996, pp. 187–209.
Levine, L. 'Rape, repetition, and the politics of closure in *A Midsummer Night's Dream*' in *Feminist Readings of Early Modern Culture*, V. Traub, M. L. Kaplan, and D. Callagan, eds, Cambridge UP, 1996, pp.211–228.
Longworth. K., 'Some like it not really', *Newcastle Herald*, 29 August 2003.
Low, L. A., 'Dreams of an explosive imagination', *SMH*, 19 July 2004.
Makeham, P., 'Framing the landscape; Prichard's *Pioneers* and Esson's *The Drovers*', *Australasian Drama Studies*, no. 23, 1993, pp. 121–34.
McAuley, G., 'The emerging field of rehearsal studies', *About Performance*, no. 6, 2006, pp. 7–13.
McCallum, J., 'Postmodern Bard matched by brilliant performers', *The Australian*, 23 January 1996.
—— 'Bard bent for a purposeful laugh', *The Australian*, 28 May 1999.
McGuire, P. C., 'Hippolyta's silence and the poet's pen' in *New Casebooks:*

A Midsummer Night's Dream, Richard Dutton, ed., St. Martin's Press, New York, 1996, pp. 139–60.

Milne, G., 'Shakespeare under the stars: a new populist tradition', *Australasian Drama Studies*, no. 33, 1998, pp. 65–79.

Montrose, L. A., '"Shaping fantasies": figurations of gender and power in Elizabethan culture' in *New Casebooks: A Midsummer Night's Dream*, R. Dutton, ed., St. Martin's Press, New York, 1996, pp. 101–38.

Morgan, J., 'Where there's a Will…', *SMH*, 21 May 1999.

——'Comics enter the character building stage, *Weekend Australian*, 20 January 1996.

Morrison, P., 'Bard true to title', *Australian Jewish News*, 2 February 1996.

Munro-Wallis, N., '*Hamlet*', 612 ABC Brisbane, 27 April 2007, http://www.abc.net.au/local/reviews, accessed 15 September 2010.

Murrie, L., 'The Australian legend: writing Australian masculinity/writing 'Australian' masculine, *Journal of Australian Studies*, vol. 22, no. 56, 1998, pp. 68–77.

Page, R., 'Stature to the pleasurable', *Theatre Australia*, no. 3, September 1978, pp. 24–5.

Parker, A. and E. K. Sedgwick, 'Introduction' in *Performativity and Performance*, A. Parker and E. K. Sedgwick, eds, Routledge, New York and London, 1995, pp. 1–18.

Parker, P., *Shakespeare from the Margins: Language, Culture, Context*, U of Chicago P, Chicago and London, 1996.

Payne, P., 'Dream of the future', *SMH*, 8 December 1989.

Perret, B., 'As you like it', *The Sunday Age*, 17 August 2003.

Prerauer, M., 'Dream becomes a reality', *The Australian*, 5 May 1982.

Rickard, J., 'Lovable larrikins and awful ockers', *Journal of Australian Studies*, vol. 22, no. 56, pp. 78–85.

Rose, C., 'As you love it', *Sun Herald*, 30 May 1999.

——'Man enough for the role', *Sun Herald*, 28 September 2003.

Rudd, K., 'Prime Minister Kevin Rudd's apology motion has been tabled in Parliament', 12 [*sic*.] February 2008, http://www.abc.net.au/news/events/apology/text.htm, accessed 31 August 2010.

Rutter, C., *Clamorous Voices, Shakespeare's Women Today*, The Women's Press, London, 1988.

Schafer, E., 'Reconciliation Shakespeare? Aboriginal presence in Australian Shakespeare production' in *Playing Australia: Australian Theatre and the International Stage*, E. Schafer and S. B. Smith, eds, vol. 9, (Australian Playwrights), Rodopi, Amsterdam and New York, 2003, pp. 63–78.

Shakespeare, W., (Complete Works) S. Greenblatt, W. Cohen, J. E. Howard and K. E. Maus, eds, *The Norton Shakespeare*, W. W. Norton & Company, New York and London, 1997.

Shakespeare, W., *The Tempest*, (Shakespeare in Production), C. Dymkowski, ed., Cambridge UP, 2000.

——*A Midsummer Night's Dream*, (The New Cambridge Shakespeare), R. A. Foakes, ed., Cambridge UP, 2003.

——*As You Like It*, A. Brissenden, ed., Oxford UP, 1993.

——*Hamlet, Prince of Denmark*, (Shakespeare in Production), R. Hapgood, ed., Cambridge UP, 1999.

——*Hamlet, Prince of Denmark*, (The New Cambridge Shakespeare), Philip Edwards, ed., Cambridge UP, Cambridge and New York, 2003.

Shurgot, M. W., *Stages of Play: Shakespeare's Theatrical Energies in Elizabethan Performance*, U of Delaware P and Associated University Presses, Newark and London, 1998.

Smith, B., *Shakespeare and Masculinity*, Oxford UP, 2000.

Stollery, C., 'Arriving at an actor's interpretation of Hamlet' in The Bell Shakespeare Company Production Notes 1992, courtesy of The Performing Arts Museum, Melbourne.

Stone, A., 'As you like it', *On the Street*, 5 February 1996.

Strube, H., 'The autonomous actor: a case study of Lindy Davies', MA thesis, Queensland University of Technology, 1994.

Styan, J. L., *The Shakespeare Revolution: criticism and performance in the twentieth century*, Cambridge UP, Cambridge and New York, 1977.

Tatspaugh, P., 'Reading: *A Midsummer Night's Dream*' in *Shakespeare: An Oxford Guide*, S. Wells and L. C. Orlin, eds, Oxford UP, 2003, pp. 540–9.

Taylor, P., 'As you like it, directed by Declan Donnellan' in *Shakespeare in the Theatre: An Anthology of Criticism*, Stanley Wells, ed., Clarendon P and Oxford UP, Oxford and New York, 1997.

Thompson, G. M., 'Miss Essie Jenyns', *Centennial Magazine*, no. 1, 1888–1889, p. 88.

Thomson, H., 'Bell's winter of discontent', *The Age*, 15 August 2003.

Tom, E., 'A man of many parts', *SMH*, 19 January 1996.

Tompkins, J., *Unsettling Space: Contestations in Contemporary Australian Theatre*, Palgrave Macmillan, Houndmills, Basingstoke, Hampshire and New York, 2006.

Usher, R., 'Playing with gender roles', *The Age*, 5 August 2003.

Ward, P., 'All the world's a pearly stage', *The Australian*, 27 May 1983.

Watson, R. N., 'As you liken it: simile in the wilderness', *Shakespeare Survey*, no. 56, 2003, pp. 79–92.

Weimann, R., 'Mimesis in *Hamlet*', *Shakespeare and the Question of Theory*, P. Parker and G. Hartman, eds, Methuen, New York and London, 1985, pp. 275–91.

Worthen, W. B., *Shakespeare and the Force of Modern Performance*, Cambridge UP, Cambridge, 2003.

——'Shakespearean performativity' in *Shakespeare and the Modern Theatre: the Performance of Modernity*, M. D. Bristol and K. McLuskie, eds, Accents on Shakespeare, Routledge, London and New York, 2001, pp. 117–41.
——'The weight of Antony: staging "character" in *Antony and Cleopatra*', *Studies in English Literature 1500–1900*, no. 26, 1986, pp. 295–308.

Interviews conducted by Kate Flaherty
Robert Alexander, interviewed 30 August 2004.
Adam Cook interviewed 21 July 2010.
Lindy Davies interviewed 19 August 2003.
Roy Luxford, interviewed 18 April 2005.
Alice McConnell, interviewed 2 August and 18 August 2003.
Aubrey Mellor, interviewed 18 August 2003.
Catherine Moore, interviewed 31 October 2003.
Simon Phillips, interviewed 14 September 2004.
Anna Volska, interviewed 9 September 2005.

Index

A Branch of the Blue Nile (play) 2
A Midsummer Night's Dream 10, 11, 161–234, 238–39
  Australia, stage history in 165–73
  authority and subversion *see* authority and subversion - staging *A Midsummer Night's Dream*
  clowns and clowning 166, 219, 222, 223, 224
  cultural authority and subversion *see* cultural authority and subversion - Titania and the Weaver
  dealing with the sky *see A Midsummer Night's Dream* (Australian Shakespeare Company - 1988, 1993, 2005)
  difficult pleasure *see A Midsummer Night's Dream* (Company B - 2004)
  gender and power *see* gender and power - Helena in *A Midsummer Night's Dream*
  Government House Gardens (Perth - 1918) 166
  Her Majesty's (London - 1900) 164
  Lighthouse Theatre Company (Adelaide - 1982/83) 169–70
  magic within *see* magic in *A Midsummer Night's Dream*
  metatheatre 184, 191, 222
  performativity 168, 179, 180, 194, 204, 209, 218
  physical magic *see A Midsummer Night's Dream* (Bell Shakespeare Company - 2004)
  rehearsal process 228, 231
  Royal Shakespeare Company (1970 and 1973) 165, 168–69, 170, 173, 189, 220–23, 225, 226
  Sadler's Wells (London - 1853) 164
  social rank and power *see* social rank and power - the Mechanicals
  stage life of 163–65
  Australia, in 165–73
  State Theatre Company of SA (1992) 171
  Sydney Theatre Company (1989) 170–71, 217
  Sydney Theatre Company (1997) *see A Midsummer Night's Dream* (STC - 1997)
  Theatre Royal (Melbourne - 1913) 165–66
A Midsummer Night's Dream (Australian Shakespeare Company

Index

– 1988, 1993, 2005) 11, 173–77, 184, 191–92, 223–25
   gender and power - Helena 205–6
   Mechanicals, the 223–25
   Titania and Bottom 214–15
A Midsummer Night's Dream (Bell Shakespeare Company - 2004) 11, 178–84, 191–92
   gender and power - Helena 204
   Mechanicals, the 227–30, 231
   Titania and Bottom 214–15
A Midsummer Night's Dream (Company B - 2004) 11, 184–91
   gender and power - Helena 206–9
   Mechanicals, the 230–34
   Titania and Bottom 214, 215
A Midsummer Night's Dream (film) 217
A Midsummer Night's Dream I (painting) 209–10
A Midsummer Night's Dream (STC - 1989) 170–71, 217
A Midsummer Night's Dream (STC - 1997) 11, 171–72
   gender and power - Helena 199–204
Aberline, Matthew 31
absurdism 213
Adam *(As You Like It)* 111, 112
Adam-Smith, Patsy 56
Adamson, Georgia (as Hermia) 179, 180, 182, 227
Adelaide Review (magazine) 46–47
adolescence *(Hamlet)* 31, 42, 55, 60
Aeneas' Tale to Dido *(Hamlet) see* First Player's Tale *(Hamlet)*
Albert Park (Brisbane) 102
Alexander, Robert 7, 79, 103, 118
Anderson, Doug 174
Andrew *(Twelfth Night)* 183

Andrews, Benedict 11, 164, 184–85, 189, 190, 209, 215, 230
A Midsummer Night's Dream see A Midsummer Night's Dream (Company B - 2004)
Anozie, Nonso 6
anti-naturalism *see* naturalism (theatre)
'antic disposition' *(Hamlet)* 37, 46, 51, 60, 63, 64, 69, 71, 72
Antony and Cleopatra 2, 75
Anzac Day 53
Anzac legend 32, 52–53, 56–57, 68, 70
The Anzacs (book) 56
war memorial 32
appropriation 2–3, 10, 13, 17, 19, 72, 98, 103, 117, 122, 128, 129, 136
Archibald Prize 148, 149
archives *see* theatre archives
Arden *(As You Like It)* 10–11, 127, 237
   Australia, re-imagining in *see* re-imagining Arden in Australia
Argue, Mark 23
Armfield, Neil 10, 11, 24, 25, 26, 34, 35, 36, 47, 64, 65, 71, 76, 86, 88, 96, 109–16, 119, 122, 123–24, 144–45
Cloudstreet (play) 112–13
   see also As You Like It (Company B - 1999); Company B (theatre company); *Hamlet* (Company B - 1994)
As You Like It 10–11, 95–158, 163, 167
   Arden *see* re-imagining Arden in Australia
authority 237–38
Cheek by Jowl (1991) 130–31
clowns and clowning 109, 140, 143, 145, 146, 149

270

INDEX

Criterion Theatre (1887) 125, 127
jazz in 104, 105, 106, 109, 140, 143
Love in a Forest (1723) 121, 128
metatheatre in 99
NIDA (1978) 101–2, 103, 118, 128
Nimrod Theatre (1983) 102–3, 118
Old Tote - 1971 100–101, 128
performativity 156, 158, 238
Queensland Theatre Company (1981) 102
rehearsal process 113, 116–18, 121, 122, 130, 131, 142, 150, 151–52
Rosalind *see* Rosalind *(As You Like It)*
Theatre Royal (Melbourne - 1863) 95, 97, 100, 106, 124
As You Like It (Bell Shakespeare Company - 2003) 11, 96, 124
an actors' Arden 116–22
Rosalind, Alice McConnell as 139, 150–57
As You Like It (Company B - 1999) 10, 96, 119
backyard Arden 109–16, 122, 146
Indigenous Australian actors in 109, 113–15, 123–24
Rosalind, Deborah Mailman as 111, 113–15, 144–50, 152, 157
As You Like It (STC - 1996) 11, 96, 110, 116, 119, 123, 145
concept of Arden 104–9
Rosalind, Anita Hegh as 137–44, 145, 146, 151, 152, 157
Asche, Oscar 165–66
Ashmead-Bartlett, Ellis 56
Astaire, Fred 77
audience
Canberra/Sydney 7–8
New York, in 7

Nigeria, in 6–8
young 37, 81, 84, 174
Australian Film Institute 147
Australian Legend (book) 54
Australian masculine identity 24, 43, 48, 52–54
Anzac legend 32, 52–53, 56–57, 68, 70
homogeneity 54
larrikinism 24, 37, 47, 53, 67–70
mateship 24, 68
social and cultural history 53–54
Australian Shakespeare Company
*A Midsummer Night's Dream see
A Midsummer Night's Dream*
(Australian Shakespeare Company - 1988, 1993, 2005)
authenticity 117, 129, 134, 151, 152
authority
cultural *see* cultural authority and subversion - Titania and the Weaver
subversion, and *see* authority and subversion - staging *A Midsummer Night's Dream*
authority and subversion - staging *A Midsummer Night's Dream* 193–234, 238
Bottom 193–94
cultural authority *see* cultural authority and subversion - Titania and the Weaver
gender and power *see* Helena *(A Midsummer Night's Dream)*
Quince 193–94
Theseus 194–95

Beat (magazine) 143
Beatrice *(Much Ado About Nothing)* 183
Beckett (Samuel) 213

Index

Beerbohm Tree, Herbert 164, 165, 190
Bell, John 10, 42, 52, 55, 59, 64, 68, 76, 77, 81, 102, 103, 118, 143
  portrait of 149
  As You Like It (Nimrod Theatre - 1983) 102–3, 118
  see also Bell Shakespeare Company; *Hamlet* (Bell Shakespeare Company - 2003)
Bell, Lucy (as Celia) 108, 137–39, 140, 143
Bell Shakespeare Company 7, 68, 78, 143, 167
  A Midsummer Night's Dream (2004) see *A Midsummer Night's Dream* (Bell Shakespeare Company - 2004)
  Hamlet (1992) 55–56
  Hamlet (2003) see *Hamlet* (Bell Shakespeare Company - 2003)
  Julius Caesar 7–8
  King Lear 147
  Richard III 7–8
  As You Like It (2003) see *As You Like It* (Bell Shakespeare Company - 2003)
Belvoir Street Theatre (Sydney) 24, 25, 28, 87, 96, 109, 123, 186
  The Popular Mechanicals (1987) 218–19
  see also Company B (theatre company)
Benedick *(Much Ado About Nothing)* 183
Bennie, Angela 88
Berlin 185
Berliner Ensemble (theatre company) 168
Berry, Ralph 47, 55, 56, 67
bestiality 186, 214
Bevington, David 213

Biddell, Kerrie 104, 143
Biggins, Penny 143
Bishop, Paul (as Orlando) 140–43
Blabey, Aaron (as Orlando) 111, 144, 145–46, 147
Blane, Sue 169
Blinky Bill (book) 182
bondage 186, 214, 215, 232
Booth, J. B. 43
Bossell, Simon (as Lysander) 179, 180–81, 228
Bottom *(A Midsummer Night's Dream)* 161, 162, 168, 181, 192, 209–34, 238–39
  Allan Wilkie as 166
  authority and subversion 193–94, 197
  cultural authority and subversion see cultural authority and subversion - Titania and the Weaver
  Jacek Koman as 185, 186, 230–31, 232, 234
  John Wood as 169
  Kevin Kline as 217
  Luciano Martucci as 217
  Ross Williams as 223–25
  see also social rank and power - the Mechanicals
Box, Kate (as Helena) 179–81, 182, 183, 204, 227
Boyd, Arthur 209–10
Brecht (Bertolt) 87, 162, 187, 209
Briggs, Tony (as Demetrius) 200, 201, 202–3
Brisbane, Katherine 27, 168
Bristol, Michael D. 16
Brook, Peter 1, 5, 225, 226, 233, 234
  A Midsummer Night's Dream (1970 and 1973) 165, 168–69, 170, 173, 189, 220–23, 225, 226

272

INDEX

King Lear (1962–64) 213
Brown, Bille
  First Player, as 77, 78–79
  Ghost of Old Hamlet, as 59
Buday, Helen (as Titania) 185, 186, 188–89
Bulman, James C. 4
Busby, Cec 143
Byquar, Bradley 113

cabaret 77, 109, 143
Cairns, Jim 101
Calderwood, James L. 184
Caliban *(The Tempest)* 3
Campbell, Marion 17
Canberra/Sydney audiences 7–8
'Caprichos' (prints) 211
Carroll, Luke (as Philostrate) 187
Cave, Nick 47
Celia *(As You Like It)* 98, 110, 111, 117, 145, 147
  Kirstie Hutton as 115, 144, 146
  Lucy Bell as 108, 137–39, 140, 143
Centennial Magazine 134
Charles *(As You Like It)* 97–98, 99
Cheek by Jowl (theatre company) 6
  Othello 6–7
  As You Like It (1991) 130–31
citational model of acting 19, 235
Clark, Jason 28
Claudius *(Hamlet)* 15, 23, 24, 27, 31, 34, 35, 36, 37, 47, 60, 82
  Anthony Phelan as 60, 61–62
  Christopher Stollery as 57
  Hamlet's relationship with 49–67
  Jacek Koman as 27, 36
Cleansed (play) 185
Clifford, Laurence (as Puck) 172
Cloudstreet (book) 112
Cloudstreet (play) 112–13
clowns and clowning

A Midsummer Night's Dream 166, 219, 222, 223, 224
  Hamlet 29, 43, 69
  As You Like It 109, 140, 143, 145, 146, 149
Cobweb *(A Midsummer Night's Dream)* 227
Cohen, W. 10
Company B (theatre company)
  A Midsummer Night's Dream (2004) see *A Midsummer Night's Dream* (Company B - 2004)
  Cloudstreet (play) 112–13
  Hamlet (1994) see *Hamlet* (Company B -1994)
  As You Like It (1999) see *As You Like It* (Company B - 1999)
Connell, R. W. 25
Cook, Adam 10, 25, 31, 43, 44–45, 46, 47, 66, 67, 69
  see also *Hamlet* (STCSA/QTC - 2007)
Cooper, Gary (as Lysander) 199, 203
Cordelia *(King Lear)* 147
Cotterill, Ralph 111
  First Player, as 89, 90
  Moonshine, as 233
  Starveling, as 230, 231, 232, 233–34
Cousins, Robert 110
Cox, Emma 173, 199
Creswick, Thomas 95, 96
Creswick, William 135
Criterion Theatre (Sydney) 125
Cullen, Adam 149
Cullen, Max 108
cultural authority and subversion
  - Titania and the Weaver 209–34, 238–39
cultural context 6–7, 9, 10, 13, 19–20, 211, 219, 220, 222–23, 235–36, 239

273

INDEX

cultural cringe 100, 191
cultural imperialism 3, 18, 19, 20, 166, 199, 200
cultural moment, notion of 4, 19, 51

Dash, Irene 164, 214
Davies, Lindy 11, 96, 116–22, 124, 150, 151, 153
  see also As You Like It (Bell Shakespeare Company - 2003)
Dawson, Anthony B. 131–32
de Jong, Sarah 173
Demetrius *(A Midsummer Night's Dream)* 188, 197, 204, 206, 207, 208
  Timothy Walter as 179, 180–81, 182, 183, 228
  Tony Briggs as 200, 201, 202–3
Dennis *(As You Like It)* 113
Desdemona *(Othello)* 6, 7
DJ (disc jockey) 29, 82–83
Doake, Michelle 179, 182
Donnellan, Declan 130, 131
doubling *see* role doubling
Dowling, Julie 199
Drama Theatre (Sydney Opera House) 109, 140
Dreamtime (Aboriginal culture) 171, 173, 182
Drury Lane (London) 128
Duke Frederick *(As You Like It)* 107, 110, 111, 114–15, 118, 138, 151
Duke Senior *(As You Like It)* 97, 98, 118, 119
  Bob Maza as 113, 115
Dunne, Stephen 120–21, 189, 190
Dunstan Playhouse (Adelaide) 31

Eastway, Paul 77
Eastwood, Laurence 30, 103
eavesdropping 1
  A Midsummer Night's Dream 183

Hamlet 40, 41, 42, 43, 44, 45
Much Ado About Nothing 183
Twelfth Night 183
Edge, Luisa Hastings 77
education, Shakespeare and 17, 18, 166–67, 178
Egeus *(A Midsummer Night's Dream)* 164, 218, 227
  Anthony Phelan as 187, 188
  Tony Poli as 179
Ehlers, Jerome (as Horatio) 29, 82–83, 84
Elizabethan period 104, 130, 154, 171, 172, 199, 200, 210, 211, 212, 216, 217, 218–19
  see also Tudor period
Elston, Glen 11, 173, 174, 184, 191, 224, 225
  A Midsummer Night's Dream (1988) *see A Midsummer Night's Dream* (Australian Shakespeare Company - 1988, 1993, 2005)
Emo 46–47, 48, 69
Empire (British) 52, 53, 167
  Shakespeare's Books: Contemporary Cultural Politics and the Persistence of Empire 17
Enoch, Wesley 199–200
Enright, Nick 112
Epic theatre 187, 209
eroticism 42, 43, 138, 156, 164, 188, 211
  see also sexuality
Examiner and Melbourne Weekly News 95
exile (re-imagining Arden in Australia) 100, 102, 105, 107, 114, 115
expressionism 184, 186, 187, 190

Fabian *(Twelfth Night)* 183
Facebook 180

274

Index

Faucit, Helen (as Rosalind) 129–30
feminine/femininity 33, 48, 126, 128, 139, 140, 155
feminism 54, 132
film 9, 75, 88, 164
First Player *(Hamlet)*
  Bille Brown as 77, 78–79
  Ralph Cotterill as 89, 90
First Player's Tale *(Hamlet)* 10, 64, 71–77, 90–91, 237
  Bell Shakespeare Company (2003) 78–81
  Company B (1994) 89–90
  Pork Chop Productions (2001) 83–85
'Flacco' (Paul Livingston) 143
Flute *(A Midsummer Night's Dream)* 227, 231
  John Leary as 232, 234
  see also social rank and power – the Mechanicals
Ford, Leon (as Hamlet) 31, 43, 48, 57–58, 59, 62, 69, 70, 77, 79, 81
Forest of Arden *(As You Like It) see* Arden *(As You Like It)*
Fortinbras *(Hamlet)* 29, 32, 55, 63
  Jeremy Sims as 83
Fotheringham, Richard 177
Fox, Mem 182
Francis Flute *(A Midsummer Night's Dream) see* Flute *(A Midsummer Night's Dream)*
Frank Dunne *(Gallipoli)* 23, 24
Freer, Wayne 112
Freud (Sigmund) 72, 226
Fryer, Kate 176

Gaby, Rose 166
Gallipoli (film) 23, 24, 56
Gallipoli (World War I) 23, 24, 52–53, 56
Gammage, Bill 56

Ganymede *(As You Like It)* 139, 141, 146, 152, 153, 154, 155, 156, 157
  see also Rosalind *(As You Like It)*
Garner, Julian 77
Garrick, David 121
Gay, Penny 68
gay activism 54
  see also homosexuality
gender 11, 13, 19, 24, 25, 53, 67, 70
  identity 98, 130–31, 136, 150, 151, 155, 156, 158
  'male role' 24, 25, 48, 237
  politics 137, 207, 208, 209
  power, and *see* gender and power – Helena in *A Midsummer Night's Dream*
gender and power – Helena in *A Midsummer Night's Dream* 197–209, 238
  Deborah Mailman (STC – 1997) 200–4, 208–9
  Kate Box (Bell Shakespeare Company – 2004) 204
  Kathryn Tohill (Australian Shakespeare Company) 205
  Rita Kalnejais (Company B – 2004) 206–9
generational conflict *(Hamlet)* 24, 37, 52, 56, 70
German expressionism *see* expressionism
Gertrude *(Hamlet)* 31, 33, 34, 47, 49, 61, 62, 66
Ghost of Old Hamlet 34, 41, 83
  Bille Brown as 59
  Company B (1994) 88–89, 91
  Hamlet's relationship with 49–67
  Ralph Cotterill as 89
Gibbs, May 182
Gibson, Mel 23, 69
  Hamlet, as 23–24, 27, 69
Gilbert, Helen 2, 16, 114

Index

Gilshenan, Darren 78
Gleckman, Jason 73
Globe Theatre (London) 31, 99, 174
Golder, John 26, 27, 86, 88, 167
Gonzago *see* 'The Murder of Gonzago' *(Hamlet)*
Goodall, Cameron (as Hamlet) 32, 43, 46, 48, 65, 66, 69, 70
Gordon-Clark, Janette 132, 134
Goth *see* Emo
Government House Gardens (Perth) 166
  A Midsummer Night's Dream (1918) 166
Goya (Francisco) 211
Gravedigger *(Hamlet)* 59
Great War *see* World War I
Greenblatt, S. 10
Grosz, Elizabeth 155
Guildenstern *(Hamlet)* 60, 63, 64, 82
Gyoerffy, Richard (as Puck) 181, 183, 184, 228

Hallett, Bryce 58
Hamer, Mary 126–27
Hamlet (Bell Shakespeare Company - 2003) 10, 25, 30–31, 55, 69–70, 76, 89
  Hamlet's relationship with fathers 57–60, 62, 64
  Hamlet's relationship with Ophelia 41–43, 48, 69
  Players, Gonzago and First Player's Tale 77–81, 91
Hamlet (character) 126, 132, 168
  adolescence 31, 42, 55, 60
  'antic disposition' 37, 46, 51, 60, 63, 64, 69, 71, 72
  Cameron Goodall as 32, 43, 46, 48, 65, 66, 69, 70
  Christopher Stollery as 55–56
  fathers, relationship with 49–67
  generational conflict 24, 37, 52, 56, 70
  J.B. Booth as 43
  Jeremy Sims as 28, 29–30, 43, 48, 60, 62, 63, 64, 69, 70, 83, 84, 85–86
  larrikinism 24, 37, 47, 67–70
  Leon Ford as 31, 43, 48, 57–58, 59, 62, 69, 70, 77, 79, 81
  Mel Gibson as 23–24, 27, 69
  'nunnery' scene 15, 35, 40, 43, 45, 60
  Ophelia, relationship with 25, 32–48, 69
  Richard Roxburgh as 27, 30, 43, 64, 69, 70, 88
Hamlet (Company B - 1994) 10, 24, 25–27, 28, 29, 41, 55–56, 69–70, 76, 90, 112
  First Player's Tale 89–90, 91
  Ghost of Old Hamlet, evolution of 88–89, 91
  Hamlet's relationship with fathers 64–65, 69
  Hamlet's relationship with Ophelia 34–36, 47–48, 69
  metatheatre, cognisance of 86–87
Hamlet (film) 23–24, 68
Hamlet (play) 23–91
  authority 236–37
  Bell Shakespeare Company (1992) 55–56
  clowns and clowning 29, 43, 69
  eavesdropping scene 40, 41, 42, 43, 44, 45
  editions, variations in 73
  First Player's Tale 10, 64, 72–77, 237
  Hamlet's relationship with fathers 49–67

Index

Hamlet's relationship with Ophelia 32–48
madness and masculinity *see* madness and masculinity (*Hamlet*)
metatheatre in *see* metatheatre
mimesis 76, 79
'nunnery' scene 15, 35, 40, 43, 45, 60
recent productions 70
rehearsal process 31, 42, 59, 65, 77–78, 81, 88
'The Murder of Gonzago' 29, 77
see also under individual productions
Hamlet (Pork Chop Productions – 2001) 10, 24–25, 28–30, 51, 69–70, 76, 87, 89
   First Player's Tale 83–85, 91
   Hamlet's relationship with fathers 60–64
   Hamlet's relationship with Ophelia 36–41, 69
   metatheatrical possibilities, exploitation of 81–83
   Ophelia's pregnancy 39–40, 41
   'To be or not to be' soliloquy 85–86
Hamlet (STCSA/QTC – 2007) 10, 25, 31–32, 65, 69–70
   Hamlet's relationship with fathers 66–67
   Hamlet's relationship with Ophelia 43–47, 48, 69
   war memorial staging 31, 32
Harding, Nicholas 149
Hastings Edge, Luisa 77
Hawkes, Terence 8, 85
Hecuba (Aeneas' Tale) 74, 78–79, 80, 84–85
Hegh, Anita (as Rosalind) 107, 137–44, 145, 146, 151, 152, 157
Helena *(A Midsummer Night's Dream)* 188, 230, 238
   Deborah Mailman as 200–4, 208–9
   gender and power *see* gender and power – Helena in *A Midsummer Night's Dream*
   Hermia, contrasted with 197–98
   Kate Box as 179–81, 182, 183, 204, 227, 228
   Kathryn Tohill as 205
   Rita Kalnejais as 206–9
Hennings (John) 95
Her Majesty's (London) 164
Hermia *(A Midsummer Night's Dream)* 200, 201, 203–4, 207, 230
   Billie Rose Prichard as 187–88
   Georgia Adamson as 179, 180, 182, 227, 228
   Helena, contrasted with 197–98
   Jane Longhurst as 175, 206
High Court of Australia 99
Hippolyta *(A Midsummer Night's Dream)* 194, 195, 197, 198, 226, 227, 239, 240
   Gillian Jones as 169
   Michelle Doake as 179, 182
Hoad, Brian 106
Hodgdon, Barbara 14
Hoffman, Michael 217
Hogan, Paul 222
Holland, Peter 130–31
Holloway, William 132, 136
Holloway company 132, 134, 135
homosexuality 131, 143
   see also gay activism
Horatio *(Hamlet)* 26, 27, 29, 47, 51, 58–59
   Geoffrey Rush as 26, 27, 87
   Jerome Ehlers as 29, 82–83, 84
Horler, Sacha (as Ophelia) 37, 40
Howard, J. E. 10
Howett, Mark 110

Index

Hughes, Ted 190
Hutton, Kirstie (as Celia) 115, 144, 146
Hymen *(As You Like It)* 107, 108, 112

identity
  Australian 53, 54, 67, 103, 112, 166, 223, 238
  gender 98, 130–31, 136, 150, 156
  group
    Mechanicals *(A Midsummer Night's Dream)* 223, 230
    Players *(Hamlet)* 78
  Indigenous *see* Indigenous Australians
  landscape, and 98, 99, 103, 112
  masculine *see* madness and masculinity *(Hamlet)*
immigration (Australia) 54, 100
imperialism (cultural) 3, 18, 19, 20, 166, 199, 200
Indigenous Australians 53, 54, 99–100, 109, 113–14, 123–24
  A Midsummer Night's Dream (STC - 1997) 11, 171–72, 199–204
  displacement and dispossession of 100, 114, 115
  Dreamtime 171, 173, 182
  'Mabo' judgement 99, 115
  reconciliation 113, 116
  Stolen Generations 115
  terra nullius, concept of 97–100, 115
  As You Like It (Company B - 1999) 109, 113–15, 123–24, 144–50

Jacobs, Sally 168
Jameson, Julietta 112
Jane Street Theatre (Sydney) 101, 128

Jaques *(As You Like It)* 103, 146
jazz *(As You Like It)* 104, 105, 106, 109, 140, 143
Jenyns, Essie 132–37
  Rosalind, as 125, 127, 136–37, 144, 147, 148, 157, 158
John, Alan 110, 119
Jones, Gillian (as Hippolyta/Titania) 169
Julius Caesar 7–8

Kalgoorlie (WA) 178
Kalnejais, Rita (as Helena) 206–9
Kane, Sarah 185
Katherina *(The Taming of the Shrew)* 147
Kean, Charles 190
Kerr, John (Governor General) 101
Kiernander, A. 68
King Lear 147, 213
King Lear (film) 213
Kippax, H. G. 101, 103, 128, 168, 169
Kline, Kevin (as Bottom) 217
Koman, Jacek
  Bottom, as 185, 186, 230–31, 232, 234
  Claudius, as 27, 36
Kosky, Barrie 147, 184–85
Kott, Jan 165, 182, 185–86, 189, 210, 211–14, 215
  Shakespeare Our Contemporary 165
  'Titania and the Ass's Head' 210, 211–12

La Boite (theatre company) (Brisbane) 147
Laertes *(Hamlet)* 42, 61, 69
Lamb, Charles 165
Lamb, Mary 165
Lanier, Douglas 9
Larkin, Aya 29, 84

Index

larrikinism 24, 37, 47, 53, 67–70
Laura *(Sea Change)* 152
Leahy, Tessa (as Titania) 173
Leary, John (as Flute) 232, 234
Lester, Adrian (as Rosalind) 131
Lethal Weapon (film) 24
Levine, Laura 195–96, 202
Lighthouse Theatre Company
  (Adelaide) 169
Livingston, Paul 107, 108, 143
Lo, Jacqueline 114
Longhurst, Jane 175
Longworth, Ken 120, 153
Love in a Forest (play) 121, 128
Lowing, Barbara 65
Luxford, Roy 6, 7
Lysander *(A Midsummer Night's Dream)* 187, 197, 200–201, 204, 207
  Gary Cooper as 199, 203
  Guy Pearce as 175, 205–6
  Simon Bossell as 179, 180–81, 228

'Mabo' judgement 99, 115
Madelaine, Richard 24, 26, 27, 33, 64, 86, 88, 167
madness
  masculinity, and *see* madness and masculinity *(Hamlet)*
  Ophelia's 'mad' scene *(Hamlet)* 5
madness and masculinity *(Hamlet)* 10, 15, 25, 27, 236–37
  Hamlet's relationship with fathers 49–67
  Hamlet's relationship with Ophelia 32–38, 69
  larrikinism 68–70
magic 6, 87
  Hamlet, in 79
  As You Like It, in 119, 120
  magic in *A Midsummer Night's Dream* 11, 161, 162, 170, 171, 173, 238
    Australian Shakespeare Company (1988, 1993, 2005) 11, 173–77
    Bell Shakespeare Company (2004) 11, 178–84
    Company B (2004) 11, 184–92
Mailman, Deborah
  Helena, as 200–204, 208–9
  Rosalind, as 111, 113–15, 144–50, 152, 157
Makeham, Paul 97
Malvolio *(Twelfth Night)* 183
Mamet, David 7
'Man enough for the role' (article) 157
Manning (Joe) (as Orlando) 156–57
margins (staging) 17, 174, 198, 219
Mark Antony *(Julius Caesar)* 8
Martin, Caroline 6
Martin Rigg *(Lethal Weapon)* 24
Martucci, Luciano
  Bottom, as 217
  Theseus/Oberon, as 179, 182, 183, 184, 227, 228, 229
masculinity
  Australian *see* Australian masculine identity
  madness, and *see* madness and masculinity *(Hamlet)*
*M*A*S*H* (tv series) 122
mateship 24, 68
Maus, K. E. 10
Maza, Bob (as Duke Senior) 113, 115
McAuley, Gay 11
McBurnie, Daniel (as Puck) 176
McCallum, John 104–5
McConnell, Alice
  'Man enough for the role' 157
  Rosalind, as 139, 150–57

Index

McKenzie, Jacqueline (as Ophelia) 35–36
McKinvern, Bruce 31
McLean, Greg 86, 87
MDA (tv series) 157
Mead, Philip 17
meaning (in performance) *see* performative meaning
Mechanicals *(A Midsummer Night's Dream)* 162, 163, 169, 186, 193
  social rank and power *see* social rank and power - the Mechanicals
  see also 'Pyramus and Thisbe' *(A Midsummer Night's Dream)*; Bottom *(A Midsummer Night's Dream)*; Quince *(A Midsummer Night's Dream)*; Snug *(A Midsummer Night's Dream)*
Melbourne Age 120
Mellor, Aubrey 101–2, 103, 118, 128
  As You Like It (NIDA - 1978) 101–2, 103, 118, 128
Mendelssohn (Wedding March) 168
metatheatre 1–3, 16, 213, 235, 236
  A Midsummer Night's Dream, in 184, 191, 222
  Hamlet, in 90–91
    Company B (1994) 86–87
    Pork Chop Productions (2001) 81–83
    see also First Player's Tale *(Hamlet)*; The Murder of Gonzago *(Hamlet)*
  As You Like It, in 99
MGM musical 170
Milne, Geoffrey 173–74
mimesis 76, 79
misogyny 212, 213, 214

Monjo, Justin 112
Montrose, Louis A. 210–11, 212–13, 216
Moonshine *(A Midsummer Night's Dream)* 233
  Ralph Cotterill as 233
Moore, Catherine 117–18
Morgan, Joyce 144
Moth *(A Midsummer Night's Dream)* 227
Mount Isa (Qld) 178
'Mousetrap' *(Hamlet) see* 'The Murder of Gonzago' *(Hamlet)*
Much Ado About Nothing 183
Muriel's Wedding (film) 222
Murrie, Linzie 54
Mustardseed *(A Midsummer Night's Dream)* 227
  Ian Watkins as 231

National Institute of Dramatic Arts (NIDA) 101, 143, 144
  As You Like It (1978) 101–2, 103, 118, 128
naturalism (theatre) 72, 140, 141, 162, 183, 188
  anti-naturalism 187, 188, 207
Newcastle Herald 106, 120, 153
Nick Bottom *(A Midsummer Night's Dream) see* Bottom *(A Midsummer Night's Dream)*
NIDA *see* National Institute of Dramatic Arts (NIDA)
Nimrod Theatre (Sydney) 68, 143
  Romeo and Juliet (1979) 68
  As You Like It (1983) 102–3, 118
Noble, Adrian 130
Nora *(Radiance)* 147

O Brave New World: Two Centuries of Shakespeare on the Australian Stage (book) 16

Index

Oberon *(A Midsummer Night's Dream)* 164, 171, 175, 182, 183, 212, 214, 215, 216, 217, 218, 226, 227, 232
  Geoffrey Rush as 169
  Glenn Shea as 173
  James Stafford as 176
  Luciano Martucci as 182, 183, 184, 228, 229
  Socratis Otto as 186, 188, 189
Old Tote (theatre company) (Sydney) 100
  As You Like It (1971) 100–1, 128
Oleanna 7
Oliver *(As You Like It)* 97, 110, 147
Olympic Arts Festival (1997) 171
A Midsummer Night's Dream (STC - 1997) 11, 171–72, 199–204
Ophelia *(Hamlet)* 28
  Anna Torv as 42
  Emily Tomlins as 44
  Hamlet, relationship with 25, 32–48, 69
  Jacqueline McKenzie as 35–36
  'mad' scene 5
  'nunnery' scene 15, 35, 40, 43, 45, 60
  Sacha Horler as 37, 40
Orlando *(As You Like It)* 98–99, 110, 111, 115, 140, 141, 153, 156
  Aaron Blabey as 111, 144, 145–46, 147
  (Joe) Manning as 156–57
  Paul Bishop as 140–43
Othello (character) 6, 7
Othello (play)
  Nigeria, performed in 6–8
Otto, Socratis (as Oberon) 186, 188, 189
outdoor productions of
  Shakespeare 100, 166, 174
  A Midsummer Night's Dream
    Government House Gardens (Perth - 1918) 166
    Royal Botanic Gardens (Melbourne – 1988) 173–84

Page, Nathan (as Snout) 232, 234
Page, Robert 128
'Pale Blue Eyes' (Velvet Underground) 187
Parker, Andrew 19
patriarchy 131, 136, 155, 156, 196, 198, 201, 206, 212, 218, 238
Pearce, Guy (as Lysander) 175, 205–6
Peaseblossom *(A Midsummer Night's Dream)* 227
People's Choice Award (Archibald Prize) 148, 149
Pepys, Samuel 163
performative meaning 4–5, 15, 18, 239
performativity 9, 11, 14, 17, 18, 19, 59, 73, 74, 107, 198, 224, 235, 237, 238
  A Midsummer Night's Dream 168, 179, 180, 194, 204, 209, 218
  As You Like It 156, 158, 238
Perret, Bill 119–20, 153
Perth 166
Peter Quince *(A Midsummer Night's Dream)* see Quince *(A Midsummer Night's Dream)*
Phelan, Anthony
  Claudius, as 60, 61–62
  Egeus, as 187, 188
  Quince, as 231, 232
Phelps, Samuel 164
Phillips, Simon 11, 96, 104–9, 110, 116, 119, 123, 137, 140, 142, 143, 171
  A Midsummer Night's Dream (1992) 171

281

Index

see also As You Like It (STC - 1996)
Philostrate *(A Midsummer Night's Dream)* 194, 227, 228, 229
   Luke Carroll as 187
Phoebe *(As You Like It)* 113
pictorialism 96, 102, 162, 164, 165
play-within-the-play 1
   A Midsummer Night's Dream 204
      see also social rank and power - the Mechanicals
   Hamlet, in 71–91
Player King *(Hamlet) see* First Player *(Hamlet)*
Players *(Hamlet)* 77–81
   see also 'The Murder of Gonzago' *(Hamlet)*
   see also First Player's Tale *(Hamlet)*
Player's Tale *(Hamlet) see* First Player's Tale *(Hamlet)*
Playhouse (Melbourne Arts Centre) 116
Playhouse (Sydney Opera House) 30, 31, 116
Playhouse Theatre (Queensland Performing Arts Centre) 31
Ploeg, Evert 148
Poli, Tony (as Egeus) 179
politics 8, 120, 150, 166, 197, 209, 211, 213, 236, 237
   gender 137, 207, 208, 209
   Post-Colonial Drama: Theory, Practice, Politics 2, 16
   Shakespeare's Books: Contemporary Cultural Politics and the Persistence of Empire 17
Polonius *(Hamlet)* 15, 28, 31, 33, 35, 37, 38, 60, 64, 73, 74, 79, 80, 82, 237
Pork Chop Productions (theatre company)
   Hamlet (2001) *see Hamlet* (Pork Chop Productions - 2001)
Possum Magic (book) 182
Post-Colonial Drama: Theory, Practice, Politics (book) 2–3, 16–17
post-colonial productions 2–3, 16–17, 20
Post-Colonial Drama: Theory, Practice, Politics 2–3, 16–17
Potra, Dan 26
power and play *see* authority and subversion - staging *A Midsummer Night's Dream;* cultural authority and subversion - Titania and the Weaver; social rank and power - the Mechanicals
presentism (theoretical movement) 8
Priam (Aeneas' Tale) 74
Prichard, Billie Rose 187–88
Prospero *(The Tempest)* 3
psychoanalytic theory *(A Midsummer Night's Dream)* 212–13, 226, 227
Puck *(A Midsummer Night's Dream)* 164, 168, 176, 188, 212, 216, 224, 227, 228
   Daniel McBurnie as 176
   Laurence Clifford as 172
   Richard Gyoerffy as 181, 183, 184, 228
Pulp Fiction (film) 232
Punch, Angela (as Rosalind) 128
Pyramus *(A Midsummer Night's Dream)* 161
'Pyramus and Thisbe' *(A Midsummer Night's Dream)* 163, 166, 221, 228, 229, 232, 233
   see also social rank and power - the Mechanicals
Pyrrhus (Aeneas' Tale) 74, 79, 80, 84

Index

QTC *see* Queensland Theatre Company (QTC)
Queensland Theatre Company (QTC)
   Hamlet (2007) *see Hamlet* (SRCSA/QTC - 2007)
   As You Like It (1981) 102
Quince *(A Midsummer Night's Dream)* 161, 227, 235
   Anthony Phelan as 231, 232
   authority and subversion 193–94, 196
   see also social rank and power - the Mechanicals

Radiance (film) 147
Raymond, Andrew 28
re-imagining Arden in Australia 10, 95–124, 237
   actors' Arden (Bell Shakespeare Company - 2003) 116–22
   backyard Arden (Company B - 1999) 109–16, 122
   concept of Arden (STC - 1996) 104–9
   exile, experience of 100, 102, 105, 107, 114, 115
   pastoral setting 10, 96, 97, 98, 100, 102, 103, 104, 105, 109, 115, 120, 121, 122, 123, 124
   terra nullius, concept of 97–100, 115
   Theatre Royal (Melbourne – 1863) 95, 97, 100, 106
   unsettling Arden (late 20th century) 100–103
realism (pictorial) 96, 102, 162, 164, 165
reality tv 180
Redgrave, Vanessa (as Rosalind) 129
rehearsal process 11, 12, 213, 236
   A Midsummer Night's Dream 228, 231
   Hamlet 31, 42, 59, 65, 77–78, 81, 88
   As You Like It 113, 116–18, 121, 122, 130, 131, 142, 150, 151–52
Restoration (England) 163
reviews and reviewers 11, 12–13
   A Midsummer Night's Dream 168–69, 174, 184, 189, 190, 200
   Hamlet 30, 32, 46–47, 86, 88
   As You Like It 95–96, 100, 101, 102, 104–5, 106, 112, 113, 116, 119–20, 123, 124, 125, 127, 128, 129, 143–44, 150, 153–54, 158
Richard III 7–8
Richelieu (play) 135
Rickard, John 68
Rider, Sue 147
Riverside Theatre (Sydney) 179
Robin Starveling *(A Midsummer Night's Dream) see* Starveling *(A Midsummer Night's Dream)*
Robinson, Keith 218
Rogers, Ginger 77
role doubling 2, 89, 169, 170–71, 226, 227–30, 231–32, 233
role playing 2, 129, 142, 158, 179, 221, 237
Romeo and Juliet 68
Rosalind *(As You Like It)* 10–11, 98, 99, 110, 111, 112, 125–58, 168, 237–38
   Adrian Lester as 131
   Alice McConnell as 139, 150–57
   Angela Punch as 128
   Anita Hegh as 107, 137–44, 145, 146, 151, 152, 157
   Deborah Mailman as 111, 113–15, 144–50, 152, 157
   Essie Jenyns as 125, 127, 136–37, 144, 147, 148, 157, 158
   Helen Faucit as 129–30
   Juliet Stevenson 130, 139, 146

Index

'Man enough for the role' 157
'Shakespeare's Rosalind and her Public Image' 126
summing up 158
Vanessa Redgrave as 129
see also Ganymede *(As You Like It)*
Rose, C. 157
Rosencrantz *(Hamlet)* 60, 63, 64, 71, 72, 82
Roxburgh, Richard (as Hamlet) 27, 30, 43, 64, 69, 70, 88
Royal Botanic Gardens (Melbourne) 173, 175, 205
Royal Botanic Gardens (Sydney) 205
Royal Shakespeare Company (RSC) 130
  A Midsummer Night's Dream (1970 and 1973) 165, 168–69, 170, 173, 189, 220–23, 225, 226
  King Lear (1962–64) 213
RSC *see* Royal Shakespeare Company (RSC)
Rush, Geoffrey
  Horatio, as 26, 27, 87
  Oberon/Theseus, as 169
Rutter, Carol 130
Ryan, Raj 108

sadism 214, 215
Sadler's Wells Theatre (London) 164
Schafer, Elizabeth 123, 147
Schlieper, Nick 104, 105
school performances of Shakespeare *see* education, Shakespeare and
Scott-Mitchell, Michael 104, 105, 107
Sea Change (tv series) 152
Sedgwick, Eve Kosofsky 19
sexual revolution 211
sexual violence 195, 202, 210

sexuality 33, 34, 37, 38, 41, 46, 47, 131, 137, 142, 143, 189, 195, 213
  see also eroticism
Shakespeare, William
  education, and 17, 18, 166–67, 178
  metatheatre *see* metatheatre
  'modern' mode of staging 163
  outdoor productions *see* outdoor productions of Shakespeare plays 140
  A Midsummer Night's Dream see A Midsummer Night's Dream
  Antony and Cleopatra 2, 75
  Hamlet see Hamlet
  Julius Caesar 7–8
  King Lear 147, 213
  Much Ado About Nothing 183
  Othello see Othello
  Richard III 7–8
  The Merchant of Venice 167
  The Merry Wives of Windsor 167
  The Taming of the Shrew 147, 167
  The Tempest 3, 108
  Troilus and Cressida 211
  Twelfth Night 97, 183, 198
  As You Like It see As You Like It
Shakespeare in the park *see* outdoor productions of Shakespeare
Shakespeare Our Contemporary (book) 165
Shakespeare's America, America's Shakespeare (book) 16
Shakespeare's Books: Contemporary Cultural Politics and the Persistence of Empire (book) 17
'Shakespeare's Rosalind and her Public Image' (article) 126
Sharman, Jim 100, 101, 128
  A Midsummer Night's Dream (1982/83) 169–70
  As You Like It (1971) 100–1, 128

Index

Shea, Glenn (as Oberon) 173
Sims, Jeremy 10, 36, 37–38, 51, 76
  Fortinbras, as 83
  Hamlet, as 28, 29–30, 43, 48, 60,
    62, 63, 64, 69, 70, 83, 84, 85–86
  'To be or not to be' soliloquy
    85–86
  see also Hamlet (Pork Chop
    Productions - 2001)
Sinatra, Frank 225
Sinclair, Jean 102
Sistrunk, Christie (as Titania) 175
Skunkhour (band) 29, 84
Smith, Bruce 70
Snout *(A Midsummer Night's Dream)*
  230, 231
  Nathan Page as 232, 234
  see also social rank and power -
    the Mechanicals
Snowy *(Gallipoli)* 23
Snug *(A Midsummer Night's Dream)*
  162
  Ian Watkin as 230, 231, 232, 234
  see also social rank and power -
    the Mechanicals
Snugglepot and Cuddlepie (book) 182
social class 129, 193, 219–20, 238
social rank and power - the
  Mechanicals 218–34
  Australian Shakespeare Company
    (1988, 1993, 2005) 223–25
  Bell Shakespeare Company (2004)
    227–30, 231
  Company B (2004) 230–34
  RSC (1970 and 1973) 220–23,
    225, 226
Spence, Bruce 143
'Spirit of Anzac' *see* Anzac legend
sport 53, 80, 177, 223
  theatre, and 177
Stafford, James (as Oberon) 176
Stanislavski (Konstantin) 162

Starveling *(A Midsummer Night's*
  Dream) 227, 229, 239
  Ralph Cotterill as 230, 231, 232,
    233–34
  see also social rank and power -
    the Mechanicals
State Theatre Company of SA
  (STCSA)
  A Midsummer Night's Dream (1992)
    171
  Hamlet (2007) *see* Hamlet (STCSA/
    QTC - 2007)
STC *see* Sydney Theatre Company
  (STC)
STCSA *see* State Theatre Company
  of SA (STCSA)
Stevens, Wallace 235
Stevenson, Juliet (as Rosalind) 130,
  139, 146
Stolen Generations 115
Stollery, Christopher
  Claudius, as 57
  Hamlet, as 55–56
Strictly Ballroom (film) 222
subversion *see* authority and
  subversion - staging *A Midsummer*
  Night's Dream; cultural authority
  and subversion - Titania and the
  Weaver
Sullivan, Barry 95, 97, 124
Sumner, Phil 176–77
Sunday Age 119–20
Sydney/Canberra audiences 7–8
Sydney Morning Herald 88, 101, 125,
  144
Sydney Theatre Company (STC)
  38
  A Midsummer Night's Dream (1989)
    170–71, 217
  A Midsummer Night's Dream (1997)
    see A Midsummer Night's Dream
    (STC - 1997)

Index

As You Like It (1996) *see As You Like It* (STC - 1996)
Sylvius *(As You Like It)* 113

Tales from Shakespeare (book) 165
Tate, Jennie 119–20, 122, 179
Tatspaugh, Patricia 163, 164
Taylor, Sean 65
Taylor, Tony 218
terra nullius, concept of 97–100, 115
The Anzacs (book) 56
The Broken Years (book) 56
The Bulletin 106
The Castle (film) 222
The Daily Telegraph 112
The Merchant of Venice 167
The Merry Wives of Windsor 167
'The Mousetrap' *(Hamlet) see* 'The Murder of Gonzago' *(Hamlet)*
'The Murder of Gonzago' *(Hamlet)* 29, 71, 77, 85, 237
   Hamlet (Bell Shakespeare Company - 2003) 77–78
The Norton Shakespeare (book) 10
The Paper Dress (painting) 199
The Popular Mechanicals (play) 218–19
The Taming of the Shrew 147, 167
The Tempest 3, 108
theatre archives 12–13
Theatre Royal (Melbourne)
   A Midsummer Night's Dream (1913) 165–66
   As You Like It - 1863 95, 97, 100, 106
theatrical force 5, 6, 20, 26, 42, 43, 64, 70, 71–91, 240
theatrical meaning 4, 8, 19, 196, 200
   'participatory' 4, 8
   'playful' 4, 60, 67, 101, 111, 112, 115, 123, 128, 139, 146, 150, 174, 176, 183, 184, 188, 190, 200, 205

   'unpredictable' 4, 63, 131, 177, 191, 196
   'theatrical seeing' 75, 80
Theseus *(A Midsummer Night's Dream)* 164, 171, 187, 194–95, 206, 226, 239
   authority and subversion 194–95, 199, 203
   Geoffrey Rush as 169
   Luciano Martucci as 179, 227, 228, 229
Thomas, Brian 100
Thompson, G.M. 134, 135, 136, 137
Thomson, Brian 170
Thomson, Helen 120
Thornton, Sigrid 152
Tis Pity She's a Whore (play) 171
Titania *(A Midsummer Night's Dream)* 164, 166, 168, 169, 197, 198, 225, 226, 227, 232
   Christie Sistrunk as 175
   cultural authority and subversion *see* cultural authority and subversion - Titania and the Weaver
   Gillian Jones as 169
   Helen Buday as 185, 186, 188–89
   Tessa Leahy as 173
   'Titania and the Ass's Head' 210, 211–12
'Titania and the Ass's Head' (article) 210, 211–12
'To be or not to be' soliloquy *(Hamlet)* 85–86
Toby *(Twelfth Night)* 183
Tohill, Kathryn 205
Tom Snout *(A Midsummer Night's Dream) see* Snout *(A Midsummer Night's Dream)*
Tomlins, Emily (as Ophelia) 44
Tompkins, Joanne 2, 103, 106
Torv, Anna (as Ophelia) 42

Index

Tovey, Noel 11, 171–73, 199
  A Midsummer Night's Dream (1997) 11, 171–72, 199–204
Troilus and Cressida 211
Tudor period 172, 173, 199
  see also Elizabethan period
Twelfth Night 97, 183, 198
Twitter 180

'unauthorised authorship' 236
Upstairs Belvoir *see* Belvoir Street Theatre (Sydney)

vaudeville 150, 218
VCA *see* Victorian College of the Arts (VCA)
Velvet Underground 187
Verfremdungseffekt (Brecht) 187
Victorian College of the Arts (VCA) 151, 157
Victorian period 31, 57, 100, 168, 189, 190, 211
Viola *(Twelfth Night)* 97, 198
violence 24, 41, 62, 64, 66, 68, 121, 162, 203, 206, 209, 238
  linguistic 10
  sexual violence 195, 202, 208, 210
Volska, Anna 11, 102, 143, 178, 179, 181, 184, 191, 227, 229
  A Midsummer Night's Dream see A Midsummer Night's Dream (Bell Shakespeare Company - 2004)
As You Like It (1983) 102–3, 118
voyeurism 186–87, 189, 190, 207, 209, 213, 215, 234

Walcott, Derek 2
Wall, Dorothy 182
Walter, Timothy (as Demetrius) 179, 180–81, 182, 183, 228
war *see* World War I; World War II
Ward, Russell 54
Watkin, Ian (as Snug) 230, 231, 232, 234
Watson, Robert N. 10, 98, 121
Weaver *(A Midsummer Night's Dream) see* Bottom *(A Midsummer Night's Dream)*
Weill, Kurt 77
Weimann, Robert 72, 76
Weir, Peter 23, 56
Wenham, David 149
Wherrett, Richard 170–71
  A Midsummer Night's Dream (1989) 170–71, 217
Whitlam, Gough (Prime Minister) 101
Wilde, Oscar 77
Wilkie, Allan (as Bottom) 166
Williams, Ross (as Bottom) 223–25
Winton, Tim 112
Wood, John (as Bottom) 169
Woods, Irma 113
World War I 26, 52–53
  Gallipoli 23, 24, 52–53, 56
World War II 171
Worthen, W. B. 4–5, 19, 75, 80, 91, 196, 235

Zeffirelli, Franco 23–24, 68

www.ingramcontent.com/pod-product-compliance
Lightning Source LLC
Chambersburg PA
CBHW031309150426
43191CB00005B/144